BRIGHT ALLIANCE

PURPOSE RISING

A Global Movement of
Transformation and Meaning

Edited by
Emanuel Kuntzelman
& Dustin DiPerna

BRIGHT
ALLIANCE

ISBN 978-0-9862826-6-9

Published by Bright Alliance

First Edition

BrightAlliance.org

Book layout and design: Brad Reynolds
integralartandstudies.com

Printed and Bound in the United States

This book is dedicated to everyone
seeking their deepest purpose.
May it help you find the way.

Editors

Emanuel Kuntzelman is a social entrepreneur, philosopher, writer and environmentalist. Over the last thirty years he has given lectures, seminars and workshops throughout Europe and the U.S. on social transformation. He is the Founder and President of Greenheart International, an organization promoting cultural exchange, fair trade, travel abroad, personal development and volunteer service (www.greenheart.org). Based in Chicago, IL, Greenheart was established by Emanuel in 1985 and is widely recognized for its work to support global leaders who connect people and planet. He is also the co-founder and President of the Fundacion por el Futuro, based in Madrid, Spain. He is a contributing author to Ervin Laszlo's book *The Intelligence of the Cosmos* (2017). His book on evolutionary wave theory, *Riding the Wave of Global Purpose*, is forthcoming. He is an initiator of the Global Purpose Movement and a lifelong spiritual seeker. More information can be found at www.emanuelkuntzelman.com

Dustin DiPerna was educated at Cornell University and Harvard University. Dustin is a visionary leader, entrepreneur, and recognized expert in world religions. He is author of the books *Streams of Wisdom* (2014), *Evolution's Ally* (2015), and *Earth is Eden* (2016), and co-editor of *The Coming Waves* (2014). Dustin is founder of the publishing house Bright Alliance. He currently teaches at Stanford University. An avid lover of art, design and nature, he lives in California with his wife, Amanda, and daughter, Jaya. More details at www.dustindiperna.com or text the word "Light" to 444999 to join his mailing list.

Table of Contents

❧

Acknowledgements

This volume is the result of an organic, purposeful team effort. Above all, we are deeply grateful to the contributing authors of this work. Their commitment to finding their own purpose and transmitting it to the general public is a testimony to what it means to find our purpose in service to humanity. We are likewise highly appreciative of the contributions of compiling and editing this work. Thanks is to be extended to Michael Stern for author coordination, Kate St. Clair for editing, Brad Reynolds for interior layout. And, finally, we extend heartfelt recognition to Greenheart and the Global Purpose Movement for supporting the publication financially, and to Bright Alliance for overall coordination of this project. With a deep bow of gratitude and hope for the future of humanity, we thank all of you for your pursuit of purpose.

PURPOSE RISING

A Global Movement of
Transformation and Meaning

Introduction

Emanuel Kuntzelman

The book you hold in your hands was created for a specific purpose. The authors contributing to this work want to change your life for good. The intention here is to give the reader a jolt of renewed inspiration, pushing each of you to a deeper understanding of the notion of purpose, no matter where you are starting from. This collection of writings is designed to help you discover an inner core of meaning and an outer orbit of social action, such that you have never before explored, so that it will transform your life in a way that will carry you through to the incarnation your soul was meant to live.

If asked whether or not we think our life is purposeful, a large majority of us will clearly say yes, of course it is. But, we might ask, to what extent is it purposeful? Many brilliant minds working in the fields of "science," whether in physics, biology, chemistry, cosmology, or others, still adhere to the view from the materialistic paradigm that our life on Earth is the end product of a long line of random and accidental mutations accumulating over millions of years of survival-driven natural selection. Materialistic scientists, even if they might say their personal life has some kind of purpose, deny that there is evolutionary purpose in the universe itself. And the debate rages on. Is our universe purposeful or is it not? That is the primary question, and the answer given herein is provided by the leading interdisciplinary scientist and philosopher of our times.

Ervin Laszlo sums it up ever so succinctly: "Purpose in the universe is a universal truth as well as a source of practical guidance." His arguments for the purposeful nature of the universe, enumerating the astonishing degree of fine-tuning that made the evolutionary process possible, leave no doubt that all this is happening with an intention in Mind. Duane Elgin's eloquent description of the universe as a living being gives literal life to that intention. If the whole world is alive, then it has a purpose within itself, just as we as individuals do.

Once that primary question of universal purposefulness is answered, the possibilities for an expanded view of our own raison d'etre take on new possibilities. Instead of seeing ourselves as an accident of the meaningless material world, we understand ourselves as the culmination of purpose itself, having come full circle to be in a position to consciously co-create ever deeper interpretations of why this is all happening and how we can best contribute to its development.

In such an ontological inquiry, there is inevitably an underlying correlation between purpose and some notion of divinity. Bryan Alvarez would say there is even a Guardian Angel with whom it behooves our spiritual selves to develop a sincere relationship. He observes that a spiritual practice should be a work of living art, yet with repeatable and effective methods that others can utilize.

This work of purposeful art could be likened to constructing a self-portrait of our souls, both as individuals and as the whole of humankind. Even for those who don't believe in the soul, or call it by a different name, there is undeniably something inside us that is painted in the image of who we are. Jonathan Gustin tells us that "living our life's purpose is an expression of the ego's realization of the soul." That soul's image, whether or not the ego wants to see itself in the mirror, is the focus at the core of Gustin's octagon of purpose. Bill Plotkin takes a deep dive (or delves) into that underworld of the soul's purpose and explores it in an ecological context. Just as animals instinctively know how they fit into their environment, we humans must also do the same and could greatly benefit ourselves and our society by discovering the ecological purpose of our existence.

This deep soul work is serious business—more so now than in any point in history—because we have the intellectual understanding of our cosmos, of evolution, and the human psyche to know that life is, indeed, highly purposeful. At the same time, we are approaching a worldwide crisis of unprecedented proportions. It is not a crisis in the sense of fighting for territory that generated wars in the past. To be sure, a struggle for diminishing resources is at stake—a fresh glass of potable water is becoming a cherished commodity in many parts of the world—but more than anything this is a crisis of purpose or, more accurately stated, the lack thereof.

If there is a purpose in the cosmos and we are the caretakers and perpetrators of that purpose, then what is it we are supposed to do? The answers readily arrive from the contributors to this volume: awaken the latent meaning in our souls to ignite the broader purpose of transforming society into a more compassionate, ecological, and cooperative global community. That is a lot easier said than done in a world that is ever more divided about the nature of our purpose, or whether purpose exists at all. It will take more than words, no matter how eloquently expressed and replete with undeniable truths, to find our purpose and change the world for the better: it will take concerted action. To that regard, Brandon Peele picks up on the work of Plotkin and Gustin and offers a veritable toolkit for discovery on the purpose journey.

And it would certainly be of benefit to adopt some version of Peele's plan for action, because one of the reasons that major change is slow in coming is that some of the spiritual soul searching we do, no matter how heartfelt and sincere, remains in the realm of searching as opposed to doing. Granted, the search is long, mysterious, and oftentimes uncomfortable. Occasionally there is a transcendental breakthrough, but then we seem to snap back to our old selves, not quite embodying that ephemeral leap into deep purpose. Terry Patten points out the critical difference between transcendence and transformation. Transcendence may be a lovely experience, but the old patterns and habits of behavior and belief need to be genuinely transformed if we hope to get on with meaningful change in ourselves.

Those patterns are most readily broken if we can learn to listen to our purpose and put it into action. Nick Jankel wisely observes that "purpose is enlightenment becoming impact." It is a kind of connector between the spiritual and material realm, which "seeks to reduce suffering before it looks to increase thriving." Given the current state of the world, let's hope this is true, because there is a plethora of material temptations that lead us astray from understanding our authentic purpose. Dennis Wittrock reminds us that if "we let profit become our purpose," then our life comes down to making money—"even at the expense of human decency, dignity, and basic compassion." These are the "imposter voices" of our cultural institutions that Patten points out, and the "substitute purpose" described by Gustin, all of which give us misleading ideas of how to validate our success in life.

Indeed, the developed world's predominantly materialistic values seem to have hijacked the goodness in our inner nature, causing the plight of purpose in the present moment, with the consequences bringing an increasing disparity of wealth and the encroaching environmental destruction of our planet. We would do well to heed the wisdom of indigenous communities, as Leela Marie Bergerud advises, concentrating on healing and shadow work to rout out the demons in our souls. Leela tells us of the Mayan prophecy of how a new consciousness will be formed when the people of the north, representing the masculine mind, unite with those of the south, symbolized by the feminine heart, in a common purpose of a planetary tribe.

The masculine, yang influence on thought (an eagle to the Mayans) that drives our quest for materiality has been prominent, with only some isolated exceptions, since the dawn of human history. So the time is overdue for the feminine force—symbolized by the condor—to fly into our consciousness and take its appropriate place. This component of the divine feminine rising is brought forth in all of its subtle, nourishing love in the contributions of Susan Lucci, Barbara Marx Hubbard, and Andrea Dennis and Carly Visk. Lucci focuses on the challenges of modern-day women when they realize that "halfway through life, one or more of a woman's roles no longer becomes her." As a woman recognizes this sense of feeling alone and overwhelmed, there is an urge to connect and explore the path back to unity in a WE space. Visk and Dennis employ their yin-inspired perspective to observe that "While at first purpose may seem to be something that needs to be discovered or achieved, nature invites us to simply remember the wisdom that we are." But they also recognize that "the drive to find purpose is pointing to a deeper yearning that requires attention and nurturing." To that extent, Barbara Marx Hubbard's autobiographical journey shows just how fully that yearning can be nurtured. Barbara's life personifies the quintessential tale of the evolutionary woman and the awakening of the divine feminine emerging in all of us—the intuitive knowledge that implores us not to simply be of help, but to take the lead and co-create a new, more potent, and purposeful reality.

Thus the feminine principle becomes a critical component of the postmaterial worldview. It lures us forward with its heartfelt compassion, providing the necessary balance to our purposeful plot. Like the condor meeting the eagle at the intersection of hemispheres, the feminine embraces the masculine drive of the past and blends its receptive, intuitive wisdom with it in the spirit of birthing a new future for humanity. Historical male dominance is not rejected, but included and then transcended, in an integral fusion that allows the evolution of purpose to become a greater whole than the sum of its genders. A new child of unique purpose is born.

Moving toward a higher, deeper, or more integral understanding of purpose, however, we bump into another obstacle: the very definition of the word *purpose*. Dictionaries all list the first meaning of the word as "an object or end to be attained." Oh my, how old paradigm that definition is, as if purpose is nothing more than another material objective to be conquered. This is the issue that Patrick Cook-Deegan addresses in discussing the shortcomings of our educational system with respect to purpose. He notes that adolescents are rather turned off by the idea that purpose is just one more thing to strive for, one more goal or object to be attained. "Work ethic and drive should not be confused with having a purpose," he sagely observes, and then explains that seeking purpose is "wayfinding," akin to the Polynesians' quests for new lands, sailing over vast distances of open sea, guided by the stars, instinct, and intuition.

Surely we need to educate our youth, and our adults for that matter, in a more profound definition of the word purpose, preferably along the lines of the soul work outlined by Gustin, Plotkin, and Peele. We need to redefine the word to suit a new paradigm of interconnected karma—of playing our best role, becoming our most precious part, in an ever-greater whole. Cortney Love addresses this need for a broader interpretation of purpose by discussing it as "Dharma," a life purpose with a moral duty to it. As she defines it, "Dharma is what we were put on this earth to do for our soul's evolution and to support the Universe." To help us visualize the concept, she displays an ikigai Venn diagram that synchronistically happens to be the same image as the Global Purpose Movement logo. It shows the overlapping intersections of what you love, what you are good at, what the world needs, and what you can get paid for.

From logos, ikigai diagrams, and the words of wisdom from our authors, we see a discernable pattern emerging—one of an integrated core of intention and motivation that allows us to move forward with practical applications to the world's needs. This we call "purpose," for lack of a better term in English. By whatever name it goes—Dharma, duty, calling, or even a second coming—it is the kernel of our soul's meaning rising into being. As that individual soul power takes root and flourishes, it meets other like-minded souls along the way and they coalesce into a new tribe with an upward movement—toward the Deliberately Developmental Civilization that Ken Wilber and Dustin DiPerna describe.

In their contribution, Wilber and DiPerna analyze the delicate interplay of states, structures, and shadows, expanding our integral understanding of development in these three dimensions. States of consciousness are the horizontal movement that we experience toward awakening, although this does not necessarily mean we have reached a higher level of development on the vertical scale of structures. And even if we do ascend to upper stages, it serves us little if we have failed to clean up our act in the process. As the authors affirm, if we have not done our appropriate shadow work, our supposed development is tantamount to trying to appreciate the beauty of a stained glass window that is dirty and broken. Thus, we have to simultaneously wake up, grow up, and clean up to achieve genuine, integral progress. If, as individuals and organizations, this can be visualized and accomplished, then what holds us back from applying this developmental model to civilization as a whole?

Well, there are still some pitfalls on the path. Cassandra Vieten and Mica Estrada warn us that "A common misunderstanding is that the best way to make change is to provide people with lots of information that supports what we want them to do differently." They reveal that information only contributes 10 percent to behavioral change and motivation only adds another 10 percent. What then, really could make us move upward to a new stage of civilizational development? Vieten and Estrada propose that it is worldview transformation. To paraphrase Buckminster Fuller, we won't change things by fighting the existing, purposeless, and materialistic reality. To change the world, we must build a new model that is a radically inclusive "invitation to join into a community of dignity and justice."

Enter the new worldview of purpose. Vieten and Estrada, and all the authors in this volume, find a common theme that encourages us to enhance our change-making ability by working on our own state of mind and way of being. Once we can individually exemplify the change we would like to see, then we can aspire to finding the supernormal capacities that Christina Grote and Pam Kramer say are waiting to emerge from our latent human potential. As their mentors Michael Murphy and George Leonard have counseled, our purpose and superpowers will only arise as a result of long-term commitment to a practice, and there is really no shortcut to reaching our soul's ultimate purpose. To us mere mortals, it might seem like superpower attributes are only in a state of "precognitive dreams of an extraordinary level of love, joy, and connection with all of life," but with an indefatigable persistence in finding purpose, the supernormal could well be our birthright.

In the end, this pursuit of purpose might be easier than it seems. In addition to all the revelatory ideas and expert advice written herein, there is a lot to be said for keeping it simple, for maintaining a beginner's mind that goes with the flow. Tazdeen Rashid's story is a reminder to follow our heart, avoiding what doesn't seem natural or true and seeking that which does. There is a pace and poetry to the path to purpose that sometimes we lose sight of in the frenzy of modern-day life. There is a rhythm and rhyme to our individual melody that our rational mind often interrupts with its nagging thoughts about accomplishing some component of the material pursuit. Without hurrying or meandering, we can attune ourselves to life's music and give freedom to our inner purpose to gradually reveal itself. Our culture inundates us with images and advertising that pounds home the message that some sort of zombie nonsense is supposed to be the ultimate form of fun. Yet at the end of the day, we go home feeling exhausted, empty, drugged out, or watered down with alcohol. How much easier is it, as Taz tells us, to "find purpose simply by being open to the Divine." There is a natural song in our hearts that longs to sing out with its mindful celebration of Bhakti energy, if only we would allow it to play its soulful sound.

Duane Elgin gives voice to the overall procession of purpose with this proclamation: "We are moving from seeing ourselves as accidents of creation wandering through a lifeless cosmos without meaning or purpose, to seeing ourselves consciously engaged in a sacred journey of discovery." Plotkin claims that we can only understand our souls in a "mythopoetical" manner. Well, perhaps we can then say that the path to purpose is the Tao of wayfinding in the ultimate Hero's journey. As such, we must approach it cautiously, just as Jankel delicately surrounds a sense of "atheistic spirituality." Purpose seems to lurk in the shadows, waiting to ambush us in wholeness at the crossroads of science and spirituality. Purpose could be a sort of creative intelligent divinity to some, or a practical worldly goal to others. However we perceive its essence, purpose is poised to pounce when we most expect it—like now, when we take the time to explore its impact on our life in all of its multifarious manifestations.

The trail ahead is still strewn with obstacles, with false signs indicating all kinds of wayward suggestions that our culture urges us to take, but deep inside there is our own personal guide who will, if we dare to listen, whisper the right directions so we can discern the straight track toward our soul's purpose and our heart's desire. In Terry Patten's words, "Integral Soul Work is thus a form of skillful means that enables our total psychophysical capacities to self-organize and make their highest art." With that evolving art form, perhaps someday "supernormal" will be the new normal.

The anthology that follows is organized into three sections: the theory, the journey, and the practice. This structure will hopefully be more helpful for the reader setting out on their own journey to discover a deeper understanding of purpose than the somewhat circuitous tale told in this introduction. No matter what order it comes in, the wisdom divulged in this book slowly seeps into the soul, giving life and light to our embryonic will to be of purposeful service to our troubled world. The contributions herein make up a rich tapestry of a vision of a new worldview. Just as it is difficult to pin down the essence of our story in a single word such as *purpose*, so too is it hard to find the focus on our life with a single formula. The answer is more like a kaleidoscopic image coming into view, as if we were able to cut to the core of Gustin's octagon and take a microscopic look into the depths of our soul. Or, it might be the vision at the center of circles in Cortney Love's diagram, where passion, mission, profession and vocation all merge as one. Or, it could be when the structures, stages, and shadows of the developmental process all fall into super-coherence, creating a holistic view into civilization's purpose-oriented future.

Whatever the models used or metaphors applied, the sagacious explanations presented in this anthology lead us to the same result: we gain a gestalt glimpse deep inside ourselves that shows us that we most definitely do have a purpose, and if we put it into practice it will lead to the best way to live out our Dharma and serve humanity in its hour of need. This compilation thus serves the purpose to which it set forth to accomplish. There is little doubt that at some juncture along the journey unveiled in these pages, readers will find precious insight that will change their lives forever. The message cannot be missed. From the beginning of time, from the primordial spark of the universe, to the turmoil of the twenty-first century, there is a constant, unwavering movement toward transformation and meaning. It gives inspiration to one and all. It is purpose rising.

PART I
The Theory

Chapter 1

TOWARD A DELIBERATELY DEVELOPMENTAL CIVILIZATION

Illuminating the Three Key Elements of
Spiritual Transformation and Purpose

Ken Wilber and Dustin DiPerna

This chapter proposes an integrative approach to spiritual transformation and purpose on a global scale. Rather than taking a "prescriptive" approach (offering a formula of what we feel ought to be the case based on our own normative opinions), we take a "descriptive" approach (articulating what we already know to be the case based on existing cross-cultural evidence).[1] In our survey of the vast array of orientations toward the further reaches of human potential, the evidence clearly shows at least three distinct elements of human transformation and development that appear repeatedly throughout various regions and cultures of the world. We refer to these three core elements of transformation as *states*, *structures*, and *shadow*. Our thesis is simple: any global, universal, cross-cultural understanding of human transformation and purpose that seeks to base its orientation on the evidence available must take states, structures, and shadow into account. Conversely, any approach to human transformation and development that leaves any one or more of these three elements out of the overall developmental picture, is by its very nature creating conditions for the development of partial/stunted human beings.

We fully understand, and in many ways agree with, the ideas of pluralism and multiculturalism—that many of the "universal ideas" taken in the past to be cross-culturally universal, found in all human beings, turn out to be merely and only culturally bound and culturally created, differing in fact from culture to culture, religion to religion, even individual to individual. But a closer inspection and finer analysis demonstrates that there are many structures, states, and shadow elements that, while their surface features vary, often dramatically, from culture to culture (and from religion to religion), often possess deep features that share a set of characteristics or patterns that are fundamentally similar cross-culturally. Certain sequences of structures of consciousness, for example, have been found to have deep features that are similar in Amazonian rain forest tribes, citizens in India, Australian aborigines, and most European countries, to name a few. We're talking not just about incommensurable differences, and not just about rigid universal identities, but about a set of unity-in-diversity features that honor both the diversities and the unities or similarities. These unity-in-diversity characteristics allow valid and fruitful cross-cultural comparisons without forcing cross-cultural (or cross-religious) identities or rigid and putative commonalities.

When states, structures, and shadow integration are honored and intentionally cultivated, humanity opens the possibility of establishing a *Deliberately Developmental Civilization*: a civilization that intentionally supports transformation through all domains of growth and development. If such a civilization can be established, we will enter into a brighter age for humankind; an age wherein awake, mature, and integrated human beings systematically create conveyer belts of developmental potential for all of us to realize our fullest potential.

The exploration of this type of *Deliberately Developmental Civilization* serves as the core of this chapter. Let's unpack the notion a bit further.

What Is Development?

To begin, let's take a closer look at what we mean by the term development. For our purposes here, we use the terms "development" and "transformation" interchangeably (with both of them intimately connected to evolution in general). In both cases, the terms refer to our innate human capacity to both grow (and heal) through predicable, sequential patterns of mental, emotional, and spiritual unfolding. Because these patterns are generally predictable and reliably progress in sequence (a sequence that cannot be altered by social conditioning), it is also the case that each higher developmental stage transcends and includes (or unfolds and enfolds) the stage that preceded it (just as organisms transcend and include cells, which transcend and include molecules, which transcend and include atoms). This process of unfoldment and enfoldment reveals a natural, nested hierarchy (or "holarchy") of developmental progression.[2] Just as evolution has touched the physical and biological dimensions—leaving each marked by sequential stages of unfolding—so evolution has touched the psychological, cultural, and spiritual dimensions as well, also leaving each marked by dependable, broad, general sequential stages of their own growth and development (as determined and demonstrated, not by dogmatic claims or assertions, but by direct and repeatable empirical studies). It is the developmental/evolutionary nature of all of those dimensions that allow the effective planning and growth of each of them—including our own overall spiritual growth and development. And it is the cross-cultural similarities, at a deep-feature level, that allow these developmental/evolutionary sequences to be a reliable map for humankind's spiritual growth and unfolding at large (with all of their relative differences and idiosyncrasies included).

What Are the Key Elements of Development and Transformation?

In order to understand development in its various parts, it is instructive to synthesize what we already know through the cross-cultural study of human potential. Let's take a look at the disciplines of developmental science, spirituality, and psychotherapy in a bit more detail.

Developmental science teaches us about our capacity to *grow up* through various developmental *structures* of consciousness. Structures of consciousness generate our internal operating system. They determine our worldview and the various ways we process information. A deep understanding of developmental science and structures of consciousness as a field of study has only been in existence for the past 100 years.[3]

One of the surprising discoveries in the overall realm of developmental studies has involved a few facts only recently uncovered: it is not the case, as had been regularly and widely assumed, that all humans possess just one major intelligence (generally called "cognitive intelligence" and "measured" by the all-important IQ); but rather, humans actually possess up to a dozen different or "multiple intelligences," including (in addition to cognitive intelligence) ones such as emotional intelligence, moral intelligence, interpersonal intelligence, linguistic intelligence, mathematical intelligence, kinesthetic intelligence, aesthetic intelligence, and spiritual intelligence, among others. But an even more surprising discovery was the fact that, despite the real differences in these multiple intelligences (also often called "*lines* of development"), all of these lines nonetheless develop or unfold through the same basic six-to-eight major "*levels*, or *structures, of development*." In other words, different lines, same levels. There are several dozen maps and models of developmental psychology, but virtually all of them present variations on these same basic six-to-eight major structures of increasing complexity and care as they move from traditional, to modern, to postmodern, to integral stages of development.

Our world's great spiritual lineages teach us something quite different. Rather than helping us *grow up* through structures of consciousness, they introduce us to our capacity to *wake up* to a series of ever-deepening *states* of consciousness.[4] States of consciousness are often referred to as "mystical experiences"—or, psychologically, as "peak experiences" or "altered states"—and traditionally, these are said to come in several varieties: they can involve *nature mysticism* (oneness with the entire gross/physical world); *deity mysticism* (oneness with a subtle/interior dimension); *formless mysticism* (oneness with an "infinite Abyss" or formless Ground of all Being); and *nondual mysticism* (or a oneness or "unity consciousness" with all realms and dimensions, manifest and unmanifest).[5]

A state of consciousness is a direct, first-person, immediate and un-mediated experience of a particular dimension of one variety or another (with "spiritual states of consciousness" involving, obviously, "spiritual" dimensions, however we wish to conceive that)—the point is simply that states are direct, immediate, conscious experiences. States of conscious-ness are obvious when one has them—when you experience "universal love-bliss" or an "all-pervading oneness with all of reality" or a "sense of loving unity with all things," you definitely know you are experiencing those. States are so obvious and hard to miss, that human beings have been aware of various states of consciousness—including so-called altered states of consciousness—for thousands and thousands of years, going back at least to the earliest shamans and their vision quests, perhaps some 50,000 years ago. And although at first, states come and go, a crucial item of development is that these temporary states can become permanent van-tage points of awareness (state-stages)—and a great number of contempla-tive or meditative systems worldwide consist of a series of state-stages of development (a developmental sequence of vantage points) said to reach from, at one end, the narrow, egoic, "separate-self sense" to, at the other, a mystical union with the Ground of all Being or the ultimate spiritual state (however it is conceived)—what the Sufis call "the Supreme Identity." This, indeed, is known worldwide as a process of "Waking Up."

Here's the key point: most of developmental science (and the entire Western developmental paradigm) has focused on *structures* of conscious-ness (and the path of "Growing Up"). Most of the world's great wisdom traditions, on the other hand, have focused on the unfolding of *states* of consciousness (and the path of "Waking Up"). In theory this may not seem like a very big dilemma, but in practice, it could mean all the differ-ence in the world. This distinction between structures and states helps to explain the difference between a fundamentalist and a saint—because what research has discovered is that, no matter what state of consciousness an individual might experience (or no matter how "high" that spiritual state might be) in their process of Waking Up, that state is still *interpreted* by the grammar or *structure* of consciousness that the individual is at in their process of Growing Up (because whatever experience you have can only be interpreted with the mental tools and grammars and structures that you have, and these develop in any line only through our processes of Growing Up). So high spiritual states of Waking Up can still be badly distorted and reduced if the individual is at a fairly low level of Growing Up. Or to bring it into our current global context, it could mean the difference between Joel Osteen and Pope Francis or between a member of ISIS and a progressive Muslim. Both Joel Osteen and Pope Francis may well have access to authentic spiritual states of consciousness, but the structures of consciousness through which each of those states is enacted and interpreted are at very different levels. (Needless to say, herein lies one of the major solutions to understanding our global "war" on terror. It's not about getting rid of religion—whether it be Islam or Christianity—it's about helping all practitioners come to express their traditions through higher and more mature structures of consciousness. Spiritual experience alone is not enough. It will be spiritual experience combined with modern, postmodern, and integral versions of each tradition that will help us find a way through.[6] We'll return to this point in just a moment with some specific examples.)

The bottom line is that our world needs human beings who are both evolved through the various structures of consciousness as well as awake to the full spectrum of states of consciousness. Up until this point these two worlds have existed side by side, as if in parallel universes, each leaving out the valuable contribution of the complementary orientation. The reasons for this are entirely understandable...

Unlike states of consciousness that show up in direct experience, structures of consciousness are much harder to spot. Structures are more like the rules of grammar than they are like the direct experience of a word or sentence (or state of consciousness). Individuals brought up in a particular language-speaking culture, for example, will grow up speaking that language quite correctly—they will put subjects and verbs together correctly, they will use adjectives and adverbs correctly, and in general will end up following quite faithfully and quite accurately all of the rules of grammar of that language. But if you ask any of them to write down just what those grammar rules are, virtually none of them can do so. Every one of them is following perfectly a set of rules, yet they have no idea that they are doing so, let alone what those rules are! The six-to-eight stages of structure development—including spiritual intelligence—are like grammar—they are six-to-eight "hidden maps" that govern how individuals think and feel about issues of "ultimate concern"; and yet, while these individuals are perfectly following the particular stage that they are at in this developmental sequence, they have no idea that they are following a hidden map that is determining a great deal of what and how they think about their religious notions. This is why not a single spiritual system, East or West, has any apparent knowledge of the six-to-eight structure-stages of spiritual growth. They understand the state-stages of Waking Up, but not the structure-stages of Growing Up. (This is why the former were discovered as far back, we saw, as 50,000 years ago; whereas the structure-stages of Growing Up were only discovered about 100 years ago—yet another reason no great wisdom tradition has any indication of them at all.)

So we have an opportunity now, as a global culture, to create a comprehensive map of development and human purpose that includes both states of consciousness and structures of consciousness, both Waking Up and Growing Up.

Finally, rounding out the survey of what we already know about our own potential for transformation beyond structures and states, advances in Western psychotherapy teach us about our capacity to heal trauma, addiction, phobia, and unconscious patterns. This means that in addition to Growing Up (through structures of consciousness) and Waking Up (through states of consciousness), we can use the incredible wisdom discovered through psychotherapeutic approaches to engage a process of *Cleaning Up*—integrating our *shadow* to become a whole human being. In addition to the psychotherapeutic tradition of the modern West, the great medicine traditions of shamanic and indigenous cultures have cultivated incredible capacity to work on more subtle levels of reality to liberate karmic patterns and bring beings into deeper wholeness. And although there is no sign that these traditions knew much about modern concepts like transference, projection, or early childhood attachment, anyone who has worked in the context of these traditions knows firsthand of their incredible capacity to reveal shadow, heal trauma, and cure addictive tendencies. In an integral approach, all of these methods of healing and integration would necessarily be included.

To be clear, here is why *Cleaning Up* and including shadow integration is of fundamental importance: even if a being has gained access to waking up (a nondual state) and a higher structure of consciousness (greater complexity, care, and perspective taking), he or she can still be victim to unconscious motivations, desires, and attachment patterns that create deep suffering for themselves and others.

We often compare this to a bright and pure light shining through a dusty (and perhaps even broken) stained glass window. The light may be real and authentic (access to a deep state), and the colors and shapes on of the glass may be complex (operating through an advanced structure), but if the glass is covered in ash, very little of the light will be able to shine through. Through interpersonal relationship with a psychotherapist and with a community of other conscious practitioners, we can begin to uproot all of our unseen patterns and heal our deepest wounds. It becomes our duty to *clean up* in this way, not only for ourselves (for in the end we aren't even aware of the patterns) but rather for all those around us (for they bear the brunt of all of the unconscious and integrated aspects of our relative self).

Any map of human growth and development that fails to include all three of these dimensions (states, structures, shadow—or waking up, growing up, cleaning up) is falling short of a comprehensive, descriptive analysis of human growth. Anything less than an inclusion of these three dimensions exemplifies a model that is partial and incomplete. Partial models will, by their nature, create human beings who are lopsided, partial, and broken. The resulting potential human pain and suffering that can come from partial maps of reality cannot be overstated. We have an opportunity in front of us to get this right, as a species, for the benefit and health of the whole.

This more complete and comprehensive view of spirituality also allows us to understand otherwise paradoxical and contradictory tendencies in religion itself. Historically, it is likely that religion has been both the source of some of the highest, most elevated, ideal, loving, and noble inspirations ever advanced, and yet it has also been the single greatest source of warfare, torture, and murderous hatred on the planet. How can that be? The answer from this more complete meta-view of religion is straightforward: higher, loving, noble motivations come from religious adepts who are at a greater number of higher structures and higher states, and have less shadow elements; while those who—with the same surface religious beliefs—are at lower levels of spiritual development, and/or experience lower states, and/or possess many shadow elements, tend more readily and exclusively to produce prejudiced, ethnocentric, murderous, and hateful motivations.

Cross-cultural evidence strongly indicates that the higher the structures of growth in spiritual intelligence, and/or the higher the states in waking up, and/or the fewer shadow elements present, then the more loving, more truly spiritual, more conscious, and more caring an individual is. Further, given this more complete and comprehensive map of an overall spiritual development, humankind can—for the first time in history—actually plan its spiritual growth in a way that aims directly for the higher reaches of spiritual realization, while minimizing the more negative, hateful, and murderous tendencies of a global humanity—something that also represents a genuine first in history.

What Is a Deliberately Developmental Civilization?

In order to understand what we mean by the phrase *Deliberately Developmental Civilization*, it's helpful to first understand the source of the phrase "deliberately developmental."

Harvard Professor Robert Kegan, well-respected developmental psychologist, coined the term Deliberately Developmental Organization (DDO) in his book *An Everyone Culture* to explain the phenomena of organizations and business ventures that take a specific approach to growth that includes the development of each employee of the organization in addition to the ever-growing bottom line. Kegan's research was able to show that those organizations that included the development of the consciousness of each person in the organization outperformed the average organization (that ignored the development of each employee) resulting in not only higher profits but also an overall more satisfying work experience.

As the startling reality of this research began to settle in, the question naturally arose, "What would it look like if we took this type of evidence seriously and apply it to our global civilization as a whole?" Similar to the way that each of Kegan's organizations examined the development of the employee, "How would we structure society and what dimensions of growth might we include if we were to optimize the growth and transformation of every being on the planet?" And finally, "If it's possible to create a deliberately developmental organization, would it be possible to create a deliberately developmental civilization?" Although acknowledging other areas of growth, Kegan's research on DDOs gave maximum attention to developmental science and the advancement through structures of consciousness. Our approach to development, as we have seen, is a bit more wide-reaching.

With a more comprehensive understanding of the various types of development in place (the articulation of structures of consciousness through developmental science, the wisdom of states of consciousness as described in our world's great spiritual traditions, and the path of developmental healing and integration as expressed in Western psychotherapy and some of the world's indigenous traditions), we can examine the notion of a Deliberately Developmental Civilization with a bit more comprehensiveness than Kegan's original research with organizations.

In our view, a Deliberately Developmental Civilization enables human flourishing through waking up, growing up, and cleaning up (states, structures, shadow). By its very nature, a Deliberately Developmental Civilization continually draws from descriptive accounts from around the world so that it remains ever fresh and constantly reiterating what it means to be a "developed" human being. Ultimately, at its core, a Deliberately Developmental Civilization intentionally creates conveyor belts of transformation (through states, structures, and shadow) leading to a universal culture of the most awake, mature, and integrated human beings possible (which also means, least domineering, least oppressive, least murderous).

For Example

Since many people might not be aware of the actual nature of items such as "growing up," "waking up," and "cleaning up," allow us to give a brief and simplistic explanation of each, showing why each is so profoundly important.

A good deal of recent research has demonstrated that most spiritual systems have both an "explanatory" branch (which consists of belief systems and often mythic narratives that purport to explain the relation of the relative, temporal, finite world to an ultimate, infinite, absolute Ground of Being), and they possess an often more "esoteric," or "hidden," branch (consisting of direct experiences of a spiritual dimension through the practice of contemplation, meditation, vision quest, and so on). The former consists of *spiritual beliefs* about reality (via structures of consciousness in the Growing Up of spiritual intelligence); the latter consists of direct *spiritual experiences* (via immediate states of consciousness in Waking Up).

Thus, the explanatory branch, as a linguistic narrative, consists of various *structures* of consciousness (and so this branch is connected directly to the multiple line of spiritual intelligence; and this means that this branch is that part of spiritual engagement that involves the common six-to-eight stages of Growing Up—in this case, growing up in spiritual intelligence). These stages of spiritual intelligence, like the stages of all multiple lines or intelligences (recall: "different lines, same levels"), progress through those six-to-eight major levels, a very simplified version of which (involving just four basic levels of overall Growing Up) consists of stages or levels that move from "egocentric" (self-focused, or "me-only") to "ethnocentric" (group-focused or "us-versus-them," or the saved versus the damned) to "worldcentric" ("all of us," or all humans, regardless of race, color, sex, or creed) to "integral" (synthesizing all previous stages). We now have empirical studies (such as James Fowler's) showing that an individual's spiritual belief system goes through all of those structure-stages of development (or Growing Up in spiritual intelligence; and Fowler demonstrated, not just those simplified four stages, but the more standard six or seven stages). This is just part of the compelling body of evidence showing that all of a human being's multiple intelligences (including our spiritual intelligence) cross-culturally develop and unfold through those basic six-to-eight levels/structures—a crucial and profound discovery that is only, as we noted, around 100 years old (and hence much too recent to be included in any of the world's great wisdom traditions).

Instead, most of the world's great religions all arose during a period of human evolution that was almost exclusively at ethnocentric stages —so that each religion originally believed that it, and it alone, had the one true way to salvation (the "chosen path" and the "chosen peoples"). Even religions that produced, in their esoteric branch, experiences of major Waking Up or Enlightenment or Awakening, still were almost entirely patriarchal (or sexist), and they embraced slavery (or racism), and so on—that is, even though highly developed in Waking Up, they were still at ethnocentric and prejudiced stages in Growing Up. That's because, even though they were quite advanced in techniques of Waking Up, leading all the way to traditional "divine unity consciousness," that was not enough to help them develop to worldcentric stages of Growing Up (they were only at ethnocentric stages of Growing Up). Research has demonstrated that Waking Up and Growing Up are relatively independent, and since the great traditions were almost completely unaware of the structures of Growing Up, they had no way to know that, even though "Enlightened," they were still poorly developed in Growing Up stages.

(When the Western Enlightenment first emerged, it was marked by a belief in the "universal rights of humankind"—that is, it moved from an ethnocentric morals to a worldcentric morals—and for that reason it largely rejected the ethnocentric beliefs of the Church. But the Enlightenment, despite its name, had no path of Waking Up at all, only a major advance in the path of Growing Up, which, profound as it was, also marked the "death of God"—and not just God as an ethnocentric, mythic-literal belief structure, but also as a directly experienced Ground of Being—the so-called disaster of modernity. This integral view of development further allows us to see why these two major cultural worldviews—generally called "East" and "West"—both have something important to offer, as well as having a major lack. What is generally called the "West" is higher in Growing Up, but almost entirely lacking in Waking Up; and the "East" is high in Waking Up, but less advanced in Growing Up—and thus the long-sought integration of East and West is also an integration of Growing Up and Waking Up....)

So this is an example of the fact that an individual (or an entire culture) can be highly developed in one path of spiritual engagement and poorly developed in another (such as highly developed in Waking Up and poorly developed in Growing Up—or vice versa). So whereas it is common to hear in religious circles that all humanity needs today is to embrace a genuine spiritual oneness or unity consciousness in order for the world to be at peace, a more integral view demonstrates that what is actually needed is a development in BOTH Waking Up and Growing Up. Leaving either one of those out—as absolutely every spiritual system in the world now does—is to leave humans only partially whole, partially complete, partially ready for peace and a genuine worldwide love.

And the same goes for unintegrated shadow elements (and Cleaning Up). Especially in spiritual circles, where individuals strive to realize and achieve the most positive and noble characteristics possible, it is common to "spiritually bypass" dealing with shadow elements by not actually healing and transforming them, but simply denying and projecting them. The "other" person thus becomes the receptacle of all of an individual's (or an entire culture's) negative, "evil" qualities, and thereafter that individual is demonized—and, in times past, were likely to be burned, crucified, tortured, or killed. Only by re-owning and re-integrating shadow elements can such extremely negative human behavior be significantly reduced.

So perhaps we can start to see the profound problems that result when either Waking Up, or Growing Up, or Cleaning Up are not included. And since it is only recently that such a comprehensive meta-map of human potentials has become available, it is only recently that the true potentials of human spirituality have truly come to the fore—as well as a clear understanding and map of how the highly "negative" aspects of spirituality that have accompanied it all-too-many times in the past can henceforth be more effectively surmounted.

What's Next?

It is our sense that the time is ripe for the establishment of a Deliberately Developmental Civilization on our planet. And central to this endeavor would be an intentional and conscious unfolding of the higher, deeper, wider, and healthier stages of spirituality (attempting to grow and develop beyond the lower, narrower, shallower stages of spiritual development so strongly involved in negative, ethnocentric, hateful impulses— thus allowing the truest and highest nature of spirituality to shine forth in all humans).

If the prophecies of our world's great wisdom traditions are to have any meaning at all, the second coming of Christ will need to be resurrected in each of our hearts; the future Buddha will need to be expressed in all of us as a global *sangha* of spiritual awakening; through *Tikkun* the world must be healed; and the hidden Imam must reveal itself in the further reaches of our own potential. As Hindu visions for the future fulfill themselves and as the Kali Yuga comes to a close, giving way to an even brighter age, our task is to find our way back home to Source and to express that Source as the evolving edge of developmental complexity in the Kosmos. A Deliberately Developmental Civilization points us in the right direction. And, at least for now, nothing less than an integral approach will do.

⌘

Endnotes

1. Using a descriptive approach to articulate the transformative potential for humanity has several advantages. First, a descriptive approach allows us to frame our theory of spiritual transformation and human potential cross-culturally, based on invariant deep structures common to all human beings. This means that even as human beings continue to exist within their particular cultural, historical, and linguistic contexts, systematic cross-cultural analysis reveals that certain aspects of transformation follow an invariant and predictable developmental pattern. Second, a descriptive approach allows us to articulate a theory based upon clear developmental stage progressions without falling victim to normative claims. Because we draw upon insider views from various traditions, allowing each to remain complete within its particular cultural setting, then judging each within the world sphere that each considers legitimate, we circumvent both the modernist error known as the "myth of the given" while also honoring the important contribution of postmodernists who have brought attention to the important distinction between emic (insider) and edic (outsider) approaches to scholarship (Wilber's zones 3 and 4, respectively). Finally, a descriptive approach allows us to take a meta-perspective, organizing our shared human wisdom about transformation into broad categories that each share common characteristics.

2. See: Wilber, *Excerpt B: The Many Ways We Touch*; www.kenwilber.com.

3. Cross-culturally speaking, there have been initiation rites in native and indigenous cultures of the world for thousands of years. And it is true that each of these initiations mark a new stage in human growth and development. But these stages of initiation

are not the same as the structures of consciousness that we refer to here. Rather than simply referring to stages/ages of life, structures of consciousness represent entirely novel lenses through which one views the world.

4. These states are known variously as Enlightenment, Awakening, *Moksha*, the Great Liberation, *Satori*, Metamorphosis, and the Supreme Identity, among many others.

5. For a detailed look at "Waking Up," see DiPerna's book *Streams of Wisdom*; www.dustindiperna.com.

6. See: DiPerna's *Evolution's Ally* for an in-depth look at how structures of development show up in our world's religious traditions; www.dustindiperna.com.

Chapter 2

IN SEARCH OF THE PURPOSE OF BEING

Cosmic Insights for Enduring
Human Life on the Planet

Ervin Laszlo

To be, or not to be—that is the question:
Whether 'tis nobler in the mind to suffer
The slings and arrows of outrageous fortune
Or to take arms against a sea of troubles
And by opposing end them.

Hamlet's dilemma is not a true dilemma. It is not nobler to take arms against our sea of troubles and by opposing end them, because "not to be" is not an alternative granted to human beings—or to any living thing in the universe. "To be" is coded into every cell, every organ, even every quantum of our body; to oppose them is arbitrary and contrary to the laws of nature—which are also the laws of human nature, of our very existence.

To be is our destiny: it is why we are here. But what is served by our being here—by our being in the world? Hamlet didn't tell us, yet it is a major question. Is there a purpose for our being in the universe?

For science, purpose is a controversial concept. Some scientists deny that it is meaningful even to ask about it. The things we encounter in the universe, they say, are the product of random processes that occur without rhyme or reason. We are the products of such processes, and there is no higher or deeper purpose for our being here.

The mainstream science community is reluctant to accept purpose for the existence of things, because purpose suggests something higher or deeper in the universe, and scientists are not ready to accept that it exists. Physicist Steven Weinberg said,

> I believe there is no point that can be discovered by the methods of science. I believe what we have found so far—an impersonal universe which is not particularly directed toward human beings—is what we are going to find. And that when we find the ultimate laws of nature, they will have a chilling, cold, impersonal quality about them.[1]

Mainstream scientists hold that the universe is the product of a long chain of random interactions. Physicist Nassim Haramein pointed out,

> The fundamental axioms and basic assumptions at the root of physical theories...presume that evolutionary systems emerge from random interactions initiated by a single "miraculous" event providing all of the appropriate conditions to produce our current observable universe, and our state of existence in it. This event, typically described as a "Big Bang," astonishingly is thought to have produced all of the forces and constants of physical law and eventually biological interactions under random functions.[2]

If the universe is a product of random interactions, things in the universe merely happen, without a meaning or purpose for their happening. This assumption, however, is not correct. It turns out that the universe is not the product of random interactions, and the things we find in the universe are not produced by random interactions.

A Coherent Universe

In the middle of the twentieth century, Sir Arthur Eddington and Paul Dirac noted curious coincidences in regard to the physical parameters of the universe. The ratio of the electric force to the gravitational force is known: it is approximately 10^{40}. This is an enormous number, but it is nearly the same as that which defines the ratio between the size of the whole universe and the size of the minute quantum particles that appear in it. This is surprising, since the ratio of the electric force to the gravitational force should be unchanging (given that these forces are constant); whereas, the ratio of the size of the universe to the size of elementary particles should be changing (since the universe is expanding). In his "large number hypothesis," Dirac speculated that the agreement between these ratios, one variable and the other not, is more than random coincidence. But if so, either the universe is not expanding, or the force of gravitation varies proportionately to its expansion.

Later cosmologist Menas Kafatos showed that many of the ratios among the parameters of the universe can be interpreted on the one hand in terms of the relationship between the masses of elementary particles and the total number of nucleons, and on the other in reference to the relationship between the gravitational constant, the charge of the electron, Planck's constant, and the speed of light.

The mass of elementary particles, the number of particles, and the forces between them display harmonic ratios. Also the microwave background radiation—the remnant of the Big Bang—is likewise coherent: it is dominated by a large peak followed by smaller harmonic peaks. The series of peaks ends at the longest wavelength physicist Lee Smolin termed R. When R is divided by the speed of light (R/C), we get the length of time independent estimates have shown to be the age of the universe. When we divide in turn the speed of light by the constant R (c/R), we get a frequency that equates to one cycle over the age of the universe. And when R is squared and divided by the speed of light (R^2/c) we get the rate of acceleration in the expansion of the galaxies.

The parameters of the universe are precisely coordinated: variations of the order of one-billionth of the value of some constants (such as the mass of elementary particles, the speed of light, the rate of expansion of galaxies, and some two dozen others) would not have produced a universe where atoms are sufficiently stable to produce enduring combinations, the basis of the phenomena that furnish our everyday world. The universe is far from being the product of random interactions. Its parameters are finely tuned to one another, and together are coherent with its overall dimensions. It is extremely improbable that such "coincidences" would occur in a random universe. It is extremely improbable that this universe would be the product of a chain of random interactions.

A World of Coherent Systems

The physical universe is not only highly coherent as a whole—also, highly coherent systems have evolved in it. This cannot be the product of chance. The large number hypothesis—that in a large ensemble of events even improbable events have a non-negligibility probability of coming about—cannot account for the findings: the search-space of the possible configuration of the elements that make up complex chemical, biochemical, and biological systems is so vast, that processes of random trial-and-error would have far exceeded the available time frames.

Biological systems are extraordinarily coherent. The human body, for example, is made up of 10^{14} cells, and each cell produces 10,000 bio-electrochemical reactions every second. Every twenty-four hours 10^{12} cells die and are replaced. Molecules, cells, and organ-systems resonate at the same or at compatible frequencies and interact at various speeds, ranging from the slow (among hormones and peripheral nerve fibers), to the very fast (along the Ranvier rings of myelin-shielded nerves). The interactions are precisely correlated, involving quantum-type "entanglements" in addition to classical physical-chemical interactions.

The evolution of coherent systems began with the emergence of quantum particles in the wake of the Big Bang 13.8 billion years ago, and the evolution of organic systems began on this planet with molecular assemblies in the hot springs of the primeval ocean four billion years before our time. These time frames, although enormous, are insufficient to explain the evolution of complex and coherent systems. The probability that even the simplest biological organisms would have come about through a random shuffling of their elements is negligible. The DNA-mRNA-tRNA-rRNA transcription and translation system, basic to living systems, is so complex and precise that it is astronomically improbable that biological organisms could have evolved through a chance combination of their genes. A random mixing of the genes of the common fruit fly would take longer than the age of the universe to come up with the DNA of that fly. According to Fred Hoyle, the probability that new species would emerge through a chance mutation of their genes is comparable to the probability of a hurricane blowing through a scrapyard assembling a working airplane.

The coherence displayed by the parameters of the universe, as well as by the structure and processes of the systems that emerge in it, are not the products of random interactions. The finding of coherence in both the universe and on Earth suggests that evolution in nature is selective and goal-directed. It is oriented toward the creation of systems of otherwise entirely improbable forms and levels of coherence.

The Intelligence of the Cosmos

The coherence of the universe, and of systems in the universe, cannot be the result of chance. But if not to serendipity, to what does the coherence of the universe owe its existence?

A coherent universe with coherence-oriented systems suggests the presence of a factor that biases the randomness of the play of interactions. This factor can be seen as a law, rule, or instruction orienting processes in a specific direction. What scientists know as the "laws of nature" are such instructions.

The laws of nature prove to be instructions for building coherent systems. The crucial instruction is the law in physics called the Pauli Exclusion Principle. The principle states that no two electrons orbiting the nucleus of an atom can be at the same quantum state at the same time.

Electrons entering the gravitational zone of the nucleus are excluded from orbits that are already occupied and are distributed into other orbits, filling up the energy shells that surround the nucleus. Due to their exclusion, the particles captured by the gravitational field of the nucleus assemble into coherent and complex structures. As a result the physical world is not a heap or conglomeration of particles, but a domain of coherent systems. It is built of the atoms that populate the periodic table of the elements, and of the structures that form as the atoms bond with each other in molecules and crystals. Molecules in turn form multimolecular structures, and these are templates for still more complex chemical and biological systems.

Other laws of nature join the Exclusion Principle in making the universe into a domain of coherent systems. Complex systems are fractal (self-similar) ensembles of cooperative parts. They embody long-range interactions that optimize connection among their elements, safeguarding and enhancing coherence through resonant relations among the parts. All parts of the systems are coherently coordinated to maintain the system in the living state. The laws of nature make for the emergence of highly coordinated ensembles of elements, highly coordinated with their environment.

The laws of nature are extremely finely tuned to producing coherence; they cannot be the products of chance. They are not here by accident. But if so, are they here on purpose? **Purpose by whom, or by what?**

Here we need to take recourse again to the idea of a higher intelligence in the universe. More and more scientists are endorsing this formerly spiritual insight. In one of his last lectures in Florence, Max Planck said, "As a man who has devoted his whole life to the most clear-headed science, to the study of matter, I can tell you as a result of my research about atoms this much: there is no matter as such. All matter originates and exists only by virtue of a force which brings the particle of an atom to vibration and holds this most minute solar system of the atom together." Behind the force that holds the particles of atoms together, Planck said, "we must assume the existence of a conscious and intelligent mind." The essentially same idea has been expressed by scores of scientists, including Einstein who said that to know the laws of nature is to read the mind of God.3

Recently Deepak Chopra and Menas Kafatos joined the groups

of scientists who attribute the laws of nature to a cosmic consciousness. Chopra and Kafatos group the coherence-creating laws under headings such as:

> *Complementarity.* Positive and negative, yin and yang—as all opposites—balance each other without abolishing or diminishing one another.

> *Creative interactivity.* As diverse elements interact, not just more of the same results; new forms and functions come into existence.

> *Evolution.* The old is the basis for creating the new, and when the new is created, it integrates the old without destroying or neutralizing it.

> *Veiled nonlocality.* Locally separate things and events are nonlocally joined together at a deeper and less evident level.

> *Cosmic censorship.* Everything is connected with every-thing else, yet local perspectives remain valid: the interconnections of the whole are kept from view.

> *Recursion.* All parts and elements of the whole share patterns and forms that mirror and repeat each other at successively deeper levels.4

Thanks to the action of these and related laws, evolution in nature builds physical entities into physicochemical structures, and these into more complex biological and ecological systems. This is a nonrandom process, and it exhibits purpose. The new, or rather merely rediscovered insight of a higher intelligence at work in nature allows us to entertain the notion that purpose is a real and fundamental phenomenon in the universe.

The Purpose of Evolution

If we recognize that evolution points to purpose, and accept the proposition that purpose is a legitimate presence in the universe, we can proceed to the next question: what is the nature of the purpose that underlies evolution?

We can seek an answer to this question by observing the direction in which evolutionary processes unfold. Such processes are at least partially irreversible, and their irreversible unfolding points in a particular direction. The direction in which they point suggests the nature of their purpose.

Evolution seems oriented toward creating systems that attain, maintain, and optimize intrinsic and extrinsic coherence. Intrinsic coherence is the responsiveness of each element in the system to every other element, whereas extrinsic coherence is the responsiveness of the system as a whole to other systems in its surroundings (and ultimately to the rest of the universe). Systems of optimal intrinsic and extrinsic coherence appear to be the goal of the processes of evolution. In the long term, the systems tend toward optimal intrinsic and extrinsic coherence: toward *supercoherence*. Supercoherence appears to be the ultimate goal of evolution on Earth and in the universe.

The above notion accords with time-honored Eastern ideas of harmony in cosmos and society, expressed in the philosophies of the Tao and in various forms of Buddhism. It matches, confirms, and elaborates the theories of a number of Western philosophers. Hegel, for example, said that the goal of evolution is the unity of mind, spirit, and consciousness achieved by a progression from primitive sensory perception toward absolute knowledge. Teilhard de Chardin identified an Omega Point of evolution where all elements fuse into a higher unity, and Jean Gebser described an entire complex architecture of goal-states informed by a mystical force he termed "the Origin."

Guidance for Our Time

If supercoherence is the ultimate goal of evolution, we and our world are far from reaching it, and even from setting out toward it.

Living and acting in accordance with the aim to reach a higher level of coherence calls for major changes in contemporary societies. In the course of the last one hundred or one hundred and fifty years, we have divorced ourselves from the rhythms and dynamics of nature. Our interests and aspirations center on maximizing narrowly conceived self-interests, disregarding the ties that bind us to each other and to the systems of life. These ties are merely the background; the foreground is occupied by our own existence, our own nation, or our own economy and business company. The popular youth-cultures instinctively seek closer ties to nature and to each other, voicing aspirations for oneness and love. But the mainstream cultures ignore the patterns of evolution in the world. They fragment our ties with each other and with the web of life. This produces unsustainability in the contemporary world, with growing stress and crises. The eruption of terrorism and war are consequences of our diminished coherence, and with it our impaired health and viability.

The current level of fragmentation of the system of life on the planet is a recent phenomenon. Until the dawn of the modern age most societies were significantly coherent both within their own structures, and with their environment. They fought each other, but did not threaten the integrity of the system of which they were a part. Today powerful subsystems in the human world act as if they were independent entities, and their competition for people, power, and resources endangers the integrity of the system of life. Today, the human community has lost its life-sustaining intrinsic and extrinsic coherence. The question is whether it can recover it.

...To Conclude

The discovery of the existence of purpose in the world, and of the nature of that purpose, offers timely guideposts for thinking and acting. We have wandered far from the coherence that characterizes viable systems in nature; we need to return to alignment with the rhythms and processes of the universe. This is not an arbitrary aspiration, but a basic imperative of our continued existence.

Purpose in the universe is a universal truth as well as a source of practical guidance. Its exploration, and the articulation of its implications for human life have become a precondition of setting forth the adventure of our species on this planet.

❧

Endnotes

1. Interview reported in Ervin Laszlo, *Science and the Akashic Field*, Rochester, VT 2007.

2. Comment by Nassim Haramein, in Ervin Laszlo with Alexander Laszlo, *What Is Reality? The New Map of Cosmos and Consciousness*. New York, 2016.

. *Das Wesen der Materie (The Nature of Matter)*, speech in Florence, Italy, 1944. Archiv zur Geschichte der Max Planck Gesellschaft, Abt. Va, Rep. 11 Planck, Nr. 1797.

3. This development is explored in more detail in Ervin Laszlo, *The Intelligence of the Cosmos*. Rochester, VT, 2017.

4. Deepak Chopra and Menas Kafatos, *You Are the Universe*. Harmony Books, New York, 2016.

Chapter 3

DISCOVERING PURPOSE
Soulwork and the Purpose Octagon

Jonathan Gustin

*Purpose denotes your soul's deep calling, the place
to which you belong and your primary reason for incarnating.*

How does one discover and embody their unique life purpose? The subject of life purpose is addressed here in light of the following: 1) There are three distinct purposes: to Wake Up, Grow Up, And Show Up,1 2) A person is born with a unique purpose that is best understood in the context of their soul, 3) The key to becoming clear about life purpose is engaging in soulwork, 4) Several forces work against purpose discovery and require attention, and 5) Eight facets comprise a unique soul-level purpose: known as a person's "Purpose Octagon."

PART 1 – Three Worlds, One Life

Through multiple roles I have played in my career—which include psychotherapist, meditation teacher, and purpose guide—I have observed firsthand how the goals of each of these wisdom streams differ. I've also come to the conclusion that the missing piece in both spirituality and psychology is a recognition of the importance of purpose. Unlike psychotherapy, which promotes healing and growth at the level of the ego-personality, and unlike meditation, which emphasizes resting as unbounded awareness, a purpose guide helps the client identify what he or she is here to do in this lifetime.

In many forms of meditation, one inquires, "Who am I?" In psychotherapy, one investigates "How do I heal and become happier?" In soulwork, one explores "What is it you plan to do with your one wild and precious life?"2 None of these inquiries yields its bounty easily. Yet, years of careful cultivation can produce robust results in each of these endeavors: enlightenment (the fruit of meditation); emotional adulthood (the fruit of therapy); and purposiveness (the fruit of soulwork)—that is, the discovery and expression of your unique purpose, the place "where your deep gladness and the world's deep hunger meet."3 (Note: soul will be defined in Part 2, and soulwork will be defined in Part 3.)

Each of these three paths constitutes what I like to call a whole *world* of human development, with each world having its own purpose. Drawing upon ancient Greek, Sufi, and shamanic cosmologies, we can refer to these three spheres as the Upperworld (nirvana, heaven, enlightenment), Middleworld (emotional adulthood) and Lowerworld (soul-purpose embodiment). Table 1 presents the three worlds and their specific inquiries, desires, paths, foci, and goals. (Note: please see the last note of this essay, *Disambiguation of the Three Worlds Map*, for two additional renderings of the map.) A different world comes into view depending upon where we rest our attention.

(handwritten margin note: Mary Oliver)

Inquiry	Desire	Path	Focus	Fruition	World
Who am I?	Wake up	Meditation	Awareness rests as Spirit	Enlightenment	Upperworld
How do I heal and become happier?	Grow up	Therapy	Awareness rests as Ego	Emotional Adulthood	Middleworld
How do I bring my gifts to my people?	Show up	Soulwork	Awareness rests as Soul	Soul-Purpose Embodiment	Lowerworld

Table 1: Three Worlds Graph

Upperworld

A different world comes into view depending upon where we focus our attention. When a meditator rests their attention upon awareness itself, he or she experiences *being* pure consciousness (which in this essay I'll usually refer to as unbounded nondual awareness). Because a taste of this awareness offers a taste of primordial freedom itself, such "upperworld awakening" (aka, traditional enlightenment) has often been regarded as the ultimate purpose of life. Indeed, there are numerous monasteries that have been filled for centuries with individuals who regard upperworld enlightenment as the primary goal of their lives.

"Waking up" in this context refers to awakening *out of* an exclusive identification with the ego/personality, and *into* unbounded awareness. To be more precise, we actually wake up *as* unbounded awareness, not *into* it. However, such awareness is *not* disembodied or ungrounded. True unbounded awakening *includes* unitive intimacy with all of creation.

A valuable synergy exists between upperworld/meditative practice and soulwork. Transcendence of discursive mind through meditative awareness has the effect of loosening the grip of the ego. This loosening aids in both the realization of spirit and the realization of soul-purpose. In both meditation and soulwork, a narrowing or softening of boundaries occurs between one's conventional self and the "other" (Spirit or soul).

Middleworld

Through psychotherapy, or what I sometimes call ego work, we bring our unclaimed parts into the fold, the shadow into the light, the unconscious into consciousness. When awareness dwells with curiosity upon our everyday personality in *traditional psychotherapy*,4 we might successfully integrate the various facets of our selves. Sustained therapeutic attention can spur us into a (mostly) stable emotional adulthood—a psychic space where we can give and receive love without undue difficulty and rest in a quiet confidence and self-possession. Middleworld work is inherently relational—both intrapsychic (between parts of the ego-personality) and interpersonal (between two or more people).

What is the connection between ego work and soulwork? The purpose for which we are born to, often lies buried under the weight of the ego's frantic efforts to obtain acceptance, love, approval and appreciation. Psychotherapy allows us to grow into emotional adulthood, which increases our capability for receiving and trusting the messages that comes from soul. When a person excavates the ego out from everything the ego thought it needed, that person is left with who he is meant to be.

Lowerworld

When awareness turns toward the soul, a rich *imaginal realm*5 of inborn archetypal figures opens up, enabling soul encounter6—a glimpse of your deep purpose. Imaginal/archetypal figures can show up as visual images, but also as a *felt sense* of purpose, where the body lights up with and aligns to our sense of purpose. Here in the lowerworld, awareness isn't concerned with unbounded nondual awareness, nor is it focused on the maturation of the ego. Instead, attention can be mysteriously drawn to your *mythopoetic identity*7: the soul-level narrative that wants to live through us and as us. Mythopoetic identity transcends common identities regarding gender, race and class. The term refers to our innate ability for myth-making (storytelling) that is generated from our depths. These personal myths arise from soul instead of being fabricated by the ego. A mythopoetic narrative is awakened when we recognize the deepest conversation we can have with life, and then live accordingly. The ego is transformed by the soul's narrative/story, resulting in a soul-infused personality. In this way, living our life purpose is an expression of the ego's realization of the soul. Answering the question of how we can attain such a realization will be the focus of the remainder of this essay. What we are building toward in this essay is the opportunity we each have to discover our eight facets of our life purpose, our unique purpose octagon. Because of the increasing threat we pose to all life (including our own species), now more than ever, all life on this planet needs a humanity that is awake to its individual and collective purpose.

Please note, that the three worlds model outlined above represents a *simplified map* of human consciousness. As such, it necessarily creates walls where none exist. For instance, the term "growing up" in *some* schools of psychology (notably Carl Jung's depth psychology and James Hillman's archetypal psychology) includes both egoic health and the journey to the soul. From the perspective of these psychological approaches, "growing up" addresses levels of maturation beyond the well-adjusted personality. It includes becoming capable of a deep and sustained attention to the inquiries of Spirit (Upperworld) and Soul (Lowerworld).

However, in this simplified three worlds map, the term "growing up" refers exclusively to Middleworld health and wholeness (aka, the maturation of the ego). At the same time my intention isn't to forward the notion that these three pathways do not overlap with one another. Rather, it is to differentiate the fields of purpose guiding, meditation, and psychotherapy, and distinguish their most elemental inquiries. I hope to clear a conceptual space where one may contemplate the questions of soul-purpose discovery without having to simultaneously work with the rather different questions associated with emotional health and enlightenment.

World Fixation

It is possible to shift attention, moment-to-moment, among the triple purposes of life. But even with this capacity to move easily among the three worlds, humans have a proclivity for becoming stuck within a single world of purpose (wake up, grow up, show up). *World fixation*8 occurs when

43

awareness focuses more or less exclusively on only one of three dimensions. Such a fixation can be understood metaphorically as having an excessive attachment to a particular topography: peaks, valleys, or plains. The transcendent *peak* represents a (disembodied) enlightenment; the depth of the underworld *valley* represents soul-purpose, and the Middleworld of daily life is the vast *plain* upon which we live (in the guise of our everyday personality/ego). (Note: Full Awakening isn't separate from anything; therefore, enlightenment isn't just the peak, it's the *suchness* of the mountain, valleys, and plains. See the endnotes for a deeper discussion on this point.)

Imagine building your home in one of these locations and rarely (if ever) exploring the other two regions. The danger of world fixation is a life spent neglecting the other dimensions of our being. A world-fixated person can become lost in the ego, or addicted to an unembodied experience of Unbounded Awareness, or consumed solely with expressing one's life purpose.

The opportunity before us is to become integrally awakened to our purpose in each world. We can roam freely among the three topographies of awareness so we wake up, grow up, and show up as part of one seamless life. In other words: we are invited to inhabit **three worlds in one life.**

PART 2 - What Is the Soul?

Soul is the part of you that whispers your true name: the story of your incarnation, your personal myth, the poetry of your life narrative and destiny... in other words, your mythopoetic identity. Soul is the essence of your specific life purpose. Soul isn't something other or different than yourself. But, from the perspective of the ego, soul can be contemplated or sensed as a deeper presence within. Soul is the mystery taking a unique human journey. Soul is the creative intelligence and imagination of a living universe expressing itself through you. Soul is the body of your gift that fills up the garment of your life. Soul is the part of you that communicates through (and as) the imaginal realm. Soul is one's *place*: one's unique niche in the habitat of the ecology of life. Soul is the source of your dream for an evolved world. Soul is the mythmaker and narrative spinner.

Alluring and complex, the soul is rich with layers of subtle meaning.

While honoring the theological dimensions of soul, this essay promotes a definition of soul closer to that of depth psychologists, especially C.G. Jung, James Hillman, Bill Plotkin, and Sufi scholar Henri Corbin. Based on these sources, as well as my own clinical experience and life experience, I believe the three key features of soul pertaining to life purpose are perception, imagination, and place.

Soul as perception. Soul is not an object or an entity, but a unique faculty of perceiving based on imagination, images, stories, sensations and symbols. We sense and perceive through the body and mind, but it is our soul that gives us a third way of knowing: deep imagination (that is sometimes connected to kinesthetic sensing, and sometimes deep imagination shows up as kinesthetic sensing). In Sufism, soul is sometimes referred to as a (subtle) "organ" of perception. While somatic sensitivity and intellectual contemplation support soul discovery, neither of these activities is able to constitute the foundation of our life purpose. The soul serves as the medium by which perception of purpose is made possible. Soul, more verb than noun, offers a unique way of looking at life. Soul as rich imaginal perceiving is the soil from which a deeply meaningful life sprouts. The soul directs us toward the aliveness, depth, and sacredness of our purpose. Many of our (especially profound) dreams can be thought of as originating from a subtle realm (or subtle body) of the imaginal/soul realm.

Soul as imagination. C.G. Jung sometimes employed the German word *seelenbild*, a composite term meaning "soul-image." Whereas the mind "sees" with thoughts, soul conveys its truth through images, symbols, and sensations that arise in awareness but are not sourced from the conscious intellect. According to James Hillman, "We are not dealing with something that can be defined; and therefore soul is really not a concept, but a *symbol*."9 Soul is a symbol for the place from which deep meaning issues forth into one's life. In this sense, soul can be seen as a *root metaphor*—a metaphorical story that shapes an individual's perception and interpretation of the world from a depth perspective.

Hillman writes, "By *soul* I mean the imaginative possibilities of our natures, the experiencing through reflective speculation, dream, image, and fantasy—that mode which recognizes all realities as primarily symbolic or metaphorical.10 Soul is a manner or mode of being (as in "His saxophone playing was especially soulful tonight"). Soul is a foundational myth from which we live our lives. Soul is a *first principle*—the creation story of our incarnation. Soul is the wondrous, mysterious wellspring of our ability to imagine and actualize our calling and destiny.

Soul as place. In his seminal book *Soulcraft*, Bill Plotkin writes, "Your soul is your true nature. Your soul can also be thought of as our true place *in* nature... At the level of soul, you have a specific way of belonging to the biosphere, as unique as any maple, moose or mountain."11 From a nondual perspective, soul isn't your true nature; it is an *expression* of your true nature, not the source itself. Still, Plotkin's words point to something important, that at a relative level, soul is the true nature of your unique self. Plotkin also offers a profound insight into the relationship between soul and place by employing the term *niche* in a novel way. A niche is the smallest unit of a habitat. A habitat is the physical space occupied by an ecosystem of plants and animals. A niche is the role the plant or animal plays in the community found in the habitat. For example, a giraffe's habitat is the savannah, and its niche consists of feeding on the canopy of trees. A squirrel's habitat is the forest and its niche includes eating acorns.

A person's niche is their soul level gift to the world. The habitat is the place in which the gift is offered. Plotkin writes, "Your soul is both of *you* and of the *world*. The world cannot be full until you become fully yourself. Your soul corresponds to a niche, a distinctive place in nature, like a vibrant space of shimmering potential waiting to be discovered, claimed... occupied."12

You are *of* a unique time and place. These external factors are not incidental to discovering your purpose. You belong to your soul's purpose, not in a decontextualized vacuum, but as influenced by the time and place in which you exist. It behooves us all to consider soul as rooted *in* the world. Modern people tend to feel uprooted given their unprecedented mobility. According to spiritual activist Stephen Jenkinson, "We are orphans when we aren't connected to the ground... Indigenosity isn't racial, it's about place. Indigenous humans have a place-based identity, and realize that *place* is our fundamental mother... Belonging (to a place) is the antidote to desire."13

Humanity's insatiable cycle of desiring is inevitable when we experience fundamental dislocation from our place (as well as from our true nature). The cessation of incessant desiring lies (in part) in the quenching of one of our primary desires: a longing to *belong*. Belonging to a community, to the planet, to life itself is found (in part) through the intimate and nourishing experience of place, the niche you were born to serve by embodying your soul's deep purpose.

Identifying soul as the seat of purpose helps lift the burden from the ego of having to discern one's destiny and calling. Once we've relieved the ego from the heavy lifting of purpose discovery, we can now focus on *what it is* that knows, inspires, holds, and supports the unfolding of our life purpose. With soul as we've just defined it, we may conclude the following: awakening to soul (through symbols, images, stories, and sensation) is *awakening to our innate imaginal perception that allows us to assume our place in the ecology of life*. When soul is understood in this way, a doorway is opened that gives us access to the knowledge of our purpose and then how to live it.

PART 3 - Soulwork

E ngagement with soulwork provides the key to becoming clear about your life purpose. Soulwork is a descent into your deep, mysterious interior. Soulwork is initiated by your longing to live a larger life and by the desire to make the world a better place. Soulwork gathers momentum through your willingness to receive your soul's guidance, rather than letting your egoic thinking dictate all your choices. Soulwork isn't a problem to be solved. Soulwork includes the process of winnowing out those symbols, images, or narratives that have grown too small to contain your life. Soulwork is the willingness to let the truth you think you know go to ruin. Soulwork is the profound act of letting your life speak.

Soulwork is a key to the embodiment of the wholeness that lies beyond enlightenment and emotional adulthood. Soulwork uncovers one's authentic place and the gift of service you were born for. Of course, there are other aims in life: the foundational desires for security, comfort, esteem, and love (our middleworld needs) that usually require attention before the spiritual inquiry into the soul's purpose can take center stage. Once those needs are at least partially met, we can inquire "What does soul ask of me?" and be guided toward finding a purpose-beyond-self.

How then do we approach soulwork? Would employing an astrologer or a psychic be considered soulwork? Would consulting the I Ching or finding our place on the Enneagram qualify as soulwork? Could some forms of psychotherapy be considered soulwork? How does one go about seeking one's purpose-beyond-self?

The approach to soulwork favored in this essay includes exploring our deep imagination as well as the engagement with the natural world for glimpses of our purpose. Soulwork practices act upon the border between ego and soul. Soulwork actually *thins* the boundary between ego and soul, allowing you to receive the images and symbols of your purpose into awareness through meditation, active imagination, prayer, and so on. Soulwork is the candle illuminating your calling that reveals your unique place and contribution.

Upon the canvas of your soul, the Mystery has inscribed with invisible ink your mythopoetic identity—the sacred narrative or destiny of your life. Soulwork makes the invisible visible. Soulwork technologies include a variety of forms of dreamwork, active imagination (aka Jungian journaling), prayer, trance drumming (aka journey work), the vision quest ceremony, and guided soulcentric meditations.14 All of these are essentially dialogues between you (as ego) and soul. Just as you can communicate with a friend through speech, gestures, mail, or phone; so too in the case of soulwork, you can communicate through a variety of methods.

PART 4 - Forces Working Against Soulwork

As stated earlier, from a soul-level perspective, one is connected to a certain *place* and occupies a particular *niche*. We feel displaced when we experience feeling disconnected from the physical location we inhabit. A parallel dislocation happens when we feel disconnected from our soul-level purpose. The persistent tug at the center of one's being is not only caused by the usual suspects (such as money, power, fame, comfort, security), or by the desire for transcendence or enlightenment—the ache stems from the longing to live in accordance with one's own purpose.

Many of us feel alienated from ourselves at a soul-level; that is, disconnected from the gifts we were meant to give. We come into adulthood knowing that we want to contribute, but not knowing where we fit in. We feel the energy of devotion and dedication, but can't quite make out what the object of that devotion is supposed to be. We want to inhabit our place (where we give our gifts) and, because we are narrative creatures, we also want to be able to describe it.

Why, then, do so many people with adequate security and comfort tend to neglect taking bold steps to discover their purpose? And, for those who do ask the bold questions, what prevents them from finding the answers?

To address this, one must consider the following forces that can impede soulwork:

Default purpose. There is a "substitute purpose" that moves our life forward when we are not living from our soul's purpose. It is best understood as our *default purpose*, which I define as a combination of bequeathed values from our upbringing and the defensive psychological positions we learn during childhood.

exterior conditioning + interior defenses = default purpose

Default purpose consists of a life script or schema usually inherited from our families and culture. This inheritance, acquired when young, often lies outside our conscious awareness, resulting in life scripts that lie partly in the shadow of our psyches. Your family has a vested interest in seeing you fulfill their purpose—instead of your own soul's purpose.

Failing to investigate the inherited, unconscious parts of our default purposes may stymie progress in discovering one's true purpose. Even when default purposes become conscious, they may end up seriously undermining purpose-discovery work due to the strong attachments we've developed to them. Other times, a purpose is *consciously chosen* (i.e., "I want to be a parent"), but then is partially outgrown (our child goes off to college). If it isn't updated, this chosen purpose can degrade into a default purpose. Many such empty nesters fail to choose another purpose-beyond-self to replace parenting.

Thus, while everyone is living purposefully (through the vehicle of a default purpose or carefully chosen purpose), *not everyone is living their soul's purpose.*

We live in a soul-illiterate culture. Few of us grew up with elders who sat us down and told us this open secret, "You have a mighty purpose, that when lived well, will bring you great joy and will serve your people too." If you didn't get this message (and few of us did), you can rectify this deficit by seeking a supportive soulcentric community.

Reasons to seek a soul-literate community, or what I like to call a soul-sangha, include the following: First, we need guidance to learn techniques of soul encounter, as neither family, school, or even religious traditions will provide the purpose-discovery technologies mentioned previously. Second, we benefit from associating with groups or guides that aid in understanding what we've learned from our dialogues with soul. Third, we'll need social and moral support to courageously live the truth of what we've learned about our purpose. A soul-sangha or a purpose community is essential for these things to occur. The journey to living our purpose is not usually a quick, easy, or a comfortable endeavor. The journey takes place on untrodden pathways—at least to us! It is best to seek community among those who are consciously working on embodying their soul's purpose.

Competing commitments. When you wake up in the morning, you might experience the following competing commitments. Commitment #1: The sleepyhead says, "I want to stay in this warm comfortable bed." Commitment #2: The responsible voice says, "Let's get going and plunge into the day." Which part to listen to?

This same dynamic arises regarding purpose discovery. One voice wants to embody your life purpose, while the other voice offers its legitimate fears regarding purpose discovery. Such concerns include: "Will I like my purpose?" "Am I worthy of my purpose?" "Is it safe to live my purpose out in the open?" "Will living my purpose cause me to go broke or lose important relationships?" I have heard these exact phrases from many people over my twenty years of purpose guiding.

There are facets of our ego-personality (referred to as "parts" or "subpersonalities") that resist soul encounter. These hidden parts of the ego include our *internal* Protector, Controller, People-pleaser, Chameleon, Skeptic, Critic, and Image Consultant.15 Each of these "voices" express a prior commitment to a particular concern, which will often compete with your commitment to soulwork. Understandably, these facets or subpersonalities experience trepidations about having us step onto the purpose-discovery path. The key to addressing these voices lies in *dialoguing* with them in ways that produce a win-win. Think of this as a form of relationship counseling for your ego's subpersonalities, which involves improving communication between the part that wants to know our purpose, and the part that fears purpose discovery. Intrapsychic multiple agendas (regarding purpose) are as common as interpersonal multiple agendas in a relationship. A skilled purpose guide can help clients with their competing internal commitments, thereby clearing the way for soul and ego to communicate freely and work as partners.

Now that we've laid out a purpose map, let's take the journey into what it feels like to know, to *really know* your purpose. Let's explore this question through the lens of what I call the Purpose Octagon.

PART 5 - The Purpose Octagon

An eight-facet purpose vocabulary.

Purpose is the indispensable concept, informing us about the way something *fits* into the world. Purpose, at the level of the human soul, is simply the reason that an individual exists to serve life. Each of us is called to the *universal purpose* of bringing more Goodness, Truth, and Beauty into the world. Within that, we are called to a unique purpose, our soul's signature offering.

I use the word *purpose* as the blanket term to denote our intended design, our soul's deep calling, the place to which we belong and our primary reason for incarnating. Yet, we could bring more precision to the inquiry of purpose if we enlarged our purpose vocabulary. For example, let's use the life of the Rev. Martin Luther King Jr. as an example.

Universal: King's purpose was to bring Goodness, Truth, and Beauty into the world.

Unique: His unique purpose was to transform America into a place where social justice could be a reality.

Specific: King fulfilled his *task* of inspiring humanity to have the courage to love and bringing civil rights to African ,Americans through the *message* "all people are created equal." He did so by employing the *gift* of oratory, and through *delivery systems* including the roles of minister, activist, speaker, and leader.

All three of these constitute King's purpose, as seen from three different perspectives. They are connected holonically 16 (a *holon* is something that is simultaneously a whole and a part, as in: an atom is a whole atom and part of a molecule, that is part of a whole cell, that is part of a whole organ, etc.). Thus, these layers are not separate/discrete purposes, but *nested purposes*, each a part of the others like a set of Russian nesting dolls as in Figure 1:

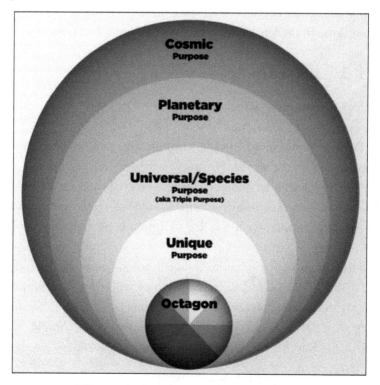

Figure 1: Wavelengths of Purpose

Let's flesh out Figure 2. Imagine the Universal Purpose of humanity as an ocean. Now visualize this ocean of purpose funneled through a pipe. The individual stream (from the pipe) represents your individual purpose. Now, imagine your stream flowing through a *purpose colander* with eight perforations, your eight-part specific purpose. These eight perforations (the Octagon) constitute the unique facets or features of your purpose. We can represent these dimensions of your soul's purpose using wavelengths of light instead of water as shown in Figure 2:

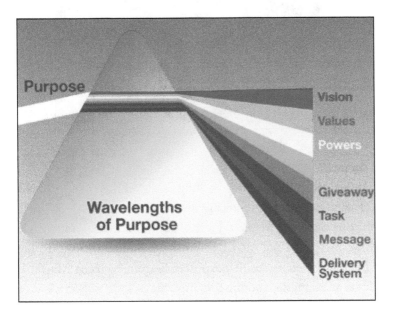

Figure 2: Wavelengths of Purpose

Through decades of working as a purpose guide, I've come to realize there are multiple facets of purpose, which I have now mapped onto an octagon. The core or hub of your purpose lies at the center of the Octagon; that is, your "Soul Image," or "Mythopoetic Identity." See Figure 3 (next page):

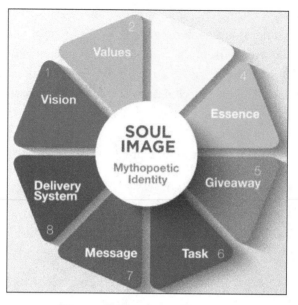

Figure 3: Purpose Octagon

To live your unique purpose fully, you will want to engage all eight facets of your calling. The following sections illustrate the multifaceted nature of your purpose. At the outset, please note that these facets unfold over time; they need not bloom instantly or simultaneously. To help describe the eight dimensions of purpose, I'll again be using Martin Luther King Jr. as an example, quoting him directly.

1. Vision: Your soul's dream (or soul's imagining or sensing) of an ideal/evolved world, were you to embody your deepest aspiration and purpose. Example: "I envision a humanity embodying their wholeness, living the triple purpose of life, to wake up, grow up, show up."

MLK—A vision of love and brotherhood: "I have a dream (Vision) that my four little children will one day live in a nation where they will not be judged by the color of their skin, but by the content of their character."

Description: A Vision is:

- **Self-implicating:** it describes what the world might be like if *you* embodied your purpose.

- **Long-term:** you may not achieve your vision in this lifetime (e.g., world peace).

- **Shared:** you share this vision with many people (some of whom you'll never meet).

- **Inspiring:** it excites and encourages you to work toward the fruition of your vision.

- **Idealistic:** it is optimistic, aspirational, often utopian.

- **Big picture:** it is not a task/mission (like the bus boycott), but a higher vision (as with social justice).

2. Values: the soul-level principles (core ideals or beliefs) that support your purpose and give shape to your efforts. Examples: equality, justice, lifelong learning, kindness.

MLK—Value of forgiveness: "We must develop and maintain the capacity to forgive. He who is devoid of the power to forgive is devoid of the power to love." Value of service: "Life's most persistent and urgent question is, 'What are you doing for others?'"

Description: A Value is:

- **A guiding principle:** educates one how to embody their purpose in the world.

- **Timeless:** rooted in eternal Goodness, Truth, and Beauty.

- **Clarifying:** helps you determine which actions to take and how to live.

- **Life-serving:** soul-level values are always a *purpose beyond self*. Example: A person can value listening to live jazz, but that musical enjoyment is not a purpose beyond self.

- **Inspirational:** values foment, incite, and inspirit Vision.

3. Powers: The soul's purpose is expressed, manifested, and supported through your inherent strengths and talents. Your Core Powers17 are your natural soul-level abilities, or native genius. When you express your genius, you come ever more deeply into your soul's powers. Examples: speaking, writing, listening, empathizing, motivating, logic, and problem-solving. A surgeon needs the power/talent of steady hands, a jazz musician needs the power of rhythm, and a psychotherapist needs the power of deep listening and compassion.

MLK—The power of *oratory* ("I have a dream" speech), the power of *leadership* (helping guide the civil rights movement), and the power of *dreaming*: "I have a dream that one day even the state of Mississippi, a state sweltering with the heat of injustice, sweltering with the heat of oppression, will be transformed into an oasis of freedom and justice."

Description: Core Powers are:

- Inherent aptitudes (abilities, capabilities, or talents) that support the fruition of your Vision.

- Strengths you discover that are already inside you waiting to be developed and honed through practice.

- Capacities that cannot be faked or learned; they must already be inside you. (Example: a high I.Q. capable of inventing new theorems in quantum mechanics, or the high spatial intelligence of an artist). Therefore, you cannot *choose* to do physics on the level of Einstein or art at the level of Picasso: you have to find your own powers, *your own genius.*

4. Essence: Is the quality of presence (at a purpose level). Though, strictly speaking, essence isn't something you do (it is the effortless radiance or transmission of your being), nonetheless it has an active transformational power. In a subtle way, your mere presence-radiance can help to transform your people. Essence18 is the core of who you are without doing anything. Examples of essence: Jesus—love, Buddha—illumination, Gandhi—justice.

MLK—Love: "Darkness cannot drive out darkness; only light can do that. Hate cannot drive out hate; only love can do that."

Description: Essence is:

- **Effortless:** you emanate your essence without even trying.
- **Radiant:** your essence is like a unique light that radiates from you.
- **Service:** your essence serves people.

5. Giveaway: What you actively do to people to transform them. This is your soul-level offering, process, or gift. The giveaway consists of the unique way in which you give your gift, not the job itself. Example: two well-known African American activists with similar Visions (civil rights) but with nonidentical giveaways: one emphasizing nonviolence, the other including more confrontational forms of civil disobedience.

MLK: His giveaway included motivating people to undertake non-violent activity at the risk of their lives in the service of advancing civil rights. Part of his giveaway (a step in the process of giving his gift) was *motivating*. He spoke to the better angels of white America and called on them to find their compassion: "Love is the only force capable of transforming an enemy into a friend."

Malcolm X: His giveaway included inspiring people to look at the difficult truth of their condition. Part of his giveaway was *confrontation with power*. He spoke unflinchingly to the power/dignity of black people and the degraded state of white America: "Our objective is complete freedom, justice, and equality *by any means necessary*."

Description: A Giveaway is:

- **Transformational:** it brings people from state *A* to state *B*.
- **Activity:** it is something you *do*, as opposed to something you *are* (as with Essence).
- **Process:** the giveaway is a series of steps, an activity you do to benefit others.
- **Multidimensional:** it is an action that can be offered to yourself, another, group, or habitat.

- **Evolutionary:** it is a process that accelerates a person's or society's growth.

- **Gift:** it is a service that betters, transforms, and evolves a person, group, or situation.

6. Task: A calling, assignment, or mission that you undertake to support your Vision. Example: The task of creating Purpose Guides Institute supports my Vision of a humanity living on purpose.

MLK—Desegregate Alabama public buses (which supports the Vision of equality for all citizens): "I want it to be known that we're going to work with grim and bold determination to gain justice on the buses in this city."

Description: A Task is a:

- **Goal:** something that has a tangible result. Examples: "End homelessness in my town." "Reduce income inequality." "Provide emergency medical services."

- **Project/product:** this is what an individual, company, or organization actually does.

- **Public Broadcasting System:** to create content that educates, informs, and inspires.

- **Google:** to organize the world's information and make it universally accessible.

- **Make-A-Wish Foundation:** to grant the wishes of children with life-threatening medical conditions to enrich the human experience with hope, strength, and joy.

- **Purpose Guides Institute:** to help people discover their life purpose.

Disambiguation: Vision, Giveaway, and Task

- Visions and Tasks are *goals*: the Vision is the *big picture goal* (*civil rights for all*) and the Task is the *tangible goal* that supports the Vision (*desegregation of public buses*). While both are aspirational, Visions are

58

long-term idealistic objectives, while Tasks are more practical and tangible.

- Giveaways are *processes*: Your Giveaway is a transformational offering, it is what you *do* to accomplish your Tasks, and Tasks move you a step closer to fulfilling the Vision.

7. Message: A single fundamental truth you were designed to propagate. Examples: Thoreau—"Rather than love, than money, than fame, give me truth." Susan B. Anthony—"Men, their right, and nothing more; women, their right, and nothing less."

MLK—Equality and respect for all. "People should be treated equally, with the same respect—no more, no less. Equally."

Description: A Message is:

- **Transmissive:** has the potential to communicate "Soul-to-Soul."
- **Inspired:** a prophetic, psychoactive message capable of inciting transformation.
- **Communication:** relays vital ideas/information that can help others.

8. Delivery System: The visible system (career, profession, vocation) through which you offer your Giveaway to the world. Think of the delivery system like a delivery vehicle: you can deliver a pizza on a bike, car or truck, and you can deliver your purpose through a variety of vocational vehicles. Each of the following triads shares the same delivery system:19 Freud-Jung-Skinner; Bush-Obama-Trump; Picasso-Monet-Warhol; Sinatra-Fitzgerald-Armstrong. Yet, each figure's Giveaway (their process of gifting) is radically unique.

MLK—minister, activist, writer, speaker.

Description: A Delivery System is a:

- **Job:** how you economically relate to the world, a form of work that is both a "survival dance" and a "sacred dance."20

- Vocation/calling: your delivery system *might* be your vocation/calling (work you feel naturally drawn toward), and it may or may not be a role that already exists in society.

I used Martin Luther King Jr. to elucidate the eight facets of purpose, because he is a great example of somebody who has deeply embodied his soul's calling. I want to offer an additional case, someone who is in the *middle* of the purpose discovery process.

Simon is a purpose guiding client of mine. We've met about half a dozen times so far. He is 38, married with one child, and makes his living as a marketing consultant. He is a "committed soccer player and passionate home cook." He is a bright, cheerful, and kind man, with a trickster glint in his eyes, who longs for a livelihood that is inline with his soul's purpose. Simon's longing for soulwork was ignited in a high school English class "where we read the Bhagavad Gita, which launched me into a 20-year exploration of what lies beyond the basics of living a typical American life."

As you read his unique Octagon, keep in the mind that, unlike Martin Luther King Jr., you do not know Simon and therefore, will not "get" everything about his purpose. Further, Simon's images will likely mean little to you. The point of presenting Simon's Octagon is to demonstrate what an *in-progress* Octagon can look like, as well as showing how images and symbols can bubble up from the depths of soul when engaging with purpose discovery methods.

Simon's Octagon

Vision: A world lit up by the sacred.
  Image: A filter over my view of the world that shows people glowing, trees glowing.

Values: Kindness.
  Image: The radiant wisdom of the gentle.

Powers: Deep listening, fearless exploration, authentic curiosity, and language that draws people into the unteachable.

Image: SmileDancer.
Essence: Bright love.
Image: Golden Belly, Golden Heart.

Giveaway: 1) Gather reliable information, 2) Fix what is in disrepair, 3) Offer new perspectives, 4) Facilitate creative thinking, 5) Illuminate with metaphor, and 6) Take their hand, light the way to their sacred dance.

   Image: Lead them to the dance floor and spin them out into their sacred dance.

Task: Show people the beauty in the everyday. Preserve sacred culture.
Image: 1) Guardian on the borderlands between the sacred and profane,
     2) Banish banality from the mouth, and
     3) Place Holy Peaches on peoples' tongues and show them how to let the juices run down their chins.

Message: You are greater than you ever imagined.
   Image: "Deep inside your heart, you've got an everlasting light, it's shining like the sun, and it radiates on every one…" (lyrics from a hippie camp song).

Delivery System: International tour guide, specifically to pilgrimage and sacred places. Owner of a tea shop that makes the everyday special. Radio or YouTube show telling stories of the everyday sacred, and stories of the cosmos, consciousness, and interconnection.

   Image: Sacred Warrior.

[*continued next page*]

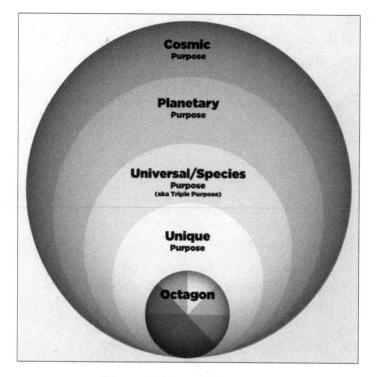

Figure 1: Nested Purposes

Let's reexamine Figure 1. It's important to notice that purpose can holonically move up (greater span) or move down (greater depth). Going up we can see that the eight facets of purpose are part of the soul's unique purpose, which is part of the triple purpose of life, which is part of the species purpose, which is part of the planetary purpose, which is part of the cosmic purpose. Going down (greater depth/specificity) we can see that each wavelength of purpose contains sub-wavelengths that enrich our experience of living our purpose. As previously stated, purpose can be imagined as *nested purposes*. For example, we could take the wavelength of the Giveaway and shine it through a second prism (see Figure 4). This would reveal the "who, what, where, when, why, and how" of your purpose.

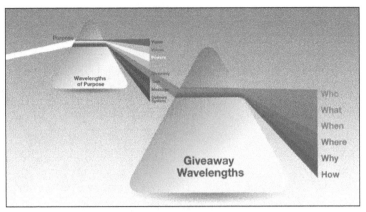

Figure 5: Giveaway Wavelengths

Who	Who are the people for whom my transformational process is intended? What is their gender, age, race, orientation, political affiliation, economic status?
What	(What state are they in): What circumstances are my people in when I meet them? How would they describe their current situation? What part of their life feels like it is in disrepair or in need of some support?
When	When is the optimum time in a person's life for me to meet them and perform my Giveaway? How long does it take me to perform the Process? Is my Giveaway something I do once or does it take multiple meetings?
Where	Where will my Giveaway happen? What is the optimal environment for my offering to unfold?
Why	What is the goal for my Giveaway? What are the signs that the target objective has been reached? When will we know the work is finished?
How	What are the progressive "rungs" of the ladder of my Giveaway? What is the first rung? How do I actually carry out the first step? What techniques and competencies will be required? What is the second rung, third rung, and so on, of my Giveaway?

Table 2: The "Who, what, when, where, why, how" Purpose Graph

It's important to realize that you do not have to know every facet (or sub-facet) of your purpose to live it. Further, it's possible to live your purpose without ever being able to fully articulate it. We live our purpose, not as experts, but always as amateurs, forever learning, growing, and deepening. Still, much can be gained by taking time to engage in soulwork practices that facilitate awareness of your deep purpose.

CODA

Imagine a soul-infused life of joyful and impactful service. Imagine a future where the most powerful political and business leaders know their high-definition, soul-level purpose. Imagine these leaders inviting us (and even expecting us!) to connect with our purpose-beyond-self. Imagine schoolteachers, professors, shop owners, therapists all living their soul's purpose.

Our species now confronts an evolutionary imperative to engage in soulwork. Future generations, countless life-forms, and the biosphere itself, depend on humanity rapidly evolving. Waking up to enlightenment and growing up into emotional adulthood will surely be a part of this evolution. And yet, maturity and awakening alone are insufficient means with which to face our collective self-inflicted dilemma.

What is required in the twenty-first century are proven pathways to address the perennial questions "What do I do with my life?" and "How do we fix this mess?" Now is the time to create modern pathways to purpose, where the profundity of meditation and psychotherapy is wedded to the domain of soulwork. The field of soulwork grows out of a rich heritage. Today, we have the opportunity to reconnect with these traditions of purpose discovery to create contemporary versions of ancient soulwork practices.

We need all hands on deck, with each citizen embodying an understanding of their purpose, so that we may (as a species) skillfully show up with our unique gifts to meet these perilous times. This proposed species-wide evolution would be a (much needed) developmental advance whereby all humans have the opportunity to tap the riches of soulful living while positively impacting the world.

Purpose Guide™ is a registered trademark held by Purpose Guides Institute and Jonathan Gustin.

Disambiguation of Three Worlds. There are six issues arising from using a simplified and reductive model such as the Three Worlds Map. They are 1) Soul-at-the-bottom, 2) Soul-in-the-middle (soul-encounter as descent vs. soul-encounter as descent *and* ascent), 3) Spirit-at-the-bottom (of the three worlds map), 4) Dimensions of consciousness vs. multiple planes, 5) Is Nonduality synonymous with Upperworld?, and 6) Tendency to tag nondual traditions as lacking Soul.

Figure 7 Three versions of the Three Worlds Map

1. Soul-at-the-bottom. Though it was Bill Plotkin's book *Soulcraft* that initiated my use of the three worlds map, my use of the term is deeply informed by Sufi and shamanic cosmologies. Let's turn first to Shamanism. I originally experienced these worlds through *shamanic journeying* to the lower and upper realms, guided by Michael Harner and his apprentices (Center for Shamanic Studies), and Tom Brown Jr. (through my studies of shamanism at his Tracker School). These two shamans spoke briefly about the three worlds, grabbed their drums, and off we went. Not much time was spent philosophizing or cosmologizing! Arising out of these journeying "sessions" (and other) experiences, I began teaching what I called the *triple purpose of life* in the early 2000s though my SoulQuest and Integral Awakening Groups. I coined the terms "triple purpose," "triple purpose of life," and "three worlds of purpose," thereby making *purpose* in its various expressions and iterations the central and guiding concept of my teaching work. The foundational concept of the *triple purpose of life* gave me a framework that allowed me to experience my work as a seamless whole, as I assumed the roles of meditation teacher (upperworld), psychotherapist (middleworld), and purpose guide (lowerworld).

In 2003, I was introduced to the terms *Three Worlds of consciousness* and *Three Worlds of identity* by Bill Plotkin (*Soulcraft*). The way Plotkin uses these terms has been hugely influential in my teaching work (as have archetypal psychologist James Hillman's writings, including *The Dream and the Underworld*). Following depth psychology and some (but not all) shamanic teachings, Plotkin places *soul-at-the-bottom* of the three worlds map, indicating that the encounter with soul is experienced as a descent, a burrowing down into our depths, a spiritual *inscendence* (a word coined by geologian Thomas Berry) as opposed to a spiritual ascent. One advantage of the *soul-at-the-bottom* map, especially for people new to the experience (or even the idea) of the three worlds, is the disambiguation between waking up to your soul-purpose and waking up to Unbounded Nondual Awareness. Discovering your soul-purpose is the experiential answer to the question, "What do I do?"—whereas, abiding as Nondual Awareness is the experiential answer to the question, "Who am I?" See Three Worlds Map #1 for a pictorial rendering of this map.

2. Soul-in-the-middle. Equally important are the teachings implied by the Three Worlds Map #2 that places *soul-in-the-middle*, between Spirit and Ego/materiality. Following Sufi and (some aspects of) shamanic cosmology, Three Worlds Map #2 renders Soul as the bridge between Spirit and ego/physicality. Map #2 renders the experience of soul-encounter as an ascending experience, *not* to Spirit (Unbounded Nondual Awareness) but to Soul. Put another way, the experience of soul-encounter can be understood as Spirit pouring itself into a unique shape (our Soul), which then is perceived further "downstream" by Ego.

My understanding of the *soul-in-the-middle* map is deeply influenced by Sufism, particularly the work of Islamic scholar Henri Corbin (*Alone with the Alone*) and his foremost interpreter Tom Cheetham (*Imaginal Love*). Corbin, drawing on the masters Suhrawardi and Ibn Arabi, offers a Sufi perspective of the "isthmus" of the imaginal realm (the realm of Soul) existing *between* the physical realm and spiritual realm. For Corbin, the imaginal exists between the material and the spiritual and so is not a "lower world." Hillman (who borrowed heavily from Corbin) seems deeply suspicious of traditional transcendent teachings. Thomas Berry (*Dream of the Earth*) and Bill Plotkin seem to carry this suspicion as well: that transcendent spirituality devoid of Soul, Purpose, Earth, or Wild Nature is a dangerous thing at any time, and especially so during our present time.

Still, we shouldn't throw the transcendent baby out with the bathwater. *Soul-in-the-middle* of the map allows for the understanding of soul-encounters as having an ascending flavor, perfume, or "directionality" from the point of view of ego. Whereas Map #1 shows waking up to our calling as *waking down to Soul*, Map #2 shows that discovery of our soul-level purpose is waking up (ascending) out of ego, into the subtler realm of soul. Both maps share this: awakening to soul-purpose is the experience of transcending ego to experience a spiritual reality that (depending on your viewpoint) can be thought of as ascending or descending, transcending or *incending*. There are shamanic descriptions more in line with Map #1 and some more in line with Map #2. My advice: go with the map toward which your *felt-sense* feels intuitively drawn. Ultimately, does it matter if your felt-sense during soul-encounter is more consistent with a burrowing down into your depths (Plotkin, Berry, Hillman, and some shamanic sources) or an experience of transcending/ascending? Personally, I have experienced soul as both a descent/incendental *and* an ascent/transcendental experience.

3. Spirit-at-the-bottom (of the three worlds map). Another way to organize the map is to have Spirit appear at the bottom of the circle. This indicates that Spirit is the primordial ground of Being/Becoming. Out of the ground of Absolute Spirit, emerges Soul. Out of soul, emerges ego. This version of the map captures the *involutionary* nature of Spirit contracting (*Tzimtzum* in Kabbalah) into Soul and then into Ego. Thus awakening to Spirit is awakening to the primordial ground that transcends all AND is the ground of both Soul and Ego. See Three Worlds Map #3 for a pictorial rendering of perceiving the three worlds in this way.

4. Dimensions of consciousness vs. multiple planes. As a depth psychologist, Plotkin (*Soulcraft*) primarily views the experience of the lowerworld of Soul as a "world of consciousness" or "a world of identity" and secondarily (or not at all?) as multiple transhuman planes of existence. I like the simplicity and clarity of Plotkin's model. But...we get into very tricky terrain here, for we are obliged to ask, "Were ancient shamans using their original terms to speak about what depth psychology would later call the psyche, consciousness, subconscious, and the underworld (like Jung, Hillman, and Plotkin), or were they pointing to transhuman realities, or did these ancient shamans hold both to be true?" To the consternation of my students, I see both views as useful and true. That said, in my writings and trainings I emphasize the "dimensions of consciousness" implications of the Three Worlds, and intentionally de-emphasize transhuman planes/realities. This allows for a smoother entryway for people to discover the wonders of the soul's deeper purpose, without having to negotiate multiple realms of reality that they may never have heard of, experienced, or that may seem to threaten prior religious belief systems. In summary: in the spirit of keeping things simple (and at the considerable expense of being reductive), I have chosen to emphasize soul-at-the-bottom instead of soul-in-the-middle, the journey to soul-purpose as a descent (rather than encounter with Soul as an ascent), and soul encounter as a confrontation with consciousness/identity/psyche, rather than as a transhuman reality.

5. Is Nonduality synonymous with the Upperworld...or not? I have used the term *Unbounded Nondual Awareness* to point toward the experience of classical/traditional enlightenment often associated with the Buddha and other sages. I come from the nondual wisdom streams of Zen and Advaita Vedanta. In this context, I've been on the receiving end of some rather disapproving looks from my nondual teachers who find the three worlds map to be "empty of any essential substance." Indeed: seen from/ as the absolute reality of Unbounded Nondual Awareness, the *story* of an ego, soul, imaginal realm, soul-encounter, or *separate* worlds is absurd. Point well taken. But, from a relative perspective, I have found the *fiction* of the three worlds (and it is a *fiction*, in the way a map of North America has three "separate" countries) to be most efficacious in approaching the three central questions of a human life: "Who am I?" "What do I do?" and "How can I be happy?" A further fiction/concession I make in this essay is to (sometimes) place unbounded absolute awareness in the upperworld of Spirit. While this move has much to recommend it, it also is technically dead wrong. Unbounded Nondual Awareness is more like the screen or paper on which (and through which) the three worlds map is written (and the eyes that see it, and the brain that processes it). Still, there is a place for simplification and reduction, which is why I've chosen to make the concessions I have. But, buyer beware of any map as simple and elegant as the three worlds map...for there is no Mexico, Canada, or United States except for the map maker, for on the ground there is only terra firma.

6. Tendency to tag nondual traditions as lacking "purpose."
The nondual lineage streams of which I am a part of (Zen and Advaita Vedanta) deemphasize Soul, purpose, calling, destiny, and the like. However, this does not mean that these are nowhere to be found within these lineages. On the one hand, you will certainly be hard pressed to find mention of Soul, purpose, and so on, in Dogen Zenji, Ramana Maharshi, or Nisargadatta Maharaj. You'd be well within reason to read what these sages wrote and believe that the "point" of spiritual life is to wake up out of the dream of the (relative) world. Paradoxically (from the ego's perspective), these nondual traditions are open to the possibility that once "awake" to/as Unbounded Nondual Awareness, it is possible that one will feel a GREAT passion to "do something" in the relative dream world that could be described as living a life purpose as an act of evolutionary service. I agree with Jon Darrall-Rew (*Earth Is Eden*): "Healthy waking up isn't just transcendence. It's transcendence PLUS intimacy with the entirety of creation as the One that is it all." Agreed! Some sages seem to live very simply *as* abiding nondual awareness without very much movement, action, desire for impact, and so on, while other sages seem to be blown off the proverbial cushion by the winds of Mystery, finding themselves on fire with an ecstatic, urgent, evolutionary impulse to transform the world. Bottom line: the nondual traditions hold both as legitimate possibilities for the enlightened life.

❧

Endnotes

1. Dustin DiPerna (*Streams of Wisdom*) coined the phrase "Wake up, grow up, clean up, show up." I've altered his term to coincide with the three worlds map.

2. Mary Oliver, excerpt from the poem "The Summer Day" (*New and Selected Poems*).

3. Quote from theologian Frederick Buechner.

4. I am using the term *traditional psychotherapy* to refer to those classical therapies and some modern therapies (such as cognitive-behavioral therapy) that focus on a limited, but essential, band of the human psyche. This is not meant as an implied criticism of therapies that "merely" help people to become better adjusted. Nor is it the author's intention to overlook the many contemporary therapies that include Soul/Purpose/Underworld elements in their theory and practice. The inevitable cost of presenting a simplified version of the psyche, with three pathways to approach three worlds (meditation, classical psychotherapy, and purpose guiding), is the possibility that the reader will be misled into thinking "therapy is never about Soul," or "meditation is never a pathway to Purpose." This is clearly not the case.

5. Henri Corbin (*Alone with the Alone*) coined the term Imaginal Realm, citing Sufi masters Suhrawardi, and Ibn Arabi as sources for the original term in Arabic.

6. Bill Plotkin (*Soulcraft*) "...soul encounter is an experience of the mysterious image you were born with..." p. 119.

7. Bill Plotkin (*Soulcraft*). Though *mythopoetic* is a term from the men's movement, circa 1970s (Robert Bly, et al.), and has roots in the terms mythopoeia and mythopoesis coined by J.R.R. Tolkien, it is Plotkin who coined the term mythopoetic identity. Note: there are potential dangers in allowing an identification with an archetypal/mythopoetic image. Carl Jung warned of the potential for a massive inflation of the ego, were the ego to be possessed by an archetype. A human is meant to actualize one's mythopoetic image, not necessarily be occupied by it.

8. I coined the term *world fixation* to describe a trend I witnessed as a therapist, meditation teacher, and Purpose Guide: a proclivity of some of my clients to attend to one of the three worlds of purpose to the exclusion of the other two. NB in the opinion of this author, this is not necessarily a bad thing: sometimes life asks us to become *world-specialists*, as opposed to *world-generalists*.

9. James Hillman (*Re-visioning Psychology*) p. x.

10. James Hillman (*Suicide and the Soul*) p. 46.

11. Bill Plotkin (*Soulcraft*) p. 41.

12. Bill Plotkin (*Soulcraft*) p. 42.

13. Stephen Jenkinson (Orphan Wisdom School): Teachings given at his farm May 3–7, 2017.

14. The Soulcentric Meditations we use at the Purpose Guides Institute are: Evolution's Purpose, Entelechy Process, 10 Years Process, Ocean Cave Meditation, Animal Guide Meditation, and Niche Tree Meditation. When thoroughly and properly prepared, I have witnessed a very high success rate amongst clients for receiving glimpses of soul-purpose, using these guided meditations.

15. I've been greatly influenced by the "parts work" pioneers Carl Jung, Hal and Sidra Stone (*Voice Dialogue*), Richard C. Schwartz (*Internal Family Systems Model*), Genpo Roshi (*Big Mind, Big Heart*), and Tim Kelly (*True Purpose*).

16. Ken Wilber uses the term (coined by Arthur Koestler) throughout his many books on Integral Theory. Wilber's theory of holons and depth/span distinctions have been influential in the creation of the Purpose Octagon.

17. Bill Plotkin (*Soulcraft*) p. 119. "Core Powers" is a phrase Plotkin uses to distinguish soul purpose from soul powers.

18. I am deeply grateful for being introduced to the Essence/Giveaway distinction created by Tim Kelly in *True Purpose* (though he uses the term blessing where I use the terms *gift* or *giveaway*..., which is a word central to the Vision Quest ceremony of Native Americans). The octagon would be diminished without Kelly's pivotal distinction. His excellent four-part model of purpose (Essence, Blessing, Mission, Message) served as both a foundation and inspiration for the Octagon.

19. Bill Plotkin (*Nature and the Human Soul*) p. 302. In his watershed books *Soulcraft* and *Nature and The Human Soul*, Bill Plotkin distinguishes between a delivery system and soul-level purpose. For instance, Plotkin writes that his soul image is Cocoon Weaver, and his delivery systems include depth psychologist, wilderness guide, and so on.

20. Harvey Swift Deer likely coined these phrases.

Chapter 4

THE REALM OF PURPOSE LEAST REALIZED

But Most Essential in Our Time of Radical, Global Change

Bill Plotkin, PhD

*...There is only one life
you can call your own
and a thousand others
you can call by any name you want.*

*Hold to the truth you make
every day with your own body,
don't turn your face away.*

*Hold to your own truth
at the center of the image
you were born with.*

*Those who do not understand
their destiny will never understand
the friends they have made
nor the work they have chosen*

*nor the one life that waits
beyond all the others....*

—David Whyte[1]

Everyone yearns for—and needs—a purpose that can be embodied, a meaning that can be lived. Our mortality demands it of us. Our love for our own life, for all living things, and for community pours itself into the world, like a prayer, through our deepest purpose. But what we mean by and experience as "purpose" depends on our stage of life and our depth of psychospiritual development. In the contemporary Western world, when people speak about personal life purpose, most everyone means a mix of social, vocational, political, and/or religious goals or intentions. A much smaller group means a desire to awaken to the divine, nondual, or the universal.

But there's a third variety of purpose that is rarely considered, that has no place or presence in mainstream Western consciousness, that is completely absent from contemporary maps of human life, even the maps of specialists in human development, including those who write about and guide "integral" development. And yet this is the single most essential realm of purpose, especially in our current critical and liminal moment in the unfolding of the world's story.

The near absence of attention to this most essential realm of purpose is not a coincidence or an oversight. For millennia, Western civilization, among others, has shaped itself in ways that suppress access to this realm. Today this realm of purpose is rarely experienced—or even consciously recognized as a possibility. Our educational, media, and religious systems and our mainstream parenting practices are shaped in ways that divert us from this vital domain of human experience. This suppression of human development has become a necessity for Western civilization in its current form; it would simply not be sustainable otherwise. Conversely, widespread access to this realm of purpose would be the single most potent factor in the termination of Western society in its present life-destroying iteration—and in the creation of a just, life-enhancing, and deeply imaginative culture with its roots in the genuine achievements of the Western tradition.

The lack of access to this particular realm of purpose is our most significant human deficit at this time. The diversity of life on Earth is now being extensively diminished precisely because of this deficit—and has been for hundreds if not thousands of years. Additionally, as beat poet Diane di Prima writes, "men die everyday for the lack of it."[2]

It is also not a coincidence that most societies and traditions that have treasured and preserved this now-rare realm of purpose have been wiped out or culturally disrupted over the past few millennia. This realm of purpose is the single greatest threat to the consumer-conformist-imperial-dominator mind, to its business as usual, as manifested not only in the contemporary West but in all egocentric societies now prevalent across the globe. If we are to survive the twenty-first century—if robust life on Earth of *any* sort is to survive—there are many things we must do in the short term (like save from extinction as many species and habitats as we can, reverse global warming, create true and universally just democracies and biocracies, and abolish nuclear weapons) but, in the long term, the single most important measure is the reshaping of all human cultures so as to support every child to grow in a way that enables the uncovering and embodiment of this particular, now exceedingly rare, realm of purpose.

The central fact that explains why this sphere of purpose is so seldom attained is this: in order to access it, what is required is a level or stage of human development rarely achieved in contemporary cultures — again, not a coincidence—despite the fact that this stage of development, in a healthy and mature Western culture, would be commonplace among 15-year-olds. No special training or preparation would be necessary. More on this below.

I hesitate to name this realm of purpose due to the likelihood you'll think I'm referring to something I'm not. I have often called it "soul purpose" but this misleads most everyone because I mean something by "soul" that almost no one else does in the contemporary Western world, including those writing about purpose and soul. Better phrases would be "mythopoetic identity" or "unique psychoecological niche" but, to be coherent, these phrases require careful unpacking and elaboration.

But before we do that, let's review some of the other, more commonly addressed and accessed realms of purpose.

Realms of Purpose through the Lifespan

As a child, I didn't think much about purpose. You probably didn't either. It's not what children *should* be thinking about. But if you had asked me what I most wanted, I probably would have said I wanted to please my parents, play with my friends, do well in school, ride my bike, and mess around outside, especially in the forests that surrounded my New England hometown.

As a heterosexual teenager, girls and sex became my foremost interest, although sports, fast cars, and playing the electric organ in rock bands became primary purposes, too. Doing well in school and being liked by my peers remained vital.

In college, much of this was still true, but by then my conscious purpose leaned more toward the exploration of nonordinary consciousness (through experiential as well as scholarly channels) and, more generally, spirituality as accessed by Buddhism, yoga, and other non-Western practices; the co-creation of a primary romantic relationship; martial arts; political activism and cultural change; the exploration of the western half of the United States, especially by motorcycle (road trips!), and of wilderness anywhere I could find it; and the need and opportunity to choose a career.

During graduate school (psychology at Colorado University Boulder), followed by my first university research and teaching position, and then a postdoctoral internship, my earlier strands of purpose continued (the common developmental pattern of "transcend and include"), but my primary conscious trajectory was to develop the skills of a research and clinical psychologist, establish a body of work of my own, make a living, and contribute something of value to society.

Although the specifics vary from one person to the next, the underlying pattern in my life into early "adulthood" is common in contemporary societies: we derive our primary meaning and purpose—if we experience them at all—through our social, vocational, political, and spiritual (or religious) pursuits. Most of these realms of experience are what I think of as "middleworld" purposes, namely those rooted in our everyday social and cultural life. A smaller subset consists of "upperworld" purposes, the desire to ascend or transcend, to experience "enlightenment" or "bliss," or to "awaken" to divine, nondual, or unity consciousness. All my examples above, from childhood through early professional life, are instances of middleworld or upperworld purposes.

But there's another realm of meaning and purpose that awaits beyond these, a deeper realm that, as human participants in the Earth community, we long for, whether or not we have a conscious connection to it, a spiritual realm entirely neglected by the mainstream world as well as by virtually all spiritual and psychotherapeutic traditions, but a realm essential to growing whole, becoming fully human, and experiencing fulfillment.

Despite my extensive early explorations in psychology and spirituality, which began in college, it wasn't until my late twenties that I had a first conscious clue that this realm of purpose even existed. It was entirely overlooked in the psychologies I studied, despite my focus on the humanistic and transpersonal. It was never considered in any of the Eastern spiritualities I read about and practiced, including Zen and Tibetan Buddhism, Kundalini Yoga, Sufism, and Taoism. There was hardly an allusion to it during the six-week summer 197³ program I attended in Berkeley on "Human Consciousness: Exploration, Maps, and Models" (cosponsored by Esalen Institute and the Association of Transpersonal Psychology), nor during my three summers, 1974–1976, as a student at the spiritually oriented, Buddhist-inclined Naropa University, in Boulder, Colorado.

Most every spiritual teacher with whom I studied in those years (and since) used the word "soul" at least occasionally and often extensively—and, among them, they meant quite a wide variety of things—but not one was referring to the realm of psyche I have since associated with soul nor of the deeper realm of purpose I am addressing here.

Breakthrough: The Underworld Passage

Before finding anyone who had written about or guided others into this realm, I stumbled into it experientially in 1980 during my first vision fast. This was a solo, self-guided ceremony conducted in a contemporary Western manner, not in imitation of Native American people or other indigenous traditions.3 But my discovery might have been made through any one of a number of other practices or ceremonies, or even sparked by seemingly random life events. What's important here is what was discovered, not how I discovered it.

What I discovered, in addition to my first glimpse of soul, was that the entire framework of purpose, meaning, and identity that I had been raised with and had been living within—and that most people in the contemporary Western world live within their entire lives—was no longer applicable or particularly relevant to me. It was over, done, bankrupt. Like a capsized swimmer in uncharted whitewater, I was navigating a life passage that relatively few people undergo in the contemporary world, into a realm of experience about which I had no previous knowledge. I had embarked upon the descent to soul, the underworld journey into the *mysterium tremendum* at the core of the human psyche.

In the course of healthy human development, we are each meant to reach this break point, this crisis, this divide beyond which we're no longer able to decisively define ourselves in terms of social or romantic relationships, or in terms of a job or career, a creative or artistic project, a political affiliation, a theory or philosophical perspective, a religious or ethnic membership, or a transcendental spiritual goal. We are propelled—compelled!—toward an underworld self-definition, a soul-infused experience of meaning and purpose and identity. True for all humans, this is our evolutionary birthright, a necessary passage on the way from psychological adolescence to true adulthood. (By "psychological adolescence," I don't mean an age range, but a developmental stage that most Western people never grow beyond.)

The mainstream currents of our contemporary cultures neither assert nor deny the existence of an underworld identity; it has simply disappeared from awareness. Even middleworld purpose has become difficult to attain. It's increasingly common for people to find themselves marooned in a world of restless emptiness with a sense of not truly or deeply belonging to anything—or with an unrelenting numbness or depression, a sense of lurching through life or just going through the motions. From age four until our midteens, middleworld purpose is all we need. But beyond our teen years, middleworld purpose alone never deeply satisfies. Even if you add upperworld purpose, there still remains a thunderous void.

This passage from a middleworld social-vocational-political-religious scaffolding of self-definition (and/or one of the universal, one-size-fits-all versions of upperworld identity) to a unique, soul-derived, underworld framework is a categorical shift in orientation. It's not a shift from one cultural definition to another. It's not a progression from one career to the next, from one romance to another, from being an addict to being a professional success, from being a Midwesterner to being a Californian, from being born into a Jewish family to becoming a Buddhist. Nor is it a shift from middleworld specifics to upperworld universality. And it's not a shift we can simply choose or make happen. It is, rather, the involuntary demise of our entire comprehension of the nature of meaning or purpose, of the ways we understood ourselves and the world through childhood and psychological adolescence, and an abduction into the depths of the psyche and the mysteries of the world toward encounters that will eventually enable us to identify "the one life we can call our own." A psychologically risky journey of many months or years, it makes a possible a personal transformation that can happen only after we reach a developmental stage that few in the West ever reach.

An Underworld and Ecological Conception of Soul

What exactly do I mean, then, by "soul" and how does this help us understand why the uncovering of what I call soul purpose has become so uncommon in the contemporary world? For an answer, we'll need to cross a threshold into a domain of discourse and experience that in the materialist precincts of the West would be considered "mystical." Otherwise you might dismiss my perspective simply because it's unfamiliar or perhaps feels dubious at first. So let's begin by reviewing how commonplace the "mystical" is in the lives and existence of *other*-than-human beings. Then, perhaps, you'll find it less surprising, esoteric, or mysterious that such extraordinary and astonishing realities apply to us humans as well.

What Every Flower, Frog, and Fox Is Born With

The mysteries to which I refer here concern, in their essence, ecological place or niche—the fact that the young of all species are *born with* an understanding of their place in the world. By "place," I don't simply mean geographical location or habitat. Rather, I mean a creature's ecological niche—its function, role, or "profession" within its community or ecosystem.[4] The young of all species, in other words, already know at birth how to be members of their species. This innate knowledge includes basic-yet-vital items such as how to move around, what to eat and not eat, how to avoid predators, and how and when to mate and with whom. But by far the most important knowledge they are born with is *how to contribute to the world their unique skill or offering*. They, in other words, are born with what we might call ecological purpose, an implicit knowledge or apprehension of their place or niche in a wildly complex and differentiated world of multiple habitats and countless species. They are born with all the capacities they need to serve the world in a way no other creature can—including how they can further develop or coevolve their own niche—and they do not have to be taught or shown "the one life they can call their own"; this knowledge and capacity is inborn. They do not have to go through an initiation process to uncover it. Although birds and mammals learn a lot of behavioral specifics from their parents and primary social group, most of the capacities that enable them to function as members of their species are innate. The newborn of species *other* than birds and mammals—95 percent of all species—receive minimal to no parenting beyond being conceived and birthed. They are born with all they need to know to have a good chance of survival, to be who they are, and to provide the "ecological functions" only they can.

This is entirely natural and ordinary, but it is also utterly astounding and miraculous, even mystical. The common-but-misguided Western philosophical impulse to try to explain this reductionistically in terms of genetics misses the most essential point. Genetics might be one piece of *how* this knowledge is transmitted (part of the "mechanism"), but the method of transmission is categorically and conceptually distinct from *what* is transmitted, and the unfathomable mystery remains that this knowledge and know-how exist and are transmitted at all.

You might say we humans, too, are born with a version of such capacities: for example, our precious innocence enables us to inspire other humans to provide the love, nourishment, and basic shelter we need; or, more mysteriously, our capacity to easily acquire human language. But it seems other species are born with a far greater innate understanding of their place in the world. And, as far as we can tell, they never have identity crises. The fact that we do, and regularly, says something significant about us as a species or about our contemporary cultures, or both.

Many examples of the innate knowledge and know-how possessed by other species are absolutely staggering. For example, consider the annual migration of monarch butterflies: They fly immense distances from their summer habitats in the eastern United States and Canada to their winter homes in Mexico, or from the Rocky Mountains to Southern California. They manage this long and wildly complex navigation even though *it takes four generations to complete a single migration.* Furthermore, they arrive at the very same trees their great-great-grandparents tenanted the year before. None of them learn how to do this from other butterflies. They are *born* with the knowledge of how to migrate thousands of miles, through countless habitats and weather systems, and end up in precisely the one spot that is theirs, something akin to finding a needle in a haystack. This is downright mystical. And, as it turns out, this sort of miracle is entirely commonplace on Earth.

Given that such mysteries are demonstrably true for other species, how could we doubt something comparable is true for us? In the contemporary world, we tend to believe that everything important that we know we learned from others—parents, other family members, teachers, books, the internet, and so on. And indeed we've learned quite a bit this way. But we, too, like all other species, are born with certain innate knowledge of our unique place in the world, of our ecological niche, of what has been called our destiny or our genius. The problem is that this knowledge is not conscious when we're born because, after all, we're not conscious of *anything* in our first couple years. And by the time our conscious self-awareness develops—somewhere between our third and fourth birthdays—we are more than busy with other things to be conscious of, like the enchantment of the other-than-human world or how to be a member-in-good-standing of a particular family and peer group, and a particular culture or ethnic or religious group.

Learning these things is the natural priority throughout our childhood and early teen years. But—and here's the rub for us humans—by the time our conscious knowledge of self and world is established in our mid-teens, we have strayed a long ways from our deeper, innate, unconscious knowledge of self and world, which is now obscured, buried, unremembered. It's still there within us, but we can't access it and we might not even know it exists. Consequently, as soon as our basic cultural and ecological education is complete, it comes time to "remember" the knowledge we were born with: our particular, destined place in the world, our original personal instructions for this lifetime. All healthy cultures provide initiatory processes (much more extensive and categorically different than a rite of passage[5]) to help their youth uncover just that. In the Western world, these initiatory processes were forgotten and lost millennia ago.

Uniqueness and Differentiation

Some people assume that individual members of other species do not have unique gifts or destinies, that whatever uniqueness there is exists on the species level, not the individual level. One flower or frog or fox, they might say, has exactly the same ecological place, niche, role, or function as any other individual of their species, more or less. If so, why would it be any different for us?

But one thing we know about evolution is that life grows ever more complex, diversified, and differentiated. This is a universal principle. Brian Swimme and Thomas Berry put it this way:

> In the universe, to be is to be different. To be is to be a unique manifestation of existence. The more thoroughly we investigate any one thing…the more we discover its uniqueness…. Ultimately each thing remains as baffling as ever, no matter how profound our understanding…. The universe comes to us, each being and each moment announcing its thrilling news: I am fresh.[6]

As life on Earth evolves, speciation accelerates. Intraspecies differentiation increases as well. From four billion years ago until less than a billion years ago, there were only single-cell organisms on Earth, although innumerable kinds of them. Now, in addition to countless species of bacteria and microbes, there are millions of complex, multicellular species and untold variations within species. Among mammalian species, there are a variety of social roles within any family or extended group. While our own innate human capacities seem minimal at birth compared to other species—we're born, after all, remarkably vulnerable and helpless—we make up for that by possessing perhaps the greatest intraspecies differentiation, something that becomes increasingly evident as we get older. Even within the same culture, even within the same family, there ends up being an absolutely astonishing degree of variation among us in talents, personal style, taste, personality, values, personal goals, and even gender embodiment.

But our individual uniqueness is not only on the social-personality-vocational-gender level. It is also, and more importantly, on the soul or ecological level. We're each born with distinct and differentiated destinies, our own unique ecological place or niche in the world, our own particular genius. This is a very old idea woven into the myths and sacred stories of all cultures. It is most likely true for all species to some degree, but it appears to be comparatively truer for us. For good or for ill.

Whether for us or any other species, the unique ecological niche for each individual creature is specific to its particular place in a particular environment. The niche of a specific fox, for example, has everything to do with the precise swath of forest in which she roams; with her relationship, for example, to the pattern of birds nests in those climbable trees and the location of rabbit warrens and rodent tunnels, as well as with her relationship to other foxes in her pack. But her individual niche is not simply or primarily a matter of how she "makes a living." It is also about how she uniquely participates in and enhances life in her forest and about the effects and influences only she can have on the local habitat and the other species there.

All this is true for us humans as well: we each have a unique set of relationships and potentials within both our local and global communities.

Soul: Your Place in the Greater Web of Life

Here's the most important thing I know to emphasize about underworld or soul purpose: this knowledge of what it is to be fully and uniquely yourself, of the gift you were *born* to bring into this world, can never be identified or described in any social, vocational, political, religious, or other cultural terms. No one is born to have a particular job or role in a particular human community. Rather, like all other species, we're each born to take a specific place within the *Earth* community, to fill a unique ecological niche in the greater web of life, to provide a suite of unique ecological functions. And *that* place is what I mean by soul, and occupying *that* psychoecological niche and providing *those* functions is what I mean by soul purpose. *This* is the realm of purpose nearly absent from contemporary discussions and most all contemporary practices and methods for uncovering and embodying purpose. And it is the most essential of these realms, especially in this time of radical, global change.

Soul and Mythopoetic Identity

Because knowledge of our place in the greater web of life is something we're born with, it is necessarily precultural and prelinguistic. As a consequence, our unique place in the world can't be identified, described, understood, or experienced in conventional cultural terms or in the direct denotative way we specify a middleworld identity. But if we can't refer to our soul's place as that of a physician, pianist, priest, president, or parent, or even more generically as a healer, artist, or leader, then how can it be done?

Here's an additional way to appreciate the difficulty: we humans possess a special realm or veneer of consciousness—our ego's conscious self-awareness—that rides on top of the more extensive consciousness we have in common with all other species.[7] Our human ego is both a great boon and a great barrier. For example, because each individual ego, unlike the soul, is a child of culture and language, we at first—in our childhood and teen years—come to understand our place culturally and linguistically, which is to say in terms of social, vocational, and religious roles. This is unavoidable, entirely necessary, and a good thing. But we're also born with an entirely different kind of knowledge, a felt-sense about our ecological place or niche in the world, knowledge that exists only within the deeper realm of consciousness that all species share, knowledge that is not linguistic but imaginal, knowledge that an immature, egocentric ego cannot access.

So the question becomes: how do we discover what this is, this innate, imagery-based, and mysterious knowledge about our ecological place in the world? How do we discover what it is when it exists at a deeper level than the ego-consciousness that dominates our experience and sense of self by the time we're in our early teens? And how do we linguistically identify it to ourselves and others once we experience it consciously?

In a word: metaphor.

When it comes to identifying soul, we can only point to it or allude to it using metaphor—in the manner of poetry or myth. We can linguistically understand our souls only indirectly, only mythopoetically. Not coincidentally, this is precisely how we learn about our souls in the first place: we discover (or remember) our innate place, our true home, our soul's purpose, when the world mirrors it to us by way of nature-based metaphors, human archetypes, or other mythic or poetic images or symbols. We don't choose these metaphors or figure them out. Rather, we're shown them in a moment of numinous vision or mystical revelation. They are shown to us by…by what? "Mystery" is as good a way as any to name our benefactor, our guide, our initiator.

Soul is a child of nature, not of culture and language.

What I mean by "soul," then, is something mystical but not upper-world mystical and not any more mystical than monarch migrations. It corresponds to what poet David Whyte refers to as "the largest conversation you can have with the world," a conversation you were born to have and that only you can have and that the world *needs* you to have for it to be whole. The seed or catalyst for this conversation has existed within you from birth or conception in the form of what Whyte calls "the truth you make every day with your own body" or "the truth at the center of the image you were born with." Take a moment to consider that these two sorts of truths—which to the Western mind seem so strange, mystical, and improbable—really do exist, and for everyone. These truths, these images, these conversations—and the niches, roles, functions, identities, meanings, and purposes associated with them—are not cultural or even merely human; rather, you were born with them, and they are ecological and mythopoetic, which is to say clothed and communicated in the metaphors, symbols, images, dreams, and archetypes of the wild world and of our own wild minds. As Diane di Prima reminds us:

> ...you have a poetics: you step into the world
> like a suit of readymade clothes...[8]

This is actually true of all creatures, not just humans: every being has its own innate poetics. And there's no better way than poetry to identify a unique ecological niche. Try describing the niche of a fox, for example. You can point to some of the primary relationships she has with other species in a particular habitat and perhaps the way her uncommon cunning allows her to carry out her distinctive calling, but her niche is something more than that and categorically different. Her niche is the sum of all the relationships she has with everything else on Earth, if not the whole universe, something we can't even get close to fully describing. The best way to understand a fox's niche is to live for several years as a native in her neighborhood while offering your daily reverent attention to her wanderings and ways. Then you'll know something of her niche but still not be able to describe it precisely or systematically. Your best option, really, for portraying her niche would be to recite fox stories, preferably outside at night around a fire or in the dark beneath blazing stars. Or fox poetry. Or vixen myth. And that of course is precisely how nature-based people have always done it.

It's no different when it comes to linguistically portraying a human's soul.

Through the journey of soul initiation, we come to understand that we each were born as something like a poem, as a unique dance, as a story in conversation with other stories, as an essential and utterly singular episode in the unfolding story of Earth, of Cosmos. As Gary Snyder writes:

> The world is made of stories. Good stories are hard to come by, and a good story that you can honestly call your own is an incredible gift. These stories are part of a bigger story that connects us all.[9]

A Few Sketches of Soul

Some examples might be helpful, even though it's impossible to communicate the numinosity of the human soul in a few words. Much better would be an intricate story or poem, something there's not space here to include. (The single best way to understand a person's soul purpose is to live in community with them and experience them in action.) That said, I'll offer here a few linguistic sketches with the hope this will at least convey a feeling for the difference between a social-vocational identity and a soul identity.

There are a great number of people whose mystical encounters with soul I've had the pleasure and privilege to learn about and to witness the embodiment of. The following are four exceedingly brief word portraits that embody the wild mysteries of such encounters and how they've been communicated mythopoetically, each of these examples being mere intimations of the genius and destiny of these four individuals:

- The overseer who guides others into the oceanic depths of the psyche.
- The one with a sparkling heart who walks the path of the bear.
- She who generates perception-expanding images and identity-destabilizing questions.
- The one who dances the Earth and dreams song to feed the longing.

Despite being so brief, you can sense how these soul-infused identities and purposes contrast with middleworld cultural roles. These are not job descriptions you'll ever see advertised. They are not the kinds of recommendations you'll get from a vocational guidance counselor. They are of the dreamtime or the mythic. And they are the kinds of purposes utterly core to our deepest, innate human identities.

Another example: The preface to my book *Soulcraft* recounts my own story of how I received, on my first vision fast at age 30, an initial glimpse of my soul identity or ecological role as the one who weaves cocoons of transformation.

Three more include:

° Malidoma Somé, the West African elder and teacher, identifies his destiny, his place in the world, as "he who makes friends with the enemy/stranger," something revealed to him (by Mystery) as a young man during a month-long initiation process.[10]

° Joanna Macy, the North American ecophilosopher, spiritual activist, Buddhist scholar, and Earth elder, experienced a life-shifting numinous image during a meditation session in the early weeks of her Buddhist practice, while living in India, at age 37:

> To my inner eye appeared a bridge, slightly arching, made of stone. I could see the separate rocks of which it was built, and I wanted to be one of them. Just one, that was enough, if only I could be part of that bridge between the thoughtworlds of East and West, connecting the insights of the *Buddha Dharma* with the modern Western mind. What my role might be—at the podium of a college classroom? at a desk in a library tower?—was less clear to me than the conviction possessing me now: I would be a stone in the building of that bridge.[11]

° Irish poet William Butler Yeats, in his mid-twenties, discovered that his destiny or soul-calling was to

> ...pluck till time and times are done
> The silver apples of the moon,
> The golden apples of the sun.[12]

In *Soulcraft* and *Nature and the Human Soul*, you'll find much more elaborate accounts of soul encounters and identities.[13]

Soul Purpose vs. Delivery System

Soul images, like these, do not tell the person *how* to embody their souls—what practices, projects, procedures, professions, arts, tools, or crafts to use, or in which settings to work. Rather, they inform the person *what* it is they are doing whenever they are doing their soul work. Their soul images reveal the deepest significance of their work and of their existence. Their conscious understanding of their soul's purpose allows them to assess to what degree their everyday actions are successful embodiments of their soul—and to make corrections as needed. These soul images are like navigational tools. They are the human equivalent of what allows monarch butterflies to migrate from New England to Mexico. The what is much deeper and more essential than the how. The how is in service to the what. The what—the soul image—is given *to* us, by Mystery. The how is determined, fashioned, and implemented *by* us, by our mature egos.

The what is what I call soul purpose. The how is what I call the delivery system for soul. The what might also be called a vision, and the how might be called a task:

> A vision without a task is just a dream.
> A task without a vision is just a job.
> A vision with a task can change the world.[14]

The what—the soul image, the navigational aid, the vision—might also be understood, metaphorically, as what William Stafford called the "thread you follow":

> There's a thread you follow. It goes among
> things that change. But it doesn't change.
> People wonder about what you are pursuing.
> You have to explain about the thread.
> But it is hard for others to see.
> While you hold it you can't get lost....[15]

Underworld Purpose vs. Middleworld Purpose—and the Sacred Marriage

Social or middleworld purpose is a perspective on personal meaning that is psychologically adolescent —again, referring here to a developmental stage, not an age range. (By calling it "adolescent," I intend no criticism or diminishment. Acquiring middleworld purpose is an essential early stage in human development.) Middleworld purpose defines us in terms of our social roles, our job descriptions, or the intended outcomes of our creative projects. Although a social or vocational perspective on purpose is necessary, appropriate, and healthy in psychological adolescence, it does not derive from the depths of the psyche or go to the depths of the world and is not enough to build a fulfilling life upon.

After being initiated into our underworld, soul, or ecological purpose, there is no longer what we might have earlier called a middleworld purpose. Now we have a middleworld *delivery system* for our true (soul) purpose. Our social roles and vocational endeavors are means to an end. Following my soul initiation, for example, I have been in the roles of psychologist, vision fast guide, author, and soulcraft facilitator, among others, but none of these social-vocational roles constitute my purpose. Rather, they have been, for me, delivery systems for the weaving of cocoons. (This essay is also an effort at cocoon weaving.) Yeats delivered his silver and golden apples with the vehicles of poetry, theater, and metaphysics. Malidoma Somé befriends the "enemy/stranger" by interpreting African indigenous wisdom for Western people through writing, speaking, community rituals, workshops, and trainings. In addition to writing and speaking, Joanna Macy embodies that stone in her imaginal bridge between the East and the West through the delivery systems of Buddhist scholarship, systems thinking, Buddhism-infused activism, and a theory and methodology for personal and social change she calls the Work That Reconnects.

From the perspective of our middleworld lives, the soul is a dream. From the underworld perspective of our soul's purpose, our middleworld lives—when disconnected from our souls—are illusions or phantasms, or drudgery.

But our middleworld lives are not incidental to the soul. Far from it.

90

The healthy, mature, middleworld ego is our means for making real our soul's underworld desires. This is why there's an ancient pancultural belief in a love affair between the soul and the ego; when they come together in partnership, this is the Sacred Marriage. Each has what the other lacks and longs for and is deeply allured by: The soul knows our true, destined place in the world, holds the knowledge of what is truly worth doing in our lives. But the soul has no means—no head or hands—to manifest that purpose. It is the healthy, mature ego that can fashion things and accomplish things in the material middleworld. The soul is captivated by this strategic capacity of the ego's to manifest, especially when accomplished artfully. The ego, in turn, is moonstruck by the soul's visions and passions. The mature ego wants, more than anything in life, to make real the dreams the soul has been weaving since before our birth—this is the deepest lovemaking. And it is life-making. The soul wants, more than anything, to be partnered with an ego with that vast desire and that elegant and artful set of reality-shaping skills. How absolutely romantic!

Upperworld and Underworld: Two Realms of the Spiritual or Transpersonal

In the Western world, the spiritual has been largely identified with the upperworld of God, Spirit, transcendence, enlightenment, or nondual consciousness. But the underworld of soul is equally spiritual, equally mystical, and equally essential to human development. Spirit and soul are both spiritual in the sense of being numinous (of the sacred or holy) and in the sense of being transpersonal (beyond the personal, beyond the realm of the ego's conscious self-awareness). The upperworld is the universal transpersonal, while the underworld is the unique transpersonal. While upperworld spiritualities focus on transcendence, the underworld journey provides for what cultural historian Thomas Berry called "inscendence," which he defined as "a descent into our pre-rational, our instinctive resources."[16] The underworld and upperworld are the two complementary realms of the spiritual. Either alone is incomplete and imperfect.

In the mainstream Western world, most religious organizations operate primarily in the middleworld of personal healing, charity, community, and morality, some in a mature and life-enhancing way, some not. In the relatively rare instances when religious people in the West truly approach the spiritual or transpersonal, it's virtually always upperworld, as is also the case in the East.

But upperworld practices alone result in an incomplete spirituality. They catalyze the life-shifting experience of oneness, of the interconnectedness or interbeing of everything, of oneself as an integral part of God or Spirit, and of the felt-sense of being unified with all of creation—along with the accompanying sense of peace, joy, vibrancy, and deep wonder about the world—but they do not help us find our unique transpersonal role in this world, the ecological niche that makes possible our greatest service to the world as well as our deepest fulfillment. Conversely, the underworld journey alone is incomplete. Living from soul, although deeply fulfilling and life-enhancing, can become too heavy, self-centered, or stressfully goal-oriented (overly attached to outcomes) when not integrated with the transcendent experience of oneness. Nondual awakening, although joyous and peaceful, can become ungrounded, purpose-less, or complacent or detached without the experience of soul encounter.[17]

Upperworld development in no way implies or requires underworld development. And vice versa. You can be an enlightened Zen master and not have a clue about your soul purpose—probably true of *most* Zen masters. And you can be a soul-initiated adult and never have had an experience of nondual consciousness.

But the universal and unique transpersonal are inextricably interwoven whether or not we've consciously experienced either one or their interconnectedness. In just two thirteenth-century sentences, Rumi—the Persian Sufi mystic—managed to sew together the upperworld and underworld or, better, showed how we can never have one without the other:

> God picks up the reed flute world and blows.
> Each note is a need coming through one of us,
> a passion, a longing-pain....[18]

The soul of anything—human, flower, frog, or fox—is a unique, God-originated passion or longing-pain pouring through one of us creatures.

Moltings: Radical Shifts in Middleworld Purpose

There is one type of change in life purpose that might be mistaken as a shift from middleworld to underworld purpose, from egocentric to soulcentric, but is actually a transition from one middleworld purpose to another. I think of this type of change, which can be quite profound, as a "molting," a metaphor borrowed from the lifecycle of moths and butterflies. The caterpillar is the larval or adolescent phase in the order of Lepidoptera. Caterpillars shed their skin several times, each time growing a larger one. Each of these sheddings is a molting. We can imagine that losing one's skin and growing a new one is a radical experience. But it does not hold a candle to the life change that occurs during the chrysalis stage when the caterpillar's body totally dissolves within the cocoon, enabling its cells to be reshaped into the adult form of a moth or butterfly. We can sense that this transition from earth-crawling caterpillar to winged butterfly is that much more profound than from one caterpillar incarnation to another.

Likewise, humans often go through a series of moltings—shifts from one social, vocational, political, religious, or spiritual role to another. This might, for example, be a transition from high school to college, or from single to married or the reverse, or from a job in advertising to a career as a psychotherapist, or from living in Louisiana to a life in L.A., or from being a closet gay to one who is out, or from being Christian to being Hindu. Some moltings are quite earthshaking, and involve extreme shifts in worldview, such as with religious or spiritual "awakenings."

For example, I recently read about a woman who, in her late twenties, had what she called a "complete emotional breakdown." She was in a dysfunctional relationship, living in a bad neighborhood, with an office job she hated. She became depressed, anxious, and desperate, and began using drugs and alcohol to dull the pain. Then she got fired. After a week or so of despair, she heard about a weeklong Buddhist meditation retreat in the desert. She packed up, left behind the life she had been living, and went to the retreat. During that week, she grieved wildly, learned to meditate, and was introduced to the Buddha dharma. By the end of the retreat, she made a vow to follow the Buddha's teachings. Clearly, this was a radical shift in worldview, lifestyle, and purpose that made all the difference in her life. (She eventually became a Buddhist teacher herself.) But it isn't a shift to underworld or upperworld purpose. It's a middleworld molting. Saying this is not in any way to diminish its significance, but rather to contrast it with an underworld or chrysalis passage, which shifts us not from one lifestyle or cultural identity to another, but from an identity rooted in the middleworld of culture to an underworld identity that is ecological and mythopoetic, an entirely different category of personal transformation.

Human moltings are major shifts or awakenings that occur before the start of the journey of soul initiation. The latter is the human chrysalis experience.

Contemporary Challenges in Uncovering Even Middleworld Purpose

Psychological early adolescence is a life stage reached by most everyone at puberty, but in the contemporary world only a small minority, perhaps 10 to 15 percent, ever mature beyond this stage due to the difficulties of completing its developmental task. That task is to fashion a social presence that is authentic and at the same time accepted by one's peer group. For an early adolescent (of any age), "purpose" is whatever might achieve that dual goal. But that goal, as simple as it might sound, is extraordinarily elusive in the egocentric and pathological environment of contemporary Western culture.

The challenges of reaching that goal are largely due to the all-too-common failures with the tasks of the two stages of childhood, especially with the nature-oriented tasks of childhood.[19] For example, it's hard to be authentic when you have trouble being present to yourself and others. Cultivating the capacity for sustained presence is the nature-oriented task of early childhood (a task that must be addressed by the parents and other family members of the young child). Presence is a prerequisite for true empathy and compassion—including self-compassion. Empathy for others and compassion for oneself have become rare achievements, and they are both essential for achieving authenticity.

Authenticity is also much more difficult when you don't feel at home in the more-than-human world (that is, the more extensive and differentiated world that includes our human world as a subset). Learning the enchantment of the larger world that enables the human village to exist at all is the nature-oriented developmental task of middle childhood. Nature connection is the evolutionary and psychological foundation for feeling at home in any other context, including your peer group.

All challenges in human development stem from the cultural disconnect from the greater Earth community. Conversely, our single greatest collective need now is for what I call eco-awakening—the somatic experience of being fully at home in the more-than-human world. Our second greatest need is the cultivation of personal authenticity and heartfelt social belonging.

Because psychological authenticity and social belonging have become so rare, they are perhaps the greatest and most pervasive longings in the Western world today. Witness the explosive growth and addictive qualities of social media such as Facebook. Being liked (or even "liked") and being authentic is what most people mean when they say they yearn for greater meaning and purpose in their lives or for the opportunity to participate meaningfully in the world. These are core middleworld desires and purposes. People want to feel more real and more a part of a real world, in greater communion with the web of life. They want their lives to make a difference. This, indeed, is the ultimate goal of the journey of soul initiation, but the necessary foundation for the soul journey is an achieved middleworld experience of *psychological* belonging (to yourself), *social* belonging (to a peer group), and *ecological* belonging (to the more-than-human world), the latter being eco-awakening. The eventual achievement of a soul-infused belonging to the world is built upon this prior three-legged middleworld foundation of belonging.

It seems what most people mean when they say they want more "soul" in their lives is actually this sense of psychological and social belonging. A smaller group also means greater *ecological* belonging. A group smaller yet means the kind of mystical underworld belonging to the world implied by the way I use the word *soul* in these pages. For yet others, "to experience soul" means to merge with the upperworld realm of Spirit or the divine.

The Journey of Soul Initiation

Although the descent to soul has largely been forgotten in mainstream Western culture,[20] there is nothing more essential in the world today. The experiential encounter with soul is the key element in the initiatory journey that culminates in true adulthood. And true adults—visionary artisans—are the generators of the most creative and effective actions in defense of all life and in the renaissance and evolution of generative human cultures.

But the encounter with soul is not a weekend workshop, a handful of imagery journeys, several entheogenic experiences, an occasional piece of dreamwork, or a vision fast. It is not something that can be achieved by simply using certain techniques or practices. It is a hazardous odyssey unfolding over many months or years. The risks to the Wanderer's sanity are great. It's a time of worry and distress for her family, too, and can be at least a temporary loss for her community. To reach the depths of soul generally requires extreme consciousness-shifting measures, practices, ceremonies, and/or circumstances.

The techniques and methods for the descent to soul are numerous but mostly unknown or forgotten in the contemporary mainstream West. I explore many of them in my books.

Whatever set of methods you use, they are your means to precipitate, quicken, and navigate the journey of soul initiation. It's entirely possible—and most always preferable—to undergo the journey in a contemporary manner that doesn't adopt or appropriate methods from another culture. Furthermore, no particular belief or faith in the journey itself is required, only a willingness to embark. Since 1980, the guides of Animas Valley Institute have woven together and cultivated a contemporary, Western, nature-based approach to the journey—a set of practices, ceremonies, principles, maps, and models.[21]

One of the most essential things we've learned is that in order to encounter your soul, you need something more than a method. As noted earlier, what must come first is the attainment of a stage of personal development that makes possible such an encounter. Until then, you can use any practices or rituals you'd like, but they will not result in soul encounter. The stage in question is absent from virtually all contemporary developmental models (including the models offered as comprehensive or integral) and is rarely attained in the Western world precisely because of its danger to contemporary society. This is the stage I have called the Cocoon, the stage in which we most fully embody the archetype of the Wanderer who constantly crosses borders into the mysteries of nature and psyche, and who hones the tools and skills of what I call soulcraft. Reaching that stage requires the wholing of the ego, self-healing, and attending to the most incomplete developmental tasks of childhood and early adolescence. I explore a great variety of practices for this preparatory work in *Wild Mind* and also in *Nature and the Human Soul*.

Harvesting the fruit of the journey of soul initiation and feeding the world with its bounty plays out over the rest of your life. When you first receive a vision, you won't know what it means or what to do with it. It takes months or years of living it into the world before you truly understand it. The vision is "only" the seed for a conversation you can begin with the world. That conversation itself is what enables you, eventually, to consciously understand your soul's place in the world and how best to embody it. Furthermore, as you embody your soul's place, you're actually modifying and coevolving your ecological niche. You are changing the world, not just yourself. You are co-imagining, co-creating, and coevolving hand-in-hand with the land, the waters, the Earth community. This is how human and Gaian evolution unfolds.[22]

Cooperating Creatively and Consciously with Evolution

We might wonder: Why do we humans need to go through an initiatory process to discover our destined place in the more-than-human world when, as far as we can tell, other species do not? This question brings us right to the heart of the matter, touched on earlier: We humans possess a power that other species—again, as far as we know—do not possess, or at least not in the way or to a degree that we do. This power is our form or mode of consciousness, our capacity for conscious self-awareness, our outlandish ability to be aware that we are aware. This ability is both our greatest strength and our greatest liability, and is perhaps the best candidate for what makes us distinctively human. It enables us, for example, to imagine possible futures to a degree or in a way that other species cannot and to manifest those possibilities, for good or for ill.[23] On the other hand, it renders us distinctively liable to suffer identity crises. And it creates a special zone of self-consciousness, the ego, that takes control of our waking lives so that we end up choosing and acting way more from this limited zone than from our larger psyche—until, that is, we've been initiated into our soul lives, "the one life that waits/ beyond all the others."

The existence of the ego is what makes us human but it also can be a catastrophic problem for us and for the rest of the Earth community if the ego is not carefully developed and matured. This is one of the most essential services a healthy culture provides: assuring that their children develop healthy, effective, life-enhancing egos. When this is done well by a human community, their youth, by their midteens, are psychospiritually prepared to embark upon the journey of soul initiation; they are ready to remember why they were born, the singular gift they possess for the web of life. Other species don't require this because they don't have egos that can get in the way of their full participation in the world. From day one, they're able to act and live in accordance with the place they were born to take.

We, on the other hand, have this exceptional capacity to become *consciously* aware of our unique place in the world, an egoic capacity that bestows us with an immense power of creativity. This is nothing less than the power to consciously cooperate with evolution. But, if we don't undergo the initiatory process and uncover our soul's purpose—distinct from our adolescent ego's purpose—then this special human capacity gives us, instead, the power to destroy the world, whether we intend to or not. Creation or Mystery has taken a great risk by sparking our species into being, perhaps an ultimate gamble. As of the early twenty-first century, there's no telling which way it will go. Again, Diane di Prima (echoing John Keats):

> ...the war of the worlds hangs here, right now, in the balance
> it is a war for this world, to keep it
> a vale of soul-making...[24]

We can see, then, that there is so much at stake within this topic of purpose, within this underworld realm of soul. A human with no purpose at all is a tragedy, a wasted life. A human with only an ego-level, psychologically adolescent purpose might realize some happiness and fulfillment, might in a variety of invaluable ways serve his or her community and the greater web of life, but could also end up being the worst kind of affliction: if he or she operates from a damaged ego and also "rises" to a position of significant economic, political, or military power, there's no limit to how much havoc s/he can wreak —as we've seen throughout history and especially in the twentieth and twenty-first centuries. But an initiated person, a true adult, whose ego is in service to soul, not to itself, whose conscious purpose is fully aligned with his or her soul's purpose, with his or her ecological niche in the web of life, this person possesses the power to enhance life in never-before-seen ways, to cooperate creatively with evolution, to participate—wildly and imaginatively—in the great work of our time.

Over the past few hundred years, Western culture has rediscovered and extended the possibilities of individual human development—an invaluable achievement—but so far this has been limited to the middleworld and upperworld realms of development. If we can now add the rediscovery and re-embracing of the underworld of soul, the West could accomplish something unprecedented in human history—something that might be necessary, as well, if we are to survive: the creation of a widespread, soul-infused culture in which full human development is culturally supported and prioritized, a resilient culture with a built-in, effective resistance to the more destructive potentials of the human species.

Endnotes

1. From David Whyte, "All the True Vows," in *The House of Belonging* (Langley, WA: Many Rivers Press, 1996), p. 24.

2. Diane di Prima, from "Rant," in *Pieces of a Song: Selected Poems* (San Francisco: City Lights, 1990).

3. Although a solo experience, my first vision fast was elegantly, wisely, and invaluably supported, through correspondence and written materials, by Steven Foster and

Meredith Little, founders of the School of Lost Borders. I recount the story of this fast in the preface to *Soulcraft: Crossing into the Mysteries of Nature and Psyche.*

4. "The ecological niche of an organism depends not only on where it lives but also on what it does.... By analogy, it may be said that the habitat is the organism's 'address', and the niche is its 'profession' biologically speaking." Eugene P. Odum, *Fundamentals of Ecology, 3rd Edition* (W. B. Saunders, 1971), p. 234.

5. A rite of passage usually lasts a day or two at the most; it marks, celebrates, and supports, but doesn't cause, the transition from one stage of life to the next. An initiatory process, in contrast, takes place over many months or years; includes a variety of ceremonies, rituals, practices, and mentorships; and, if all goes well, results in (causes) a psychospiritual transformation, such as the passage into true, initiated adulthood— which then deserves to be celebrated and supported with a rite of passage. Initiatory practices, in other words, take place during life stages and support developmental progress during that stage. Rites of passage, on the other hand, take place during the transition from one stage to the next and support those transitions.

6. Brian Swimme and Thomas Berry, *The Universe Story* (New York: Harper Collins, 1992), pp. 74–75.

7. In many spiritual circles, the ego is thought to be the primary problem, public enemy #1, something to rid oneself of. But without an ego, we're not human. The actual problem is not egos but *immature* egos (egocentric egos), by far the most common type of ego in the Western world today. The goal is not to get rid of the ego but to mature and deepen it, and deepen it by rooting it in the underworld of soul.

8. From "Rant," in *Pieces of a Song*, ibid.

9. Gary Snyder, *Back on the Fire* (Shoemaker and Hoard, 2007), p. 160.

10. Malidoma Somé, *Of Water and the Spirit* (New York: Arkana, 1994).

11. Joanna Macy, *Widening Circles* (Gabriola Island, BC: New Society Publishers, 2000), p. 106.

12. From "The Song of Wandering Aengus" in Richard J. Finneran, ed., *The Collected Poems of W. B. Yeats* (New York: Scribner, 1996), pp. 59–60.

13. Bill Plotkin, *Soulcraft: Crossing into the Mysteries of Nature and Psyche* (Novato: New World Library, 2003); Bill Plotkin, *Nature and the Human Soul: Cultivating Wholeness and Community in a Fragmented World* (Novato: New World Library, 2008).

14. Source unknown, although attributed to a variety of people including Chief Seattle, Winston Churchill, and Anonymous.

15. William Stafford, "The Way It Is," in *The Way It Is: New and Selected Poems* (Saint Paul, MN: Graywolf Press, 1998), p. 42.

16. Thomas Berry, *The Dream of the Earth* (San Francisco: Sierra Club Books, 1988), pp. 207–208. Berry saw inscendence as essential to human survival at this time: "We must go far beyond any transformation of contemporary culture.... None of our existing cultures can deal with this situation out of its own resources. We must invent, or reinvent, a sustainable human culture by a descent into our pre-rational, our instinctive resources. Our cultural resources have lost their integrity. They cannot be trusted. What is needed is not transcendence but 'inscendence.'"

17. For more on the relationship between underworld (soul) and upperworld (Spirit) and the three realms of human development, see chapter 2 of *Soulcraft* (ibid.), which can also be found online at http://www.natureandthehumansoul.com/newbook/chapter2_sc.htm.

18. Jelaluddin Rumi, *The Essential Rumi*, trans. Coleman Barks (San Francisco: Harper, 1995), p.103.

19. See: *Nature and the Human Soul*, ibid., chapters 4 and 5; or "A Brief Introduction to the Eco-Soulcentric Developmental Wheel," a link to which you can find under "What's New" on http://www.animas.org.

20. I say "largely forgotten" rather than "entirely forgotten" because what I think of as "soul" and the "descent to soul" are actually found in many places in Western culture, hidden in plain sight, but very rarely recognized as such. Although not articulated in terms of psychoecological niche, something like an underworld conception of soul can nonetheless be detected in such Western habitats as the cycles of Greek and Arthurian legends, the sacred mythologies of the Celtic-speaking peoples, the work of authors and artists from Dante to D.H. Lawrence, or the stanzas of Romantic poets like Coleridge and Wordsworth, as well as my favorite resources of Rumi, Blake, Goethe, Rilke, Yeats, Hesse, Jung, Eliot, Hopkins, Hillman, Stafford, Thomas Berry, Jean Houston, James Hollis, Mary Oliver, Clarissa Pinkola Estes, Michael Meade, and David Whyte.

21. See: Bill Plotkin, *Wild Mind: A Field Guide to the Human Psyche* (Novato: New World Library, 2013); Soulcraft, ibid.; Nature and the Human Soul, ibid.; www.animas.org; www.wildmindbook.com; www.natureandthehumansoul.com; see: "The Story of Animas," a link to which you can find under "What's New" on http://www.animas.org.

22. For this and other ecological and eco-cultural perspectives incorporated in this paper, I am grateful for the help of Kevin Fetherston, Ph.D., riparian forest ecologist; Nate Bacon, M.A., cultural ecologist and wildlife tracker; and Julian Norris, Ph.D., ecopsychologist and leadership coach.

23. Geneen Marie Haugen, "Awakening Planetary Imagination: A Theory and Practice" (PhD dissertation, California Institute of Integral Studies, San Francisco, 2015).

24. From "Rant," in *Pieces of a Song*, ibid.

❧

Chapter 5

THE POWER OF FEMININE PURPOSE

Carly Visk and Andrea Dennis

When the Divine Feminine asks a question, she does not go hunting for the answer. Instead she invites the answer to find her.

—Author unknown

For many years, the predominant approach to our human experience has been expressed in a masculine way. We have sought to compete, achieve, and transcend. This is not a reference to traditional genders—that is, male and female, although that continues to be an area of our societal human experience being called into balance. Rather, this refers to the energetic qualities of masculine and feminine, both of which rely upon each other—the yin and the yang. The masculine energy is important for thrusting forth what we manifest, while the feminine energy focuses on the being rather than the doing, a remembrance of our interconnectedness. While both qualities are equally important and sacred, we invite you to consider that calling forth the feminine side of purpose is vital to restoring balance both within ourselves and on our planet at this time. Like the power of Mother Earth and her sacred waters, the Divine Feminine within each and every one of us is a guide to the harmony and radiance that is our true nature. Surrendering to this fierce and loving grace is an essential part of opening to one's purpose, and this chapter aims to explore how and why.

Most concepts, programs, and literature in the purpose field are focused on the outward expression of achievement-oriented purpose. However, this imbalance in favor of the masculine flies under the radar since our society rewards masculine expressions of accomplishment. In fact, masculine pursuits such as achieving, transcending, and gaining tend to be continuously reinforced while feminine traits such as receptivity, softness, and vulnerability are often not valued and therefore difficult to nurture and sustain. Indeed, there is often no tangible reward for embracing these resplendent yet subtle feminine qualities, perhaps only the support of those aiming to do the same. Therefore, the unique contribution of this chapter is to explore a feminine approach to purpose and reflect on how the gifts of the Divine Feminine unfolding on our planet now can be fully received and integrated.

Through sacred space and ritual, we have aspired to channel the words on this page from the Divine Feminine Herself. We have aimed to embody the received teachings as fully as possible during the writing process and we invite you to read this chapter from a place of embodiment as well. Feel into the words and invite them to move beyond the mind, and cognitive understanding, into the heart.

Begin with Gratitude and Remembrance

Gratitude is the memory of the heart.

—Jean Baptiste Massieu

As we write these words, we realize that it is not only us, Andrea and Carly, expressing our insights and intuitions on feminine purpose, but also our ancestors, our mothers, and all those who have given us life. It is the lineages of wisdom that have evolved and guided us since the awakening of human consciousness. It is Mother Earth and her waters from which all life on this beautiful blue planet come from. It is this feminine power and love that connects all of us.

And this is where we begin, with remembrance for where we come from and gratitude for this sacred and mysterious life. While at first purpose may seem to be something that needs to be discovered or achieved, nature invites us to simply remember the wisdom that we are. And once we connect to this innate purpose, gratitude flows like a river, effortlessly. With the same inner knowing as a bird soaring upon the wind, we have the opportunity to dance with the divine unfolding of life in each moment. And so it is, with remembrance and gratitude, we listen and take one breath at a time.

Our purpose can be felt in the light of the stars as well as in myths and stories that have been passed down to us from generation to generation. The Jewish myth of the angel Lailah reminds us that our purpose is already within our being and it has only been forgotten:

> According to this midrash, there is an angel, Lailah, who brings the soul and the seed together and then sees to it that the seed is planted in the womb. In doing so, Lailah serves as a midwife of souls. While the infant grows in the womb, Lailah places a lighted candle at the head of the unborn infant, so he or she can see from one end of the world to the other. So too does the angel teach the unborn child the entire Torah, as well as the history of his or her soul. Then, when the time comes for the child to be born, the angel extinguishes the light in the womb and brings forth the child into the world. And the instant the child emerges, the angel lightly strikes its finger to the child's lip, as if to say "Shh," and this causes the child to forget everything learned in the womb. Still, the story implies, that knowledge is present, merely forgotten.1

A second part of this myth was told to us verbally by a beautiful and wise singer named Peia. She told the story during an intimate concert and went on to say that the tradition of lighting birthday candles comes from this myth. Each year on the day of our birth, we light a candle to remind us of the inner knowing of our soul's purpose. And like this, through ritual, perhaps rituals already present in our lives, we are able to create space to hear the whispers of the universe within. After telling this story, she continued on to sing:

> Blessed we are to dance on this ground with the rhythm of saints to carry the sound. We hold a prayer for the Earth, for the ones yet to come. May you walk in beauty and remember your song.

In Native American traditions, it is said that we are here today because our ancestors prayed for it to be so. Just as those who have walked before us paved the way for our lives, now it is our responsibility to do the same for our future generations.

Though society's dominant modern worldview and unsustainable way of living has disconnected many of us from nature and her inherent intelligence, we are being called to return to the truth of our interconnectedness. Joanna Macy and Chris Johnstone write:

> Could the next leap in evolution arise out of a shift in identification, in which we shed the story of battling for supremacy and move instead into playing our role as part of a larger team of life on Earth? Could the creativity and survival instinct of humanity as a whole, or even of life as a whole, act through us? Here connected consciousness stems from a widening of our self-interest, where we are guided by the intention to act for the well being of all life... We stand at an evolutionary crossroads, and we collectively, could turn either way. Our own choices are part of that turning... When our central organizing priority becomes the well-being of all of life, then what happens through us is the recovery of our world.2

We are, at the same time, a drop of water and the entire ocean. We are children of the Earth and co-creators of the future. We are here together as a united family of light. Let us remember to greet the dawn every morning and give thanks for the abundance around us and the guidance within us. As we acknowledge and nurture the beauty of all life, we allow the purpose of each and every one of us to unfold. We invite you now to close your eyes for a moment, feel the intelligence of life within you, and reflect on your interconnectedness to everything that is, everything that has been, and everything that ever will be.

A Process Of Awakening

Beautiful dreamer, wake unto thee. Undreamed of love awaits for thee...

—Song lyrics adapted from Stephen Foster

In this moment, here we are. Like life, our purpose is unfolding and evolving. It is a process of awakening. Breathing in and breathing out, we are continuous rebirth. With a foundation of gratitude and remembrance, we now cultivate awareness of the present moment to support this unfolding process. When we release the mind's grasp on the past and the future, we let go of the desire to achieve an outward purpose through the overcoming of obstacles. Instead, we connect to a deeper inner purpose in the present and become vessels for the flowering of consciousness. Eckhart Tolle speaks eloquently on this concept:

> A new heaven and a new earth are arising within each of us at this moment. So awakening to your life's purpose is not to try to look to the future and expect fulfillment there but to stay in the moment, allowing the ego to dissolve. Your life's inner purpose is primary, and your inner purpose is to awaken, to be conscious. In whatever you do, your state of consciousness is the primary factor.3

We strive for clarity and peace of mind, for as within, so without. The world we live in is a reflection of what is inside of us, so tending to our inner landscapes and staying in the present moment may be the most powerful tool we have for manifesting change in alignment with spirit.

When we quiet the mind, we begin to hear the voice of something beyond our rational intellect. We allow ourselves to be guided by intuition. It is the voice of our ancestors, of our spirit guides and helpers, and of the God of our own unique understanding, whether that be Great Spirit, our Highest Self, the Great Mother, our Father, the force of evolution, or by any other name. With a calm mind and open heart, we can hear the secrets of infinity-eternity beyond the familiar domain of time and space. We surrender to our deepest truth of being one with everything.

In the current whirlwind of information on the internet and social media, it is more important than ever to be able to discern what we know to be true. We can cultivate this knowingness by returning to our instincts and internal compasses. As Carl Jung writes:

> Your vision will become clear only when you look into your heart... Who looks outside, dreams. Who looks inside, awakens.

We invite you to take a moment and turn inward: Start with your breath. Notice the pauses in between the inhalation and exhalation. After a few breaths, allow a question you've been reflecting on lately to arise. Then ask yourself: *Where is my internal compass pointing?*

Jung believed that an individual's purpose was to achieve Self-realization, or the highest potential of human awareness, by following the guidance of the inner soul and also by exploring archetypes and symbols of the collective unconscious. Given that the process of opening to inner purpose is aided especially by feminine qualities such as allowing, receiving, nurturing, and listening, we suggest that connecting to feminine archetypes is a fruitful way to cultivate this awakening. In doing so, we also become vessels for the expression of the Sacred Feminine that is needed now to bring the dream of the modern world back into balance. For example, meditating with the archetype of the Wise Woman, often symbolized by the High Priestess of the Tarot, may help us connect to the knowledge that is hidden within the mysteries of the universe to understand our world in new and unique ways. Similarly, meditating with the archetype of the Great Mother, often represented by the Virgin Mary, may help us to become more compassionate. Cultivating greater compassion, which Osho describes as the "highest expression of love," may be the greatest collective purpose we share as humans. Let us be vessels for this immense love that our world so greatly needs, by whichever way our heart guides us.

Embrace the Tension

Serenity comes when you trade expectations for acceptance.

—Unknown

There is a consistent dance in the human experience to both create and let go of attempting to control. This too applies to the concept of purpose. How can we embrace the tension of living our purpose in day-to-day life, while also practicing nonattachment from achieving what the mind believes our purpose to be? It is a balancing act of effort and ease. On one hand, straining to define or achieve our purpose can create an overexertion of energy and psychological entrapment. On the other hand, when we lack direction in our lives, we risk becoming lost in existential confusion, which can lead to a denial of the gift of life itself. While recognizing that purpose is not something to be accomplished through force, we must still acknowledge that the drive to find purpose in our lives most often is pointing to a deeper yearning that requires attention and nurturing. This reminds us again that living our purpose is a process of awakening that requires both patience and discernment. It is a journey of learning to allow purpose to move through us in a nonattached way.

A place to start is to consider how we label life events. If we consider them to be "bad" or "good," positive or negative, we create a story or context that can detract from a total acceptance of them as part of our life's expression of purpose. The importance of moving forward while practicing nonattachment and nonjudgment is illustrated in the following Sufi parable, *Fatima's Journey*:

> Fatima was the daughter of a thread maker. One day her father asked her to join him on a sea journey for business so that she could find a husband and settle. During the

journey came a great storm, killing her father and washing her ashore. While wandering the new shores, destitute and depressed, a family of cloth-makers found her. Although they did not have many resources, they took her in and taught her their trade. Within a few years, Fatima became happy again in her new life.

One day while she was on the seashore, slave traders abducted Fatima. She was taken to another country to be sold as a slave. Her sadness and depression had no bounds. At the slave market, a man looking for a slave to work in his woodshop came across Fatima. Upon seeing her impoverished disposition, he decided to buy her, so he might give her a better life than that of the others. When he took Fatima home, to be a servant for his wife, he discovered that all his money has been stolen. Now penniless, he and his family, including Fatima, were forced to work the long and arduous hours in the wood yard making masts for great ships. Fatima worked tirelessly to show her gratitude *for his* kindness, and she became his trusted aide. In her third life, Fatima again found happiness.

The man later asked Fatima to embark upon a journey for business. She readily accepted and during the voyage a giant typhoon upended the ship. Yet again, Fatima became shipwrecked and cast ashore alone. She wept and become despondent to life. "Why is it," she cried, "that whenever I try to do something it comes to grief? Why should so many unfortunate things happen to me?" Of course she received no direct answer.

She finally arose and started walking inland. She had landed in a place with a great legend that a foreign woman would one day enter the land and build a tent for the Emperor, since no one in the country had yet made a tent. Every year, the Emperor sent his staff to all the cities in order to find the foreign woman, and it was in this that Fatima arrived. She was taken to the Emperor. He asked her to make him a tent. She thought that perhaps she could do it and asked for rope. When they said they had none, she remembered learning to spin thread from her father and made rope. She then asked for cloth; seeing that there was no cloth, she recalled living with the cloth-makers and set out to make cloth. She did. The last piece she needed was the tent poles, and again there were none to be found. She thought of the wood yard, and how she had been trained, and with great artistry she fashioned tent poles.

When the completed tent was presented to the Emperor, he granted Fatima anything she requested. She chose to happily settle in the new lands with her partner and live in peace for the rest of her days.4

Fatima's journey reminds us of the need to embrace both the tension of having purpose in the moment and practicing nonattachment to a certain outcome. Trusting in the unfolding of life does not mean a passive complacency or sidelined efforts. It does not mean we cannot have goals. It is a total embrace of what transpires in the present moment without being weighed down by the past or attempting to control the future. We can set goals to express our personal purpose, and then practice nonattachment from the outcome and live in the present moment—nothing else will lead to the future except for the now. No matter where we find ourselves, this is exactly where we are meant to be. And as Sufi poet Rumi writes, "If all you can do is crawl, start crawling." Take a moment, and considering Fatima's story, ask yourself: *If I could release the need to define my purpose, and live in the present moment—now—what does that feel like?*

There is value in letting go of the need to always understand and to have certainty. While being certain of something is often preferred over ambivalence, it can actually be harmful in that it limits new possibilities and may create a devastating effect if the certainty does not play out in reality. A friend of ours describes this as the *violence of certainty*. When we consider life from a perspective of certitude, it overlooks the tension of the known and unknown. This is also true in the expression of purpose. Throughout life, we have many roles to play, and our soul's purpose fluidly dances with our earthly manifestation. The freedom comes in knowing that all we need to do is be in the present moment allowing all that arises to exist in the same breath. Let us tread lightly on any sense of certitude or absolute as we hold the tension of being both purposeful and nonattached. In the following passage, Aldous Huxley encourages us to remember this:

> It's dark because you are trying too hard. Lightly child, lightly. Learn to do everything lightly. Yes, feel lightly even though you're feeling deeply. Just lightly let things happen and lightly cope with them. I was so preposterously serious in those days… Lightly, lightly—it's the best advice ever given me… So throw away your baggage and go forward. There are quicksands all about you, sucking at your feet, trying to suck you down into fear and self-pity and despair. That's why you must walk so lightly. Lightly my darling.5

As we walk gently upon the Earth embracing both the light and the darkness, may we trust that we are all exactly where we're meant to be.

Allowing Purpose To Flow

> *I don't believe people are looking for the meaning of life as much as they are looking for the experience of being alive.*
>
> —Joseph Campbell

Many of the Great Wisdom Traditions spring from the intention to reveal our interconnectedness, or the philosophical, spiritual, and scientific understanding of non-separation and intrinsic oneness, otherwise known as nonduality. We all come from the vast field of consciousness moving through us, and there we shall return. As the great teacher, Pierre Teilhard de Chardin expressed, "We are not human beings having a spiritual experience. We are spiritual beings having a human experience."

In this truth, we are already living our purpose. We are exactly where we are meant to be, no matter our current situation. Yet, from a relative perspective, we can reflect on our individual journey and begin to align our lives more fully with purpose through the practice of gratitude, remembrance, presence, and nonattachment. And as this journey unfolds, our creative force and the artistry within us continue to emerge. In our interconnectedness, we are all part of a joyous odyssey as co-creators, mirroring each other's growth and transformation.

We choose to allow purpose to flow through us in every moment, and when we are in need of guidance, we are gifted with an internal compass and a wide range of approaches and teachers for support. For some of us, the masculine approach to strive and achieve is our calling. This indeed has been the prominent meme. And yet, the opportunity to simply allow our unique journeys to unfold and evolve is also present. Rainer Maria Rilke speaks to this with grace:

> Have patience with everything unresolved in your heart
> and to try to love the questions themselves as if they were
> locked rooms or books written in a very foreign language.
> Don't search for the answers, which could not be given
> to you now, because you would not be able to live them.
> And the point is to live everything. Live the questions now.
> Perhaps then, someday far in the future, you will gradually,
> without even noticing it, live your way into the answer.

Herein lies the feminine approach—the power in feminine purpose—the receiving, the listening, the inner knowing. It is not a mountain we need to climb or a valley we need to enter, it is the very moment we are living right now.

❧

Endnotes

1. Schwartz, H. Mysteries of the Angel Lailah. Retrieved from jbooks.com/interviews/index/IP_Schwartz_Lailah.htm.

2 Macy, J. & Johnstone, C. (2012). *Active Hope: How to Face the Mess We're in without Going Crazy*. Novato, CA: New World Library.

3. Juline, K. "Awakening to Your Life's Purpose." Retrieved from eckharttolle.com/article/Awakening-Your-Spiritual-Life's-Purpose.

4. http://www.ideas-and.com/sufi-parable-fatima.

5 Huxley, A. (1962). *Island*. New York, NY: Harper Collins.

Chapter 6

PURPOSE AND THE WESTERN MYSTERY TRADITION

Bryan Alvarez

In this chapter, I describe one of the most important spiritual ritualistic practices within the Western Esoteric Tradition: the Knowledge and Conversation of the Holy Guardian Angel. It is my hope that the elucidation of this ritualistic work, considered the classic method of attaining personal religious experience as exemplified in the West, will uncover that which is hidden and shine light onto the darkness of Western culture's spiritual birthright. By placing it within the context of purpose, history, art, and trance consciousness, we may be able to see it from a different angle, thereby unraveling its spiritual mysteries in a more modern and meaningful way. The different levels of purpose, from the personal to the cosmic, give a deep insight to this most arcane ritual practice.

Introduction

It has been called many things by many people. It is Christ to the Christian, Atman to the Hindu, the personal God to the Bhakti Yogi, and the Higher Genius to the psychotherapist. It is the Philosopher's Stone to the alchemists and the Daemon to the Greeks. It is the Holy Guardian Angel. Within the Western esoteric tradition the ritual of the Knowledge and Conversation of the Holy Guardian Angel has long stood as a signpost of spiritual achievement amongst magical adepts. While many traditions have similar concepts and practices, this ritual exemplifies the Western spiritual heritage. The higher self shines like the Augoeides of the heavens, that luminous light from the ocean of spirit. In essence, it is a spiritual practice of becoming aware of one's purpose on a number of different levels, from the personal to the cosmic.

The phrase Holy Guardian Angel in this context was purportedly first used by Abraham von Worms, a German rabbi, in 1458 in the influential *Book of the Sacred Magic of Abramelin the Mage.* This text gives ritualistic instructions on how to achieve this knowledge and conversation. Along the way the spiritual practitioner is expected to confront the shadow of their psyche and tame personal demons before they are able to ascend to the heights of the angels. It is a work of purification, consecration, and empowerment. The result is inspiration, insight, enlightenment, and the knowledge of one's purpose.

First, I would like to define and give a short history of Western esotericism. It is important to understand the lineage of thought that has brought us this particular work by placing it within a historical context. Then I will talk a bit about the varieties of purposeful experience the practitioner may expect to come in contact with in this type of work. Finally, I will talk about how through the lens of purpose this type of spiritual work can take on new meanings. It is important not only to understand this work, but how modern thought plays a role in understanding it. What was once understood as demons and spirits has become reinterpreted as imbalanced structures within the psyche in the modern era. Yet the goal has stayed the same, which is to heal the self and synergize with the transcendent.

A Short History of Western Esotericism

Western esotericism, otherwise known as the Western Mystery Tradition, is a term designating a collection of spiritual practices that have developed within Western society. While this umbrella term first found its use in seventeenth-century Europe, the practices that make up this tradition date back to late antiquity. In the second and third centuries CE, we see arising three major pillars of thought that are the foundation of Western esotericism. These are Hermeticism, Gnosticism, and Neoplatonism. In short, what these three schools have in common is that the main purpose of life is to transcend the self to achieve spiritual union with the divine.

By the Middle Ages we start to see the development of the Kabbalah, as well as the publication of a variety of grimoires. These are magical texts containing alchemical formulas to not only achieve gnosis but to also work miracles in the physical world. One particularly important aspect of the Kabbalah is the model it uses showing how all levels of existence, from the gross to the subtle, are interconnected holistically. When we begin to talk more about purpose in relation to a spiritual practice this will become a very important concept.

By the Renaissance and early modern period many were synthesizing these ideas together, as they were considered "pagan" philosophies. Two of the most prominent were Heinrich Cornelius Agrippa, who used Christian Kabbalah as a framework to explore philosophical and scientific traditions of antiquity; and Paracelsus, who brought together various traditions of folk magic and the alchemical tradition. It is in these works that much of modern-day Western esoteric practices originate. In this time period we also see the rise of trance states as developed by the works of Franz Mesmer, with Animal Magnetism; and Allan Kardec, with the Spiritualism movement. What we see here are practices that heal, manifest, and induce trance, or visionary, states of mind. These are important concepts to consider as we begin to discuss modern esotericism in the light of purpose.

By the eighteenth and nineteenth centuries, "occultism" had emerged fully as a third way between Christianity and science. Here we see the rise of major occult science thinkers, such as Helena Blavatsky, with the Theosophical society, and Rudolf Steiner, with the Anthroposophical Society. By the twentieth century, with the rise of secret esoteric orders such as the Hermetic Order of the Golden Dawn (HOGD), to the new esoteric thought of G. I. Gurdjieff, we've seen those three pillars of Western magical thought create an entire family of spiritual practices. The

HOGD is also known for their work creating systems of correspondence wherein vastly different spiritual and religious traditions are brought together because of common experience or underlying philosophy. This underlying foundation stems from the branches of those three original pillars of Western esotericism. Despite the many different branches of practice, the ultimate goal of achieving a sense of transcendence has seemingly stayed the same in all this time. These systems of correspondence show the commonality of ideas and practices. British occultist Samuel Liddell MacGregor Mathers founded the HOGD. His translation of the *Book the Sacred Magic of Abramelin the Mage* still stands as one of the more important versions available.

Finally by the 1960s and 1970s, with the rise of the New Age movement, Wicca, Chaos Magick, modern Paganism, and the shamanic revival, it would seem that we have come full circle, reinterpreting the ancient techniques of gnosis for a technological age. By this time, magical consciousness, visionary experience, alchemical healing, and the transcendent self has manifested in a wide variety of practices. What is particularly interesting about this is how many practitioners in the West have begun to bring together a wide variety of different cultures into one space to heal, to manifest, and to induce trance or magical consciousness. This is a continuation of the correspondences of the occult orders of the eighteenth and nineteenth centuries, but with an even greater reach by including modern technology, environmentalism, and indigenous techniques.

As we can see, the Western Mystery Tradition has come a long way to be what it is today. Containing various disciplines from many people and places from around the world, we find aspects of philosophy, science, religion, art, literature, music, and so much more. It is a full study of the human experience. Yet, at the center is this transcendent self, this Holy Guardian Angel to encounter, which requires searching beyond the rational mind toward that divine unity at the heart of it all.

Art and Magick

We've talked about the history of Western esotericism, but what exactly is this magick they speak? Why is it spelled with a *k* sometimes? What is the difference, if any, between art and magick? According to infamous nineteenth-century British occultist Aleister Crowley, *"Magick is the Science and Art of causing Change to occur in conformity with Will."* This is a powerful definition in that it allows both sides of the human experience, the subjective and the objective. A spiritual practice by this definition should on one hand be a work of living art, including both the art and the process. Yet it should have repeatable and effective methods that other practitioners can utilize in their personal development. In this sense then, this type of magickal practice is akin to art therapy or sound healing in many ways. It is a practice of becoming one's self, entering into one's purpose, and a system to communicate the methodology behind the process.

Crowley is also the one to begin spelling magic with a *k* so as to differentiate it from the stage magic of the day. His influence is so great on modern Western esoteric practice that to not include him would be to neglect a piece of magickal history. What is significant about his work is the philosophy that underlined all of it. This philosophy can be summed up in the phrase "the method of Science, the aim of Religion." Despite occultism being considered a "third way" between Christianity and science in the eighteenth and nineteenth centuries, the scientific method played a large role in Crowley's spiritual work. While the HOGD created systems of correspondences between esoteric traditions, Crowley included the scientific discoveries of his time to develop his map of the universe.

However, there is another individual who certainly needs to be discussed when talking about art and magick as a system of self-discovery and purpose. While Crowley's definition of magick is still commonly the one you hear about, there is another variation of it put forth by Dion Fortune. While lesser known in popular culture than Crowley, Fortune is one of the nineteenth century's greatest female magicians. Her works have been incredibly influential in many ways, spanning many powerful topics such as Hermetic Qabalah, Scientific Illuminism, gender in an esoteric practice and much more. She defines magick as "the art of causing changes in consciousness in conformity with the Will." Fortune was a psychologist by trade, and so here the emphasis is on changes in consciousness. This is an important distinction to be made when we start to consider modern magick in its many forms. She was bringing magick into the twentieth century in ways that would not be fully understood until the 1980s and 1990s

When we look at the main goals of the Western esoteric traditions, that of healing, manifesting change, and trance consciousness, all culminating in that transcendent self through ritual action, we see the ultimate point of change in this magickal definition as starting from within the individual. This practice is about becoming one's true self and fully entering into one's purpose. It is not enough to cause change to our environment if we are not willing to change ourselves first. We're now edging a bit closer to what it means to have Knowledge and Conversation with the Holy Guardian Angel.

It is now necessary that we talk about the idea of purpose and how it functions within the Western esoteric philosophy. We can see from the above definitions of magick that there is a specific direction of change from the inner to the outer in the Western esoteric practice. As the practitioner begins to work in this way, ideas like Truth, Purpose, and Will take on entirely new meanings.

Perspectives and Purpose

Purpose simply defined is the reason for which something exists or is done, made, or used. Within the scope of this chapter, we can see how purpose can take on a much larger definition. As the veils of self are lifted through methods of artistic expression, framed within archetypal spiritual awakenings, the individual is brought face to face with the deepest aspects of their psyche. But the magician is never isolated from the greater context of society, environmental conditions, and the universe at large.

Purpose through this lens can be seen as a unifying force for humanity. As individuals align with their purpose we will see deeper synergy and collaboration across diverse regions of the human experience, technologically, culturally, and biologically. Purpose can be seen from a variety of different levels. Within the context of this chapter I will talk about many layers of purpose. This includes personal purpose, soul purpose, absolute purpose, and cosmic purpose.

A magickal practice as defined by the parameters of the Western esoteric tradition will fall under different levels of purpose over time as the individual works toward the transcendent self. As the practitioner begins working from the inner to the outer, causing change in conformity with the will, we see how the mechanism of change is associated with the individual and their environment. Here environment is defined as the aggregate of surrounding things, conditions, or influences to which the individual interacts. Let us see how this idea of purpose moves from the inner transformation of the individual outward and upward to the transcendent self.

First is **Personal Purpose**. Life results in a unique set of self-identifying experiences for each person. Each life is unique and contains a story of awakening unto itself. It is both nature AND nurture that play roles in our personal purpose. Cultural and biological factors can be strengths in some ways and limitations in others. By knowing our strengths and limitations, we are able to direct our attention to healing imbalances and becoming more actualized within our abilities. When we become familiar with our strengths and limitations, we are able to find our place within the greater planetary society.

Next is **Soul Purpose**. This deep reservoir is home to our brightest light and our darkest shadow. It is through these concepts that we discover our soul's purpose. As we begin to dance with nonduality these concepts take on new meaning and importance. Here the individual begins working with the magickal exercises to induce an alchemical transformation within the identity of the self in relation to the universe. The deeper we go into our *Soul Purpose*, we begin to pay very close attention to those things in our lives that have shaped us into who we are. Practices such as meditation, yoga, art, and science are all methods for the individual to operate within their soul purpose. The result of this type of spiritual work is to harmonize the imbalances within the psyche and body of the self within a given environment. Here the individual learns what they are indeed capable of achieving.

Then we have **Absolute Purpose**. This is the spiritual impulse to "wake up" and realize the nonduality of existence. This drive is important, as it relates not to the subjective experience of the individual to their environment but rather to the objective nature of the universe. This impulse to awaken into our higher genius is answered by the magickal practice. It is the promise of change for the better. The environmental conditions here are the self within the universe.

Finally, at the largest scale of being, the mechanism of evolutionary consciousness itself, we have **Cosmic Purpose**. Once again we are brought to the very mechanism that was hinted at within the absolute purpose. It is not just a subjective environmental relationship with the universe as object, but rather the universe as a process of which we are a part. This level of consciousness is at the very heart of causing changes in consciousness in conformity with will. This is the type of consciousness unimpeded by psychological or physical imbalances within the individual. The imbalances of the self have been realigned and the limits of our potential have been expanded to include change we never thought possible. This cosmic purpose consciousness is created by the Knowledge and Conversation with the Holy Guardian Angel. While we may traverse many different relational levels of purpose throughout this journey upward and outward toward the transcendent self, each path is leading to the same destination.

So, what exactly is this Holy Guardian Angel and what does it mean to have knowledge *of* and conversation *with* such a thing?

The Ritual

The Knowledge and Conversation of the Holy Guardian Angel (HGA), otherwise known as the Abramelin Operation, is considered to be the pinnacle work of the Western mysteries. It opens the magician up to even greater perspectives of purpose, truth, and meaning. We have talked about definitions of magick (and a variety of traditions within), varying levels of meaningful purpose, and the movement of experiential consciousness from within outward to encompass the whole of the universal process. In this way I hope to have given the reader an idea of what to expect from this type of work in preparation.

The *Book of the Sacred Magic of Abramelin the Mage* is written in three sections. The first section consists of the author's travels and the miraculous experiences he had while performing this work. Much advice is given regarding general magick practice. The second section consists of the methods by which the operation is carried out. This includes varieties of magickal practice, considerations, preparations, astrological information, orations, and conjurations of a vast array of angelic and demonic entities. The final section consists of practical applications of working with these spirits through the use of magickal talismans.

The ritual itself is a long and winding work that takes place over the course of many months and even years for some. Depending on the translation of this text, or the variation of it as interpreted by others, you may find a minimum range of 6 to 18 months of magickal work and spiritual cultivation to complete. Coming from a more arcane form of magickal tradition, much of what is in this ritual as written would likely be difficult for a modern practitioner in the West. The magician is expected to pray daily at sunrise and sunset. During this time they must avoid alcohol, sex, and any other distractions that may lead their concentration from the goal at hand. For these reasons, isolation in nature is thought to be the most conducive to this work. This includes both family and friends, save for those that may be there to assist (though isolation is best).

The magician in this work will have many meditative and visionary experiences. There is an aspect of *dharana*, or concentration of the mind, to it in that the magician is fully immersed in the visionary experience but without the trappings of attachment. The phantasmagoric landscapes of the mind have a tendency to lead the individual to and fro without having led them anywhere at all. A level of discernment is required if they are to find this balance between what is truth and what is distraction. "Illumination consists in the introduction of the mind to a higher mode of consciousness than that which is built up out of sensory experience," says Dion Fortune in her most famous work *The Mystical Qabalah*.

As this work continues, the vision becomes clearer through the help of gnostic trance techniques, while the internal voice of the magician begins to come from a place beyond egoic limitations. The truth and success of the experience is such that the magician will know beyond a doubt that the connection has been made. Occultist, psychotherapist, and onetime secretary for Aleister Crowley, Israel Regardie wrote in his popular work *The Tree of Life*: "It may be that with the third and last period this Dark

Night of the Soul will pass slowly and imperceptibly, and then will arise the soft rose and pink grandeur of the Dawn, to be followed by the bright daylight of the Knowledge and Conversation, with the beatific vision and the perfume so sweet and sustaining to sense and soul, of the Holy Guardian Angel." Regardie wrote much about this ritual process from both magickal and psychological perspectives. His work would lay the foundation for modern esoteric thought.

With the connection made, the magician must then begin to harmonize the imbalances of the self that are deeper. This is done through a series of conjurations of a variety of spirits, both good and evil. Whether one sees these spiritual entities as separate from or part of one's self is irrelevant. The goal is to heal the imbalances of the self. The subject of spiritual entities having an existence wholly beyond the self is a large debate within the magickal community and much larger than the scope of this particular chapter. I shall leave the subject with a quote from Carl Jung, "We discover that the 'other' in us is indeed 'another,' a real man, who actually thinks, does, feels, and desires all the things that are despicable and odious... A whole man, however, knows that his bitterest foe, or indeed a host of enemies, does not equal that one worst adversary, the 'other self' who dwells in his bosom." Working under the guidance of the HGA, with its perfected voice and pure vision, the mind of the magician is brought to realms beyond the rational and the egoic to achieve balance.

Once complete, the magician has after long last entered the realm of the adept. This is the end of this particular work, but as it should be expected there comes a new set of trials to push through.

Analysis through the Lens of Purpose

In all of its detail, we see how the practitioner must learn to move beyond rational mind if they are to succeed. Looking at this from Fortune's definition of magick as the "art and science of causing changes in consciousness in conformity with the will," and from the different levels of purpose touched upon prior, we can begin to look at this work in a different way. We talked of personal purpose, soul purpose, absolute purpose, and cosmic purpose. I would like to go through and show how these different levels of purpose can give deeper insight into the experiences when performing this work.

Personal purpose, that vocation of self that gives back to the society in which it is born, is one of the biggest aspects of this ritual, and the Western mystery tradition as a whole. We are the products of a variety of cultural and biological influences. Yet, to find one's personal purpose is to understand one's strengths and limitations and how through vocation we can contribute back to society. As it is written within the initiations of the HOGD, "I seek to learn that I may serve." This is greatly exemplified within the ritual through the spiritual incantations to commune with the angelic and demonic aspects of the self. We are products of a number of environmental and social conditions that become symbolized by the various spirits. To confront these entities as either real or as symbols is to begin this process of understanding our abilities.

Soul Purpose, the reservoir of pain and passion, shadow and light, is the real work within this ritual. It is a continuation of personal purpose to which after identifying imbalances we seek to remedy them. The conjuring and working with angels and demons, while dressed in an arcane form, gives a very transformative and healing experience to the magician. This is the heart of soul purpose. Phil Hine, writer and modern-day chaos magician, sums up this concept in a down-to-earth way, "Personal demons are latent structures within the psyche, unresolved complexes and repressed 'voices' thrown up by the ego as a defensive measure... It can be useful to identify these intrapsychic structures as 'demons' for purposes of working with and integrating them." Here we see a form of anthropomorphizing the spirits to proactively work with them. This is where the discernment of the visionary experience becomes crucial to its success. It's important to reiterate that it's not about viewing demons as psychic structures or as real, but to successfully heal the self as a whole. It is one of the many ways modern magical practitioners are moving this work forward into the future.

Absolute Purpose is the spiritual impulse to "wake up" and realize the nonduality of existence. In most spiritual traditions, this impulse is what influences the practitioner to start in the first place. Western esotericism is no different. Using our subjective experience to understand the objective is something that is developed over the course of time. They engage with the visionary aspect of the mind to such a degree that discernment becomes absolutely necessary. The difference between a true objective magical reality and the egoic interpretation of the experience is meant to be understood. The absolute purpose is what drives us forward in a spiritual practice. In the end, the magician is expected to overcome this and know for certain the legitimacy of the experience through a sense of absolute purpose. Regardie sums up this idea quite succinctly, "Hitherto the eyes of the soul were closed, and blind, affrighted, and ignorantly dumb, the individual was whirled on the ever-moving wheel of life and pain. With the attainment of the angelic splendor, the center of consciousness having been forever exalted beyond the empirical ego, a flood of ecstasy causes the realization that it is only the Angel who is and always has been the Ego, the Real Self never previously known." The absolute purpose realized is the manifesting of the transcendent self.

Lastly we have **Cosmic Purpose**. This is that ultimate state of being wherein consciousness itself is in a synergistic flow with the universal evolutionary process. This is the philosopher's stone of the alchemists. It can be difficult to truly describe this experience without attaching to it a number of descriptions, which we know (despite trying our best) can sometimes be even further from the experience. This leads to another incredibly useful aspect of magick as a whole. Within the practice we are given a language to describe otherwise ineffable experiences. We as a fully realized person become co-creators within the dynamic evolutionary process of the universe. The realization that the HGA is not fully separate or fully you is the blossoming of cosmic purpose. The attainment of the Knowledge and Conversation of the Holy Guardian Angel results in understanding the depths of self and how we are co-creators within the evolutionary process itself.

Modern Magick

There is a new growing movement that cultivates and researches a state of consciousness that is in line with both the Western esoteric tradition and cosmic purpose: flow state consciousness. According to Steven Kotler and Jamie Wheal in their new work *Stealing Fire* flow state is defined as an "optimal state of consciousness where we feel our best and perform our best... Action and awareness start to merge. Our sense of self vanishes." Flow states of consciousness are seen as ways to enhance creativity. In their work, Kotler and Wheal have found there to be a number of different ways to create flow states, including through the use of art, psychology, technology, and pharmacology. Flow state, while not a new concept, gives a name to that cosmic consciousness achieved through ritual work. The type of consciousness that is cultivated through contact with the HGA can then be seen as a flow state, wherein the magician develops a sense of cosmic purpose. When achieved through the use of ritual and flow, this type of consciousness can be utilized to cause change in conformity to will

Through the model of purpose we can see the dimensions of Western esotericism and its ritual practices in a more specific light. The esoteric spiritual practice of the West is a vast tree with many limbs, each with many variations. Yet, at the root we can see that even if the techniques change, the goals remain the same.

Closing Remarks

So here we are. Now that we have achieved union with the holy of holies, what do we do now? Well, we continue the work started so long ago by our spiritual forefathers and foremothers. It is my hope that through an understanding of arcane magical techniques, states of consciousness, and purpose we can all become the best version of ourselves possible.

This type of practice is the spiritual birthright of the West with an aim of uniting (while also respecting) practices from around the world. This spiritual adventure is one that shows the capability of bringing people together into new and meaningful levels of purpose and experience. As this esoteric work continues to be brought forward into the present moment and beyond, we as humans come that much closer to that great purpose behind it all.

The initiation never ends.

❧

References

Carl Jung *Collected Works of C.G. Jung, Volume 7: Two Essays in Analytical Psychology* 1972. Princeton University Press. Second Edition.

Dion Fortune *The Mystical Qabalah* 1999. York Beach, Maine. Samuel Weiser Inc.

Israel Regardie *The Golden Dawn* 2002. St. Paul, MN. Llewellyn Publications. Sixth Edition.

Israel Regardie *The Tree of Life: An Illustrated Study in Magic* 2006. Woodbury, MN. Samuel Weiser Inc. Third Edition.

Lon Milo DuQuette *The Magick of Aleister Crowley* 2003. San Francisco, CA. Red Wheel/Weiser, LLC.

Phil Hine *Condensed Chaos* 1996. Tempe, AZ. New Falcon Publications.

S.L. MacGregor-Mathers *The Book of the Sacred Magic of Abra-Melin the Mage* 1986. Wellingborough, Northamptonshire, UK. The Aquarian Press.

Steven Kotler and Jamie Wheal *Stealing Fire* 2017. New York, NY. HarperCollins Publishers.

Chapter 7

HUMANITY'S JOURNEY HOME
Learning to Live in a Living Universe[1]

Duane Elgin

We are pilgrims together, wending through unknown country, home.

—Father Giovanni (1513)

Humanity's Most Urgent Challenge

Humanity is experiencing both a collective identity crisis as well as evolutionary crisis. Critical challenges to our future confront us with fundamental questions: Who are we? What kind of Universe do we live in? Where are we going? Do we continue our rapid march into materialism, grounded in the assumption that we live in a Universe that is indifferent to humanity and comprised mostly of dead matter and empty space? Or, do we open to transforming insight from the combined wisdom of science and the world's spiritual traditions: the Universe is not dead at its foundations but is profoundly alive and we humans are an integral part of that larger aliveness. In the words of Plato, "The Universe is a single living creature that contains all living creatures within it."

Our view of the Universe profoundly impacts how we live in the world. If we think we live in a nonliving Universe without larger meaning and purpose, then it makes sense to exploit that which is dead on behalf of ourselves, the most visibly alive. Alternatively, if we have the direct experience of touching the aliveness of nature and the world around us, then it is natural to respect and care for the abundant expressions of aliveness. These are two radically different ways of looking the Universe and, in turn, produce dramatically different views of our identity and evolutionary journey. This leads to a startling conclusion: the most urgent challenge facing humanity is not climate change, or species extinction, or unsustainable population growth; rather, it is how we understand the Universe and our intimate relationship within it. Our deepest choices for the future emerge from this core understanding.

At the Evolutionary Crossroads

How have we come to such a critical crossroads in our evolutionary journey? First, in the last several hundred years, we have been spectacularly successful in exploiting the abundance of Earth's resources to create a short period of unprecedented material prosperity for a minority of the Earth's population. This burst of affluence emerged from a worldview described as "scientific materialism," which regards the Universe as nonliving at its foundations and comprised mostly of empty space and inanimate matter. Second, based on this worldview, we have been consuming Earth's resources far beyond her rates of regeneration. Short-term material prosperity is being gained at the cost long-term ecological ruin. As Wendell Berry reminds us, nature "has more votes, a longer memory, and a sterner sense of justice than we do." We are creating by our own hand a long-term future that is unforgivingly inhospitable for advancing human civilization.

We are being compelled by circumstances to come together—collectively and rapidly—to cope with climate disruption, massive human migrations, unsustainable population growth, critical shortages of key resources such as water, the threatened extinction of nearly half of all animal and plant species, and much more. As world-changing trends of enormous magnitude converge and amplify one another, the people of

Earth will confront the unyielding reality that, unless we wake up and work together, we have only the legacy of a grievously wounded Earth and impoverished future to leave to our children and grandchildren. We require a new pathway ahead and are reminded of Einstein's famous words: "We cannot solve our problems with the same thinking we used to create them."

We are moving through a perilous phase of planetary transition. Hopefully we will have the wisdom to make deep, structural changes in our manner of living and turn toward a more sustainable and promising future. The alternative is the collapse, and even extinction, of human civilizations. It is unwise to be complacent about our future, as collapse has happened numerous times. More than 20 major civilizations have collapsed over the millennia, including the empires of the Romans, Mayans, Aztecs, Easter Islanders, Anasazi, Mesopotamians, and the Soviets. Importantly, many examples of collapse involve climate change as a key contributing factor.

Although collapse has occurred numerous times throughout history, today is different in one crucial respect: there are no frontiers left. *The circle has closed.* The entire world has become a single, integrated system—economically, ecologically, and socially. Never before has the entire planet been at risk of collapse and taking all the world's civilizations down at the same time. Humanity has never experienced the collapse of an embryonic, but truly global, civilization such as exists today. Our time of planetary transition is truly a great transition, unprecedented in human history and deeply formative in shaping the long-range future.

To move swiftly through this perilous time of planetary transition requires unprecedented breakthroughs in how we live and relate to one another. Yet, cooperation is difficult and slow in a world that is unraveling and where most people are coping with chronic, planetary-scale, traumatic stresses. A natural tendency is for people to separate and seek islands of safety to ride out the disruptive storms of transition that are beginning to blow through the world. However, if we pull apart and seek only our personal security by retreating from the world and isolating ourselves, then systemic problems are certain to escalate and produce the very future of ruinous collapse we most fear.

Immense suffering can be a positive force for evolution *if* it burns through our denial and distraction and awakens humanity to our collective task of transition. The unrelenting suffering of millions, even billions, of human beings could penetrate through our complacency and isolation and awaken us to engaged action. Needless suffering could become a psychological and psychic fire that burns away surface differences to reveal a collective intelligence and shared human identity with sufficient wisdom to guide us into a sustainable global civilization.

The Remarkable Invitation

Being unflinchingly realistic, it does not seem likely we will turn away from our current path of separation—with its growing inequities, overconsumption of resources and deep injury to Earth—unless we discover, *together*, a pathway into the future that is so truly remarkable, transformative, and welcoming that we are drawn ahead by the scope and intimacy of its invitation. Just in time, that pathway is being revealed by insights converging from science and the world's wisdom traditions. In a sentence: *We are discovering that, instead of struggling for meaning and a miracle of survival in a dead Universe, we are being invited to learn and grow forever in the deep ecologies of a living Universe.* To step into the invitation of learning to live in a living Universe represents a journey so extraordinary that it transcends the wounds of our past and invites us to begin a process of healing and reconciliation to realize a remarkable future we can only accomplish together.

The Nature of Our Cosmic Home

In contemplating a great turn toward this new pathway of development, it is important to ask: Is the Universe truly as Plato described—"a single living creature" that contains all living creatures within it? Seeing the Universe as a super-organism with a permeating aliveness is not new—this was humanity's basic understanding for thousands of years until gradually replaced by the worldview of scientific materialism roughly 300 years ago. Since then, the scientific community has been employing its ever-more-powerful tools to explore the nature of reality and has discovered a Universe of astonishing depth and subtlety. In turn, the ancient intuition of a living Universe is now being reconsidered as science cuts away

132

superstition to reveal the cosmos as a place of unexpected wonder, depth, and sophistication. Here are six key attributes emerging from science that point toward a living Universe:

A Unified Whole: In the last several decades, scientific experiments have repeatedly confirmed "nonlocality" and the discovery that the Universe is a deeply unified system at the quantum level that communicates with itself *instantly*, across impossibly vast distances. To illustrate: At the speed of light, it takes more than eight minutes for a photon to travel from the Sun to the Earth, and more than 14 billion years to travel across our visible Universe. Yet, quantum physics demonstrates these unimaginably vast distances are traversed and transcended, *instantaneously*, in the quantum realm. Science no longer views the Universe as a disconnected collection of planets, stars, and fragments of matter. Instead, the Universe is fully unified and connected with itself at every moment. In the words of the physicist David Bohm, the Universe is "an undivided wholeness in flowing movement."

Empty Space Is Not Empty: For centuries, scientists thought empty space was "empty." Recently, scientists have discovered that an extraordinary amount of background energy permeates the Universe! This invisible energy accounts for an estimated 96 percent of the known Universe. In turn, the entire visible Universe—atoms, people, planets, stars, and galaxies—constitutes only 4 percent of the total Universe. Two kinds of invisible energy are known to exist: *dark matter* (a contractive force) accounts for roughly 23 percent of the invisible Universe, and *dark energy* (an expansive force) accounts for approximately 73 percent of the Universe. We are immersed within a vast sea of largely invisible, subtle but astonishingly powerful energies with an array of capacities we are only beginning to discover and understand.

A Co-Arising Universe: At every moment, the entire Universe is emerging freshly as a singular orchestration of cosmic expression. There is one grand symphony in which we are all players, a single creative expression emerging freshly at each moment—a Uni-verse. While an evolving Universe provides a stunning narrative of "horizontal" unfolding across "time," the insight of an emerging Universe adds the "vertical" dimension of the Universe continuously arising into time. Despite outward appearances of solidity and stability, the Universe is a completely dynamic system. Nothing endures. All is flow. Max Born, a physicist who was instrumental in the development of quantum mechanics wrote, "We have sought for firm ground and found none. The deeper we penetrate, the more restless becomes the Universe; all is rushing about and vibrating in a wild dance."[2] In the words of the cosmologist Brian Swimme, "The Universe emerges out of an all-nourishing abyss not only fourteen billion years ago but in every moment."[3]

Consciousness at Every Scale: Scientists are finding evidence for consciousness or a knowing capacity throughout the Universe. From the atomic level to the galactic scale, a self-organizing, centering capacity is at work that is fitting for each scale. In turn, the capacity for centering self-organization points to the presence of some level of knowing consciousness. The physicist and cosmologist Freeman Dyson writes that, at the atomic level, "Matter in quantum mechanics is not an inert substance but an active agent, constantly making choices between alternative possibilities... It appears that mind, as manifested by the capacity to make choices, is to some extent inherent in every electron."[4] This does not mean that an atom has the same consciousness as a human being but rather that an atom has a reflective capacity appropriate to its form and function. Max Planck, developer of quantum theory, stated, "I regard consciousness as fundamental. I regard matter as derivative from consciousness. We cannot get behind consciousness. Everything that we talk about, everything that we regard as existing, postulates consciousness."[5] An ecology of consciousness permeates the Universe.

Freedom at the Foundations: Quantum physics describes reality in terms of probabilities, not certainties. This means that uncertainty and freedom are built into the very foundations of existence. No individual part of the cosmos determines the functioning of the whole; rather, everything is interconnected with everything else, weaving the cosmos into one, vast interacting system. In turn, it is the consistency of interrelations of all the parts that determines the condition of the continuously emerging whole. We therefore have great freedom to act within the limits established by the larger web of life.

Able to Reproduce Itself: A vital capacity for any living system is the ability to reproduce itself. A stunning hypothesis emerging from cosmology is the idea that our Universe reproduces itself through the functioning of black holes. In this view, a black hole represents the seed from which a new Universe can blossom and grow. Physicist John Gribbin writes, "Instead of a black hole representing a one-way journey to nowhere, many researchers now believe that it is a one-way journey to somewhere—to a new expanding Universe in its own set of dimensions."[6] Given the presence of billions of black holes in our Universe, there could be countless other cosmic systems continuously being born by "budding off" from our Universe through the birth canal of black holes. Gribbin writes that Universes are not only alive; they also evolve as do other living systems: "Universes that are 'successful' are the ones that leave the most offspring."[7] The idea that there have been countless Universes evolving through time is not new. A precursor can be found from 1779 when David Hume wrote, "Many worlds might have been botched and bungled, throughout an eternity, ere this system was struck out; much labour lost, many fruitless trials made; and a slow, but continued improvement carried on during infinite ages in the art of world-making."[8]

When we bring these attributes together, a clearer picture of our remarkable Universe comes into focus: The Universe is a completely unified system that is continuously regenerated by the flow-through of phenomenal quantities of life energy whose essential nature includes consciousness, or a knowing capacity, that enables systems at every scale of existence to center themselves and exercise some measure of freedom of choice. In addition, the Universe appears able to reproduce itself via black holes within a vastly larger cosmic garden or multiverse, where our Universe is but one among countless others. Overall, the vision of our Universe emerging from science is that of a magnificent superorganism evolving in complexity and consciousness.

How Wisdom Traditions Regard the Universe

How does the emerging, scientific view of a living Universe fit with the originating insights of the world's major wisdom traditions? Is there a place of meeting in their respective views? Despite their many differences, when we penetrate the depths of the world's major spiritual traditions, a stunning understanding about the Universe emerges that is in accord with insights from the frontiers of science: we live within a living Universe that arises, moment-by-moment, as an undivided whole in an unutterably vast process of awesome precision and power. The following quotes illustrate how this remarkable understanding is expressed across the world's major religions (excerpted from my book, *The Living Universe*):

- **Christian:** *God is creating the entire Universe, fully and totally, in this present now. Everything God created...God creates now all at once.*[9]
  —Meister Eckhart, Christian mystic

- **Islam:** *You have a death and a return in every moment...Every moment the* *world is renewed but we, in seeing its continuity of appearance, are unaware of its being renewed.*[10] —Rumi, thirteenth-century Sufi teacher and poet

- **Buddhist:** *My solemn proclamation is that a new Universe is created every moment.*[11] —D.T. Suzuki, Zen teacher and scholar

- **Hindu:** *The entire Universe contributes incessantly to your existence. Hence the entire Universe is your body.*[12] —Sri Nisargadatta, Hindu teacher

- **Taoist:** *The Tao is the sustaining Life-force and the mother of all things; from it, all things rise and fall without cease.*[13] —Tao Te Ching

- **Indigenous:** *...there was no such thing as emptiness in the world. Even in the sky there were no vacant places. Everywhere there was life, visible and invisible...*[14] —Luther Standing Bear, Lakota elder

Beneath the differences in language, a common vision is being described. The Universe is continuously emerging as a fresh creation at every moment. All point to this same, extraordinary insight. The Universe is not static, nor is its continuation assured. Instead, the Universe is like a cosmic hologram that is being continuously upheld and renewed at every instant.[15] A universal encouragement found across the world's wisdom traditions is to *live in the "NOW."* This core insight has a clear basis in physics: the present moment is the place of direct connection with the entire Universe as it arises continuously. Each moment is a fresh formation of the Universe, emerging seamlessly and flawlessly. When we are in the present moment, we are literally riding the wave of continuous creation of the cosmos—reality surfing.

A Living Universe In Everyday Human Experience

How does a living Universe perspective fit with our everyday human experience? If the unity of existence is not an experience to be created but an always-manifesting condition waiting to be appreciated, then how widespread is this experience in people's lives? Do many people experience the everyday world around ourselves as "alive"? Scientific surveys give us insight into this key question:

◊ A global survey involving 7,000 youths in 17 countries was taken in 2008. It found that 75 percent believe in a "higher power," a majority say they have had a transcendent experience, believe in life after death and think it is "probably true" that all living things are connected.[16] These views are in accord with a paradigm of aliveness.

We can secure further insight from scientific surveys conducted in the United States that show a measurable transformation in mainstream consciousness is underway.

◊ In 1962 a survey of the adult population in the United States found that 22 percent reported having a profound experience of communion with the Universe. By 2009, the percentage of the population reporting a "mystical experience" had grown dramatically to 49 percent of the adult population.[17]

◊ In a national survey of the United States in 2014, nearly 60 percent of adults reported they regularly feel a deep sense of "spiritual peace and well-being," and 46 percent say they experience a deep sense of "wonder about the Universe" at least once a week.[18]

◊ A 2002 national Gallup survey asked respondents to rate the statement, "I have had a profound religious experience or awakening that changed the direction of my life." A stunning 41 percent of Americans (about 80 million adults at the time) said the statement *completely* applies to them.[19]

◊ A 2009 Pew survey of a national sample of Americans found that roughly 3-in-10 Americans (29 percent) say they have felt in touch with someone who has died and a quarter say they believe in reincarnation.[20]

◊ Another trend suggestive of cultural awakening is the

growing use of psychedelics such as mushrooms, ayahuasca, and LSD. In a US survey published in 2013, an estimated 32 million adults, or just over 10 percent of the adult population, said they have used psychedelics.[21] These drugs can awaken mystical experiences marked by feelings of unity with the Universe, a sacred sense of reality, and an expanded sense of self. Psychedelics are being used to treat depression and posttraumatic stress in war veterans, so the healing potential of the experiences they facilitate is well established.

These surveys show that experiences of spiritual communion with the aliveness of the Universe are not a fringe phenomenon but, instead, are familiar encounters for a large portion of the public. Humanity is measurably waking up to a larger view of ourselves and the Universe.

Awakening to an intimate connection with the unity and intelligent aliveness of the Universe is often accompanied by feelings of great joy, boundless love, and the presence of a subtle, radiant light. To illustrate, below is a classic account of a spontaneous awakening experience. While an undergraduate student, F.C. Happold had this experience of communion with the permeating aliveness of the Universe:

> There was just the room, with its shabby furniture and the fire burning in the grate and the red-shaded lamp on the table. But the room was filled by a Presence, which in a strange way was both about me and within me, like light or warmth. I was overwhelmingly possessed by Someone who was not myself, and yet I felt I was more myself than I had ever been before. I was filled with an intense happiness, and almost unbearable joy, such as I had never known before and have never known since. And over all was a deep sense of peace and security and certainty.[22]

Turning from spontaneous awakening to the intentional exploration of consciousness, for more than two thousand years, pioneering individuals have been investing their lives in solitude and sustained meditation

to investigate directly the nature of reality. What these explorers of consciousness have discovered is not a grey, machinelike hum of a nonliving
Universe but, instead, an ocean of unbounded love, light and creative intelligence whose nature is beyond the reach of words.[23] When our personal aliveness becomes transparent to the aliveness of the living Universe,
transformational experiences of wonder and awe emerge naturally. As we
open into the cosmic dimensions of our being, we feel more at home, less
self-absorbed, more empathy for others, and an increased desire to be of
service to life. These shifts in perspective are immensely valuable for building a sustainable future.

Given the many psychological and social benefits of meditation, it
is understandable that as people are confronted with an unraveling outer
world, a growing number are turning inward in search of a more direct
and felt connection with life—and this has helped produce a rising wave of
interest in meditation around the planet. For example, a 2012 study in the
United States found that 8 percent of adults, or roughly 18 million persons,
meditate regularly.[24] Ancient wisdom traditions are being rediscovered and
adapted to modern conditions. People are developing a new literacy of
consciousness in their everyday lives. For example, the elevated experience
of "flow consciousness" is now recognized not only by meditators but also
by high-performance sports teams, jazz ensembles, business-project teams,
farmworkers, classrooms, community groups, and more.[25] Humanity is developing a basic literacy of consciousness.

Humanity's awakening is being further accelerated by virtual reality technologies that immerse people in alternative worlds of experience
and expand how we view, and think about, the "ordinary world" around
us. Inexpensive headsets with a computer interface are making immersive
experiences in alternative realities widely available for education, medicine, games, urban planning, and much more. In a simulation, nothing real
"really" exists—except as a computer program, and yet when we put on
a VR headset, within seconds our sensory experiences and reactions feel
incredibly real. What is "reality"? By directly experiencing our immersion
within an alternative reality that feels real to our senses, our curiosity can
be awakened regarding the reality of our everyday experience. Because
virtual reality so vividly creates the felt-experience of entering alternative

worlds, it loosens our attachment to a singular view. Virtual reality technologies are an evolutionary catalyst, awakening mainstream cultures to viewing the Universe as a continuously refreshed, cosmic hologram that can be known consciously and directly because we are an integral expression of it.

As these diverse streams of awakening converge, they are forming a river of wisdom that is transforming global consciousness and culture.

Our Bio-Cosmic Identity and Evolutionary Journey

Summarizing: Powerful trends are converging to awaken the paradigm of a living Universe in mainstream global culture: astonishing new attributes of the Universe from scientific discoveries, confirming insights from the world's wisdom traditions, measurable growth in awakening experiences from around the world, accelerated learning through virtual reality technologies, and much more. What does this combined wisdom tell us about our identity and evolutionary journey?

Bio-Cosmic Identity: From a living Universe perspective, our identity is immeasurably larger than our biological self. We are vastly more than a skin-encapsulated bundle of chemical and neurological interactions. Our physical existence is permeated and sustained by an aliveness that is inseparable from the larger Universe. Seeing ourselves as part of the fabric of creation awakens our sense of connection with, and compassion for, the totality of life. Cosmologist Brian Swimme explains that the intimate sense of self-awareness we experience bubbling up at each moment "is rooted in the originating activity of the Universe. We are all of us arising together at the center of the cosmos." We once thought that we were no bigger than our physical bodies, but now we are discovering that we are deeply connected participants in the continuous arising of the entire Universe. Awakening to our larger identity as both unique and inseparably connected with a co-arising Universe transforms feelings of existential separation into experiences of subtle communion as biocosmic beings. We are far richer, deeper, more complex, and more alive than we ever thought. To discover this in our direct experience is to enter a new age of exploration and discovery.

Cosmic Purpose: To be born as a human being is a rare and precious gift. Our bodies are biodegradable vehicles for acquiring soul-growing experiences. As compostable conduits for channeling learning experiences, our bodies are the current expressions of a creative aliveness that, after nearly 14 billion years, enable the Universe to look back and reflect upon itself. While we have the gift of a body to anchor our experience, it is important to recognize our biocosmic nature. In the Gospel of Thomas, Jesus says, "Take heed of the Living One while you're alive, lest you die and seek to see Him and be unable to do so." An ancient Greek saying speaks even more directly, "Light your candle before night overtakes you." If the Universe were nonliving at its foundations, it would take a miracle to save us from extinction at the time of death, and then to take us from here to a heaven (or promised land) of continuing aliveness. However, if the Universe is alive, then we are already nested and growing within its aliveness. When our physical body dies, the life-stream that we are makes its passage to a fitting home in the larger ecology of aliveness. We don't need a miracle to save us—we are already inside the miracle of sustaining aliveness. Instead of being saved from death, our job is to bring mindful attention to our ever-emerging aliveness in the here and now.

We are moving from seeing ourselves as accidents of creation wandering through a lifeless cosmos without meaning or purpose, to seeing ourselves engaged in a sacred journey of discovery in a Universe of vast depth and richness. An old saying goes, "A dead man tells no stories." In a similar way, "A dead Universe tells no stories." In contrast, a living Universe is itself a vast story continuously unfolding with countless characters playing out gripping dramas of awakening, inseparable from the artistry of world-making. The Universe is a living, unfolding creation. Saint Teresa of Avila saw this when she wrote, "The feeling remains that God is on the journey, too." If we see ourselves as participants in a cosmic garden of life that has been growing patiently over billions of years, then we feel invited to shift from feelings of indifference, fear, and separation to feelings of curiosity, love, and participation. In the words of Annemarie Schimmel, "Once the journey to God is finished, the infinite journey in God begins."

Natural Ethics: If we are no more than biological entities, then it makes sense to think we could disconnect ourselves from the suffering of the rest of life. However, if we are all swimming in the same ocean of subtle aliveness, then it is understandable that we each have some measure of direct experience of being in communion with the larger fabric of life. Because we share the same matrix of existence, the totality of life is already touching each of us and co-creating the field of aliveness within which we exist. A felt ethics emerges from our intuitive connection with the living Universe in the form of a "moral tuning fork." We can each tune into the nonlocal field of life and sense what is in harmony with the well-being of the whole. When we are in alignment, we experience a warm, positive hum of well-being as a kinesthetic sense that we may call "compassion." In a similar way, we can also experience the dissonant hum of discordance. When we are centered in the life current flowing through us, we tend to act in ways that promote the well-being of the whole. In recognizing we are partners in the unfolding story of cosmic evolution, we shift from a sense of existential isolation to feelings of intimate communion. With life is nested within life, we treat everything that exists as alive and worthy of great respect. We recognize that every action has ethical consequences that cascade instantly throughout quantum-linked cosmos.

Sustainable Living: The Earth cannot sustain humanity's current levels and patterns of resource consumption. We are moving rapidly beyond the long-term carrying capacity of the planet. The paradigm of materialism is leaving a devastated Earth as our legacy to our children. The perspective of a living Universe offers a very different understanding and future: *Aliveness is the only true wealth.* Nothing is more precious than learning to live in the deep ecology of the living Universe. If we focus our attention on growing our experience of aliveness, it is only natural for us to choose simpler ways of living that afford greater time and opportunity to develop the areas of our lives where we feel most alive—investing our time in nature, nurturing relationships, caring communities, creative expressions, and service to others. In seeing the Universe as alive, we naturally shift our priorities from an "ego economy" based upon consuming deadness to a "living economy" based upon growing aliveness. An aliveness economy seeks to touch life more lightly while generating an abundance of meaning and satisfaction.

Eco-Villages and New Communities: A deep change in perspective finds natural expression in how we construct our everyday lives. As we learn to live sustainably while creating lives of greater satisfaction and fulfillment, new forms of community will be a natural outcome. As the world unravels, smaller communities can provide lifeboats of resilience to weather the storms of transition. Communities of the scale of a "village" (roughly one or two hundred people) are small enough to support a rich array of personal relationships and large enough to support a vibrant microeconomy and diverse social activities. Large-scale breakdowns will produce local breakthroughs in patterns of living. Cities could be decentralized rapidly into thousands of relatively self-reliant and highly resilient "ecovillages," each with distinctive adaptations of architecture, culture, and expressions of sustainability. Common to most would be a childcare facility and play area, a common house of some kind (for community meetings, celebrations, and regular meals together), a community garden, a recycling and composting area, solar energy systems, a bit of open space, and a workshop. Each could offer a variety of services to the surrounding ecovillages as well; for example, organic gardening, green building, conflict resolution, healthcare, home schooling, eldercare, and so on. Ecovillages could replace the alienating and insecure landscape of massive urban regions with countless, small islands of sanity, security, and resilient community. Ecovillage living would offer a path of separation and retreat from the world were it not for the internet and social media creating an intensely interconnected and interdependent planet that is ever more transparent to itself.

Awakening to our conscious connection with the living Universe naturally expands our scope of concern and compassion—and brightens the prospect of working together to build a sustainable future. However, making the turn from separation to connection does not end our journey of learning. As we discover the astonishing depths and subtlety of the Universe, we recognize we have as much to learn on our journey of return as we have on our long journey of separation. This is humbling news. Instead of the current era representing the pinnacle of human evolution, we appear to be approaching a midway point in the journey of awakening as we turn from separation toward community and cooperation. We still have far to go and much to learn to reach our initial maturity as a dynamically stable species-civilization.

Humanity's Choice

Our first task as a human community is to recognize the remarkable choice directly before us. On the one hand, if we regard the Universe as dead at its foundations, then feelings of existential alienation, anxiety, dread, and fear are understandable. Why seek communion with the cold indifference of lifeless matter and empty space? If we relax into a dead Universe, we will simply sink into existential despair, so better to live on the surface of life. On the other hand, if we live in a living Universe, then feelings of subtle connection, curiosity, and gratitude are natural. When we see ourselves as participants in a cosmic garden of life that has been developing patiently over billions of years, our regard for the universe shifts from indifference, fear, and cynicism to curiosity, love, and awe. Humanity's future pivots on which understanding prevails and the choices that naturally follow.

The well-being of humanity and the Earth depends upon this generation waking up, growing up, and moving from our adolescence into our early adulthood as a species, and thereby establishing a new relationship with nature, other humans, and the living Universe. If we do not welcome the miracle of life around us and within us, the alternative seems likely to be our effective extinction as a species. Climate chaos, sea level rise, mass migrations, species extinction and more are accelerating and moving past critical tipping points, producing irreversible changes to the Earth, and making humanity's turn toward a sustainable future immensely more difficult. Would we choose ruin over life? As unthinkable as it may be, it seems painfully realistic to conclude that, *unless the great diversity of humanity can find an awe-inspiring bridge to the future that is grounded in a commonly felt experience of tremendous, untapped evolutionary potential, we will not have the soulful motivation needed for turning from separation and survival to community and co-evolution.*

Our situation is unprecedented: *We are being pushed by Earth-sized ecological necessity and pulled by Universe-sized evolutionary opportunity.* If we lose sight of where we are (living within a living Universe), we profoundly diminish our understanding of who we are (beings of both biological and cosmic dimensions), and the journey we are on (learning to live within the depths of cosmic aliveness). *Ultimately, in learning to live in a living Universe, we are learning to live in the deep ecology of existence—in eternity. This is such an astonishing call to our soulful nature from the deep compassion of a living Universe that we would be spiritual fools to ignore this unmeasurably precious invitation.*

We are in an early "establishing phase" of conscious evolution where we are just beginning to recognize ourselves in the mirror of reflective consciousness. Although the Universe has been growing us through countless lifetimes, only now are we waking up to who and what we truly are. As we use the internet and social media to collectively witness our planetary journey, it is helpful to view the path as a reflexive loop that turns back upon itself. We are in the process of realizing our self-given name as a species: *Homo sapiens sapiens* or the being that "knows that it knows." In becoming "doubly wise," we turn the knowing faculty back upon itself and, ultimately, become aware that we are awareness itself—an invisible knowing-presence at the foundations of the living Universe.

As the push of outer necessity meets the pull of untapped inner capacity, humanity is beginning to awaken. And yet, adversity trends such as radical climate change are accelerating so rapidly there is a real danger that humanity's responses could prove to be too little and too late—and we may veer off into a new dark age. If we are distracted and in denial, and overlook the urgency and importance of the great transition now underway, we will miss a unique, never to be repeated, evolutionary opportunity. Each generation is asked to make sacrifices for the next, to be a caretaker for the future. This generation is being pushed by an injured Earth and pulled by a welcoming Universe to make a monumental gift to humanity's future: working together with equanimity and maturity to consciously realize our evolutionary potential and purpose of learning to live in a living Universe.

⸎

Endnotes

1. This essay was developed for the forthcoming book *Global Purpose Movement*, November 2017. See: https://globalpurposemovement.com and was adapted from my forthcoming book on the theme of "learning to live in a living Universe."

2. Max Born, *The Restless Universe*, New York: Harper & Brothers, 1936, p. 277.

3. Brian Swimme, *The Hidden Heart of the Cosmos*, New York: Orbis Books, 1996, p. 100.

4. Freeman Dyson, Infinite In All Directions, New York: Harper & Row, 1988, p. 297.

5. Max Planck, *The Observer,* January 25, 1931.

6. John Gribbin, *In the Beginning: The Birth of the Living Universe,* New York: Little Brown and Co., 1993, p. 244.

7. Ibid, p. 252.

8. David Hume, "Critique of the Design Argument," http://philosophy.lander.edu/intro/introbook2.1/x4211.html

9. Matthew Fox, Meditations with Meister Eckhart, Santa Fe, New Mexico: Bear & Co., 1983, p. 24.

10. See, for example, Coleman Barks, The Essential Rumi, San Francisco: HarperSanFrancisco, 1995.

11. D. T. Suzuki, *Zen and Japanese Culture,* Princeton, NJ: Princeton University Press, 1970, p. 364.

12. Sri Nisargadatta Maharaj, *I Am That,* Part I (trans., Maurice Frydman), Bombay, India: Chetana, 1973, p. 289.

13. LaoTsu, *Tao Te Ching* (trans. Gia-Fu Feng and Jane English), New York: Vintage Books, 1972.

14. Luther Standing Bear, quoted in Joseph Epes Brown, "Modes of Contemplation Through Actions: North American Indians," *Main Currents in Modern Thought,* New York, November-December, 1973, p. 194.

15. The view of our universe as a "cosmic hologram" is described in a recent book by Jude Currivan, *The Cosmic Hologram,* Vermont: Inner Traditions, 2017. Also, see Michael Talbot, *The Holographic Universe,* New York: Harper, 1992 (first edition).

16. *With Their Own Voices: A Global Exploration of How Today's Young People Experience and Think About Spiritual Development,* Eugene C. Roehlkepartain, Peter L. Benson, Peter C. Scales, Lisa Kimball, and Pamela Ebstyne King, 2008 by Search Institute, www.spiritualdevelopmentcenter.org. Also, see article by Jane Lampman in the November 6, 2008, edition of the *Christian Science Monitor.*

17. See: Andrew Greeley and William McCready, "Are We a Nation of Mystics," in *New York Times Magazine,* January 26, 1975.

18. Pew Research Center, "U.S. Public Becoming Less Religious," November 3, 2015, http://www.pewforum.org/2015/11/03/u-s-public-becoming-less-religious.

19. George Gallup Jr., "Religious Awakenings Bolster Americans' Faith," Gallup Organization, January 14, 2003. http://www.gallup.com/poll/7582.

20. http://www.pewforum.org/2009/12/09/many-americans-mix-multiple-faiths/#ghosts-fortunetellers-and-communicating-with-the-dead.

21. "Over 30 million psychedelic users in the United States," Published online March 28, 2013; https://www.ncbi.nlm.nih.gov/pmc/articles/PMC3917651.

22. F. C. Happold quoted in: Greeley and McCready, op. cit., January 26, 1975.

23. See, for example, descriptions of the generative source of the Universe; *The Living Universe*, op. cit., pp. 86-89.

24. "Use of Complementary Health Approaches in the U.S.," National Health Interview Survey, See 2012 study, https://nccih.nih.gov/research/statistics/NHIS/2012/mind-body/meditation.

25. Duane Elgin, "*Collective Consciousness and Cultural Healing*," a report to the Fetzer Institute, Kalamazoo, MI, October 1997; http://duaneelgin.com/wp-content/uploads/2010/11/collective_consciousness.pdf.

Chapter 8

INTEGRAL SOUL WORK
Personal and Global Purpose

Terry Patten

Ours is an era of unprecedented change. The fabric that binds us culturally and as individuals is disintegrating and being rewoven before our eyes. For many of us, the unquestioned assumptions by which we've lived for generations are being upended. That includes everything from the structure of our government, to the trajectory of our careers, to warp-speed advances in technology. Most challenging is a massive ecological crisis of such breathtaking scope that most of us are ill-equipped to even begin to fathom its implications.

The discussion of finding one's unique purpose against this backdrop of overwhelming social, ecological, and political challenges can seem quaint, or even tone deaf. "Impractical" and "self-absorbed" are also descriptors that come to mind. For this reason, at times I've found myself reluctant to participate in the "purpose" conversation. Then too, there are our suffering brothers and sisters whose "purpose" is abundantly clear, driven as it by the necessities of survival. When starvation threatens, one's purpose is to find food. Notions of self-discovery and personal development can seem like fluff in comparison.

And yet, such soul investigation is inherent to the human experience. Saints, sages, and philosophers throughout recorded time have explored ideas of purpose, destiny, and the unique soul nature of the individual. These individuals may be more sensitive to the reality of suffering than are most of us—and they also see how this awareness can enable us to grow. Given the space and time, the most "ordinary" of us intuits that the world wants something from each of us, and we in turn want something from life. Those pushed to the brink by extreme circumstances often emerge newly oriented by some sense of purpose, or least the drive to make sense of their ordeal and prevent its reoccurrence for others. In fact, being involved in an ordeal of survival, or witnessing the sufferings and ordeals of others or loved ones, often activates a deeper and clearer sense of purpose—one that more clearly accesses eternal truths, and spontaneously lets go of the more superficial, ego-based planning and comfortable certitudes of a typical middle-class Western life. When life becomes less certain and pre-dictable—when nothing can any longer be taken for granted—it becomes possible to resort to the mysterious and sacred reality that animates us.

It would seem that the "strange attractor" of a future higher order is calling human beings to discover the narrative thrust and arc of our lives. Indeed, a major category of human spirituality focuses on the experience of being a unique and separate individual, deepening our locus of experi-ence and identity, exploring these depths and engaging its subtle dynamics to actualize our richest expression of "beingness."

This broadly adopted approach asserts the unique soul nature of the individual, and also suggests a journey across a lifetime (or multiple lifetimes) of progressively fulfilling the soul's continually unfolding destiny. This is "soul work" as contrasted with transcendental spirituality.

Quieting Imposter Voices

But how do we recognize our destiny? How can we know when we've arrived at our life's work, that shining thread of meaning, which is peculiarly our own? The task becomes a matter of tuning in to our "still small voice" through a cluttered array of "imposter voices" and ingrained cultural agreements. The loudest voices for most of us—from our family of origin, the media, school, church, and other cultural institutions—have imprinted ideas upon us about what constitutes a life well lived and how to validate ourselves and our success. These are "imposter voices," inauthentic voices that echo influences superficial to our deepest source of guidance from our soul or daemon.

Consciousness researcher Charles Tart memorably dubbed this "the Consensus Trance," characterized by "automatic and conditioned patterns of perception, thinking, feeling, and behaving." A conscious and healthy self-assessment can be subsumed by this conditioned "reality." The psychic space needed to awaken from limited identities and hear the voice of one's soul can get crushed beneath the weight of the cultural agreements into which we were born.

Even those who present themselves as purpose coaches, guides, or counselors—many of them sincere, caring people—can subtly put us off the scent by suggesting that purpose can be reduced to a mission statement or sound bite, easily rattled off before the elevator doors close. Often only a superficial sense of purpose is possible under such conditions, rather than the rich, dynamic, and embodied transformative process that many of us have found to be possible.

The flight from meaninglessness and the terror of wasted days can also be a pitfall in the journey to discovering our purpose. If we flee toward purpose, hoping it will be the salve to assuage these fears while failing to remain present and notice ourselves and the world around us, then we risk becoming trapped in a cycle of endless seeking, enacting a self-fulfilling prophecy.

I must surrender even my desperate yearning to have my life matter, if I am to listen clearly with the "ear of the heart" to the particular call of my soul. Then relaxing my ordinary verbal mind's chatter and my personal strategies, I might begin to rest profoundly enough to be able to hear that deeper level of my being, the "still small voice" of my soul. This is perhaps one of the ultimate of human privileges. It is one of the highest achievements of the inner life of the most privileged people, even more sublime than their education, contemplative practice, personal growth work or psychotherapy. So it is often treated as one of the highest kinds of personal actualization. But, as mentioned above, this kind of surrender sometimes comes from suffering or disillusionment in which the ordinary course of one's life is radically disrupted. Suffering can produce a kind of grace. Of course, it can also overwhelm and defeat our spirit. How one benefits from experience depends on what one brings to it. In any case, when I arrive in contact with my soul's voice, one of my soul's most powerful messages is a clarification of why I have been born, of the purpose of my life.

Encountering Your Daemon

Deeper, more psychologically sophisticated soul work in the West is influenced by the view that comes to us from the ancient Greeks. Before drinking the hemlock, Socrates described the following version of what happens between lifetimes: each soul drinks the water of Lethe and forgets all the details of the life just ended and all past identities. What remains is our essential character, shaped by the virtue we cultivated in our previous life (or lives).

On the basis of our character, we are assigned our daemon, our life's soul companion, the carrier of our deeper flavor, our soulful nature and guiding spirit. Next, we go before the Fates: Clotho, Lachesis, and Atropos.

Clotho considers our character and our daemon, then proceeds to spin our "spindle destiny"—the unique circumstances of our birth—including everything we ordinarily associate with both heredity and environment. These include the time and place of our birth, including whether our life takes place in war or peace, prosperity or famine, health or sickness, and how tall we are, how attractive, whether extraverted or introverted, and countless other inheritances. She chooses the womb of our mother, the life of our father, their relationship, our siblings, community, region, and our world. She decides all the consequential details of our genetic inheritance, the nature of the time we live in, and all kinds of details of our health, personality, and appearance.

Next we go before Lachesis, who assigns us our luck, the subtle magnetism that surrounds us, and attracts and repels the coincidences, people, places, blessings, and opportunities that we attract and repel. This too is responsive to our character, and like character, this magnetism remains malleable as we continue to practice and cultivate virtue.

The last fate, Atropos, assigns the moment of our death, before we are even born. Her assignation was thought to be inflexible. *Atropos* means "she who cannot be turned."

In this ancient Greek view, a soul's task is to cultivate virtue, to develop character, and build a relationship with one's daemon, to learn to listen to the voice of the daemon with the "ear of the heart," and to realize one's soul's highest destiny, or what we might in the present context call "purpose." This is the basis for Jungian psychologist James Hillman's "acorn theory" (1996). Like an acorn that eventually becomes the unique oak it is potentiated to become, if we actually are able to live out true character, the soul will gradually reveal and realize its unique character across the trajectory of our life.

The Integral Yoga of the Soul

Though the search for purpose and destiny reaches back to the ancient Greeks and beyond, we moderns have at our disposal a rich array of tools and perspectives that were not available to the ancients, including access to an unparalleled range of intellectual, scientific, philosophical, spiritual, and cultural knowledge that even includes formerly secret, esoteric teachings of the world's great wisdom traditions. A manifestation of my life's purpose has been the development of Integral Soul Work, which integrates many of these philosophical and scientific tools and perspectives while drawing upon the world's great spiritual teachings. This body of work emerged directly from a period in my life when I came to revisit the deep and subtle practice of soul work in a new, humbling, and very human way.

By that time I had already spent decades as a serious spiritual practitioner. The core of this process was arriving at a deeper and more radical trust—trust of life itself, and of my deepest self, or soul. To truly trust my life, I had to choose, again and again, to trust. Anxiety would surface, and I chose instead to trust. To do this I had to go deep, tuning in not just to the nondual Suchness and the causal Self privileged by the spiritual communities in which I participated, but also to hear the voice of my soul. I needed to relate to my key life decisions in a way that allowed them to be guided by its wisdom.

This required me to get in touch with an underlying current of ex-tremely subtle anxiety that had previously been invisible to me. Though my dedicated practice had enabled me to transcend this anxiety, it didn't transform the pattern tendency. And this is the main distinction between transcendental spiritual practice and soul work. The psychic alchemy of subtle soul work has the potential to actually transform our karmic, ener-getic, and psychological patterns.

This drew me to emphasize subtle soul sadhana as a much more central dimension of practice. The term "spiritual bypassing" is used to critique the tendency of spiritual practitioners to use spirituality as a substi-tute for a full embrace of their ordinary human drives and challenges. But there's another spiritual bypass that is worth addressing. There is a strong tendency among practitioners of transcendental spirituality to bypass the subtle dimensions of our lives and our soul-level experience. Reclaiming it is an enormously powerful—and underemphasized—dimension of spir-itual practice. It can be done with rational discernment, transcending the magical thinking that so often finds its way into subtle New Age spirituality and egocentric framings of the soul. But our soul organizes the resonant power of our deepest resources. The soul's rich reservoirs of guidance and depth are essential to our fullest excellence and empowerment.

The path of transcendental spirituality can be viewed as analogous to space, in that we continually awaken from limited identities, expanding into our ultimate identity as the universal Self and Suchness, transcending suffering and experiential limitations. It is as if identity ascends into the light.

Soul work gives us a practice path analogous to time, in which we are a traveler, on a "hero's" journey—receiving a call, being tested, fighting battles, being transformed, and thus engaging an adventure of deepening wisdom and love and self-actualization. It is as if identity descends into the underworld of the deep psyche and body, and then the DNA of the sap rises in us from our depths to our heights.

I shared my process of learning with my students, and in that pro-cess Integral Soul Work emerged, integrating both of kinds of mystical experience. Grounded in a radical nondual view, I teach an approach

156

that opens into a relationship to the "strange attractor" of our daemon or soul, and the field of subtle energies, influences, and experiences. It is a self-transcending path, rather than being directed toward the illusory goal of fulfilling the limited, perceived ego, or self-sense.

It is a very happy way of life, but it is not directed at seeking happiness. Again and again, the practitioner acts on and affirms their understanding that personal happiness comes through awakening from false identifications, resting in the inherently happy nature of reality, through loving service to others, and through devoting oneself to what is greater than the self.

Practitioners discover the happiness of devotional surrender, the disposition summarized in the great Christian prayer, "Not my will, but thine, be done" (Luke 22:41–42). Practice involves the continual conscious, natural reorientation of attention—a continual rediscovery of freedom, a continual reawakening of joy, and a continual return to love. This life of practice orients the practitioner to the inherently happy "true north" of self-transcending love and service. In the context of such a life of self-transcending practice, the practitioner is not concentrated in the self-oriented motivations that animate conventional soul-oriented spirituality. He or she is no longer craving to be fulfilled by life's experiences. Of course, most of us would appreciate better health, more money, and more fulfilling relationships—but we do not focus on attaining these things, nor do we assume they will lead to fulfillment in life.

There is a recognition of the essentially sacrificial nature of life. Sacrifice means "to make sacred," and the very word points to the fact that in relation to the great Mystery, the act of taking toxifies us. We cannot "consume" holiness. We receive spiritual nourishment only as the natural response of a living universe to our unselfish self-giving. Sacrifice in this sense acknowledges that it is through giving that we receive the blessings of life. It is only in self-transcending devotional service to others that we have a healthy experience of the kind of wholesome thriving and fulfillment that life can truly offer. In our surrender of our defenses and symbols of imaginary security, we become attractive offerings to Life itself, grateful conduits through which grace can flow into the world.

Now it is no longer the story of the separate soul as if it were the center of its universe. Rather than being impractical or self-absorbed, the discussion of finding one's unique purpose becomes part of the story of how our soul's unique expression finds its way into the world of relations, enabling us to make a bigger difference in the lives of others and our world. We do this through the archetypal enactment of our individual stories. Our souls "dance" with each other on many levels, co-creating the heroic action of our collective soul, and fulfilling our collective purpose.

This is the domain of Integral Soul Work. It is the wide-ranging poetry whose vocabulary is the mythic structure of archetypal stories—the hero's journey, the divine romance, giving birth and nursing, the saga of death and rebirth, and the story of growing up.

As we begin to allow ourselves to participate in the mythic, soul dimension of our lives, we learn to conduct a whole symphony of animating poetic energies through our bodies and psyches. We become lightning rods to the greater energies of the anima mundi, or world soul. This is the field in which we learn the yoga that teaches our material life how to resonate with the subtle realms of soul in a new way, with a new dimension of creativity. It involves really letting go into a bigger force that wants to find its way through us to enact a heroic or tragic or tantric hero's journey or other archetypal story.

Slow Dancing with the Soul of the World

How do you come to know the narrative thrust and arc of your life? A visioning process must enact itself. In Integral Soul Work, you drop down into whatever it is that glows in your bone marrow, and ask from the heart, and from the very bottom of your being, for help to align you to your Soul, to help you learn to hear its voice. Knowing that you cannot come to know its unique contours simply via nondual recognition of everything that arises as none other than the Self, (critically important as that is), you begin to feel into the pulse of the sap that rises through your body and soul. You wait to hear a new, deeper, previously hidden voice. You open your feeling to learn what is being said to you by the DNA of the protoplasmic informational energy that surges, nurtures, and replenishes your very consciousness, the actual nerve spark in your cerebrospinal fluid.

Your soul or daemon is recognizable because it speaks in chorus with your heart and blood. Life wants to live. That which has always animated evolutionary emergence is still alive in you and wants to keep evolving. And it wants to more fully express this right now through your body, your emotions, your mind, your imagination, your relationships, and your creativity. Our body-minds are structured to experience this somatically. We learn to mobilize a coherent somatic embodiment of our highest gross, subtle, and causal possibilities by a kind of "method acting," inhabiting a new role in a narrative, enacting a new story.

Powerful resonances arise when we inhabit a character playing a particular role in an archetypal story. It neatly enlists a wide range of hidden abilities because it reverse-engineers the neurological cues that trigger the highest capacities of the brain, the nervous system, and our biochemistry. Without believing in mythic narratives the way a "primitive" magical or mythic mind would, we freely discover and inhabit these roles and let this, with remarkable efficiency, organize and liberate our highest spiritual, mental, physical, and emotional capacities.

Integral Soul Work is thus a form of skillful means that enables our total psychophysical capacities to self-organize and make their highest art. Consciously living a new story is tremendously powerful. And it is unavoidable in any case, now that we have entered an era when our world drama has flashed its apocalyptic teeth and stopped making sense. The absurdity of our slumbering world ecological crisis and the many complex political and cultural global issues at hand grant us a new degree of artistic license to take theatrical poses, to assume the mantles of our archetypes, to lovingly and playfully unleash their power through a kind of ceremony of transformation—a magical dance—whose intent is to conjure our emergence into a higher structure, a better story.

There are larger subtle dynamics, an impulse in the soul of the world that is trying to express a new level of intelligence through each of us. Seen thus, soul work opens up a political practice, a form of subtle activism. Each aspirant explores and learns how to make his or her way back energetically (and thus shamanically and ceremonially, ritually and mythically) to learn their unique art, their way of entering and inhabiting that wild new world creatively. We each do the art of showing up face-to-face with the soul of a world that has summoned each of our souls to its unique destiny, in play with other souls, to become new human beings in a new kind of human culture. This culture is one that naturally co-creates a healthy future for each of us, for our species, and for all our other relations on this planet.

Practicing in Mutuality—You Don't Have to Go It Alone

Certain aspects of the soul work journey—such as the soul's journey to the underworld and its battle with the nemesis—are intensely personal ordeals, events that occur only in a profound existential depth, in the solitude of the soul. The greater context of the Integral Soul Work journey, however, can only be lived fully in relationship, in mutuality. We need to share the process with fellow practitioners who are authentic, vulnerable, and passionate—people who can be trusted and who are on a similar trajectory of awakening.

Cooperative mutuality and intimacy teach us much, of course. But what is most essential is that integral soul-and-spiritual fellowship allows us to experience the anima mundi, the World Soul who is incarnating through us all together. A presence and intelligence arrives that is more than the sum of the presence and intelligence of the individuals. And its character, passion, and heroism are a necessary source of strength, inspiration, and guidance.

Mutuality is a key ingredient in what makes it possible for a community of practice to break new ground. Who do we think we are to assume that we can actually be the change we want to see in our world? That question can only be answered with another question: Whom do we think we are if we do not make the attempt to do it to the best of our abilities? This is Integral Soul Work—a capacious art form, grounded in self-transcending practice and lived in mutuality.

Living the Question

In his *Letters to a Young Poet*, Rainer Maria Rilke issued the invitation to "love the questions" and to "live the questions." I issue that same invitation to you here even as you embark (or continue) on this journey to discover your purpose, whether practicing with Integral Soul Work or some other approach. The hard truth of this matter is that purpose is a dynamic, ongoing revelation, rather than something discrete and well defined. And there is something inherently, "purposefully" elusive about it.

If you are really rigorous with yourself, you'll admit that there is a sense in which you will never fulfill your total soul purpose. You will practice and close the gap all your life, but the project will never be finished. The adventure will never end. To feel the call, to choose to trust the process of your life, to be humbled, to deepen and listen and wait until your heart breaks open to the lower octave where that deeper voice of soul truth resides—this path fulfills itself with every step, and yet it never ends.

We now face questions that are so profound and existential that they can deepen us into new levels of intimacy with the world and with each other. But it is a deep yoga of inquiry. Most people can't abide in such open questions and the discomfort they create long enough to be transformed and reshaped by them. But we can practice to build our capacity. Perhaps if we can learn to hold our exploration of our personal and collective purpose like a Zen koan—an impossible question that stops the mind, a question we have to live with over time, one that cannot be answered with our ordinary consciousness, the answers to which are all provisional and temporary—then we will be able to tolerate that fire and even learn to thrive within it, as we tune in ever more deeply to the voice of the Soul.

PART II
The Journey

Chapter 9

FINDING PURPOSE AS AN EVOLUTIONARY WOMAN

Barbara Marx Hubbard

I am an Evolutionary Woman. In my writing and teaching I've developed a new worldview of Conscious Evolution as the fundamental context for the next stage of human evolution. Throughout my life, I have written eight books and 195 volumes of Journal begun in 1948 to be communicated over Deepak Chopra's ISHAR, a new communication system and archive for evolutionaries. I founded and led the Foundation for Conscious Evolution (since 1993) and am the co-chair of the Center for Integral Wisdom, cofounder of the Association for Global New Thought and the World Future Society, a member of Evolutionary Leaders Group, the Club of Budapest and more. I have found my purpose.

Let me share with you how I got here...

Evolutionary Women fall in love and are attracted by shared purpose to fulfill their greater destiny.

In 1948, I was sitting at a small café on the left bank in Paris, where I was on my Junior Year abroad from Bryn Mawr College.

A handsome American came in and sat opposite me at the little wooden table. The chestnuts roasted in the fire. The November day was cold. I had been trying to be an existentialist, to believe there was no deeper meaning but what I gave it. I wore my beret, smoked Gauloises, and had half a bottle of red wine for lunch. I was depressed. Soon I gained my courage, smiled, offered him some of my wine and asked him my fundamental life question:

What do you think is the meaning of all our new scientific, technological, and industrial power that is good?

He amazed me by saying, "I am an artist seeking a new image of man commensurate with our powers to shape the future."

He told me that when a culture loses its story, it loses its greatness. We had lost our grand narrative. We could no longer believe in the Renaissance story of progress after the two world wars, the Holocaust, and the loss of millions of lives. At that time in Paris the worldviews were existentialism, nihilism, absurdism, materialism. No one at the Ecole des Sciences Politiques where I was in school had any hope, yet I was innately hopeful. But about what? That was my question.

He enthralled me. He told me it was up to the artist to help humanity find its new story. As he spoke it flowed through my mind, *I'm going to marry you.* And I did!

I married Earl Hubbard in 1951 in New York City and we had five children. I wrote and edited several books with Earl, engaging in deep morning breakfast dialogues as we sought to understand the next step in human evolution as a "cultural humanity" now being born into the Earth/space environment.

Gradually, I realized that something profound was missing in my life. I loved my husband, my children, and was following all the requirements of the 1951 women: *Get married, have as many children as possible, and care for your husband and home.* I did it all with love, yet I became deeply depressed, feeling I was literally turning into stone.

Inspired by the great American dream that we are seeking "life, liberty, and the pursuit of happiness," I set out to discover who was happy in Lakeville, Connecticut. To my dismay, I found a sort of mildew of depression coating the comfortable lives of this community. Something was missing. What was it?

During the 1960s, I found the answer through Abraham H. Maslow's *Toward a Psychology of Being.* As a psychiatrist studying wellness rather than illness, he discovered that all *Self-Actualizing* happy, beneficent people had one thing in common: *Chosen work they found intrinsically self-rewarding and of service.*

He advised everyone to "Be bold. Do what attracts you."

What attracted me was Dr. Maslow, so I was bold, called him up, asked him for lunch, and he came!

That was the beginning of my emergence as an Evolutionary Woman. It happens when a woman learns that her depression is a signal for something more to be expressed, and learns to say YES to the impulse of attraction within her. The "something more" begins to be revealed.

At the lunch, Dr. Maslow gave me a list of 300 people, his "Eupsychian Network of Good Souls," that he had collected over a lifetime. Many of them became founders of the human potential movement. My YES had brought me in touch with the newly emerging network of evolutionary transformation.

I returned from the New York luncheon determined to transform my life with this precious list. I wrote a letter to all 300 people, asking them what they thought was "The Next Step for the Future Good." I offered to publish their key responses in the "Center Letter," which I created myself.

In the early 1960s, I read Teilhard de Chardin's *The Phenomenon of Man.* I was thrilled to discover evolution has a purpose. For billions of years it has been moving from single cell, to multicell, to animal, to human, and now to us. The inner drive, the consciousness force, the divine in nature had a direction toward higher consciousness, purpose, and more complex and synergistic order. The epiphany was the amazing realization that the direction of evolution and my own are one.

The Evolutionary Woman gains a new identity. She is "the universe in person." Her passion to grow, to love more, be more, create more, is the Eros of the Universe itself animating her.

Teilhard intuited the next stage of evolution. Before the internet, he declared that the noosphere, the thinking layer of Earth would one day "get its collective eyes". When enough love and creativity entered that field of the planetary nervous system, (now growing rapidly through internet, Facebook, Twitter, etc.), people would be changed, not one by one, but all at once. He called it the *Christification of the Earth.*

I was deeply excited. In some intuitive way I realized that it was my mission to help the "noosphere" get its collective eyes and to help the nervous system of the planet to be filled with innovation and love. I realized it was like the nervous system of a newborn baby, about to wake up to a new planetary consciousness. A "vocation of destiny" was born. I yearned to become a communicator of evolutionary potential.

Evolutionary Women are animated by a unique expression of the Impulse of Evolution as their own calling to evolve.

Through the great Indian Sage Sri Aurobindo's magnum opus *The Life Divine,* I learned that the impulse of evolution, the "supramental genius" of evolution was arising in evolving humans. At some point, he prophesied, we would become "Gnostic Humans," a new species, beyond the animal/human life cycle.

Evolutionary Women often feel we are not getting older but getting newer. Something new is being born in us.

Then came Buckminster Fuller. He told us that *SpaceShip Earth came without an operating manual,* so that we would *have* to learn how to guide the system. He informed us we have the technology, resources, and know-how to make the world work for all... if we learned synergy and cooperation.

These four great pioneers, with others, laid the foundation for the Evolutionary movement. I had learned the evolutionary code. Evolution has direction, purpose, and intent. The intent is more consciousness, creativity and love by means of ever-greater complexity or synergy.

I discovered that this was my intent. I and the Impulse were one.

I became a conscious Evolutionary Woman!

The next great breakthrough for my emergence was meeting Dr. Jonas Salk in the early '60s. I read something he had written on a Theater of Man, wrote a piece on it, and sent it to Jerry Piel, editor of *Scientific American* and on Jonas's board. Jerry gave it to Jonas, who called me one sunny day in the fall in New England. I had had my fifth child, and was sitting on the lawn with them all in the sun.

The phone rang, "Mrs. Hubbard? This is Jonas Salk." The minute I heard his voice I realized something new had happened. Even though I didn't know it then, he was an evolutionary man. It was coded in his voice – exciting, inviting, charged with vitality.

He said, "Mrs. Hubbard, You have written my vision better than I could have. We are two peas in the same genetic pod. Can I take you to lunch?"

I said yes!

He came the next week to drive me from Connecticut to New York. It was a magnificent fall day; the apple orchard sparkled with red and gold, the sun burned warm on the grass. The doorbell rang. My heart skipped a beat; I opened the door to him. He smiled that incredible, magnanimous smile and said: "Mrs. Hubbard, this is the Garden of Eden."

"Dr. Salk," I said, "You're right. I'm Eve and I'm leaving!" He looked startled. It startled me too.

During the ride to New York I told him everything that was wrong with me: my love of the future, the yearning to do more, the sense of deep vocation, a vital task that I was to perform.

He said, "Barbara, this is not what is wrong about you. This is what is right about you. You are a mutant! And I will introduce you to the few others I have been able to find in twenty-five years." This was the next step in my emergence as an Evolutionary Woman.

I had met another evolutionary being. The Evolutionary Impulse became self-aware in me.

He turned up the frequency of the inner code of evolution within me by resonating with it with his own being.

I wrote in my Journal in 1964
:

This Christmas of 1964 is the best of my life, not because I have achieved my ideals, but because the problem of identity has disappeared. I can never again say, as I once did, "in my own eyes I'm nothing," for, as all people are, I, too, am the inheritor of the evolution of the ages. In my genes are the generations. Every cell in my body identifies me with the great and terrible adventure of inanimate to animate to human and every desire of my being sets me passionately to work to further the rise of humanness out of humanity. I am what was and what will be. If I am nothing, life is nothing; that it cannot be—and be.

The rise of the Evolutionary Woman is awakened by the incarnation of the Impulse of Evolution as one's own inner drive to become one's unique self.

Your life purpose becomes the unique expression of the "irreducibly beautiful impulse of creation," as Marc Gafni writes in *Becoming Your Unique Self.*

With this often comes the disruption of past life patterns of the exclusive role of wife and mother, housekeeper, and caretaker. The Evolutionary Woman is not seeking to be equal to men in a dysfunctional world, but to join with men and women to participate in the emerging world.

One day my husband Earl was speaking in a talk I had arranged for him. I stood behind a tree and wept. He came to me and said, "Darling, why are you crying?"

I dared to say, "Earl, I want to speak too!" My heart sank. I knew it would hurt him.

He was crestfallen. "Then I can't make you happy." "That's true," I said, "No one can *make* another happy."

I told him I had to go forth and tell the story my own way. He said, "I'm the genius. You're the editor." I nodded, with tears of love, but there was no going back. We didn't know how to grow the relationship as younger people often do now.

The Evolutionary Woman is not merely a co-equal. She is a co-creator, becoming a new archetype. "The Feminine Co-Creator." She is incarnating the impulse of evolution as her own passion to create, motivated by the Creator within her to become a co-creator with the divine. She is moving toward the next stage of human evolution as a conscious co-evolutionary.

I sadly had to ask for a divorce. After loving each other, having the five beautiful children, writing and editing his books, cherishing his paintings and securing a major show at the Gallery of Modern Art, I realized that I had to go forth and tell the story myself.

It was then that Lt. Col. John J. Whiteside entered my life. He was Chief Officer of Information in New York for the Air Force. He loved the book I edited for Earl called *The Search Is On* and spread it to the news media and the generals of the Air Force. In it he had declared: "We are being born as universal humans."

John told me he had been totally committed to covering the Apollo Program live, sensing it had great meaning, while others were reporting, as he told me, as if they were telling the story of the birth of the Christ child, as to how much the infant weighed and the labor conditions at the inn.

John said, "Now I know why I wanted it to be covered live. It was a birth!"

The Evolutionary Woman becomes aware that we are entering a new stage of evolution, not only personal but collectively.

I was alive with the aspiration of a universal impulse of creation, as though I was being born anew.

John told me that if I attempted to make my husband the spokesperson for my mission, I would fail. So I took the radical step as an Evolutionary Woman to break out totally from the role of wife and of mother.

In 1970, as an Evolutionary Woman, I became a new kind of mother.

I told my 9-year-old son that his mother was a pioneer and that I wanted him to come too. He wrapped his little arms around me and said, "We know, Mom, that you love us. You are doing what mothers are meant to do. You are creating a future for your children. I want to come with you."

And so it was. Earl and I separated. John had told me that if I tried to make Earl the voice for my mission, I would surely fail. That was the key. I could not let that happen.

We were divorced in 1970. I moved my five children to Washington, DC. My sister lent me her home, the Greystone Mansion in Rock Creek Park, as she and her husband, Wayne Barnett, had moved to Stanford University where he was teaching law.

Together, John and I founded the Committee for the Future in 1970, to bring positive options for the future into the public arena for decision and action.

One day he took me to meet the head of CBS News.

"Tell him the news," he said to me. I said, smiling, knowing how strange it would sound to him: "The news is humankind has been born into the universe."

He looked at John as if he were crazy. But then he nodded, "It's true," he said, "but we can't say it."

"Why not?" I asked. He shook his head.

Gradually we developed a powerful new global Earth/Space Human Development Goal: "New Worlds on Earth, New Worlds in Space, New Worlds in the Human Mind." The idea was that after the lunar landing we should have a *social* lunar landing, guiding the military/industrial complex toward a new evolutionary goal to restore the Earth, free the people, and explore the infinite regions of spirit and the universe beyond our mother planet, as later written up in my book *Conscious Evolution: Awakening the Power of Our Social Potential.*

Soon thereafter we went to meet with Congressman Olin Teague of the Science and Technology Committee of the US Congress and told him about the new Earth/Space goal. He said ruefully, "I completely agree with you. But we can't do it in the Congress. There is no way for the various committees to come together to look at any long-range goal. YOU DO IT!"

Amazed, John and I considered how to do it. We began to speak of the goal to business leaders, politicians, and space scientists. They all agreed it was good but said the others would not get it. I went to see Mr. Rockwell of Rockwell International in his giant office. "Mr. Rockwell," I said, "Why don't you call together a design team to design the first Earth/Space Human Development program." He looked stricken. He nodded and said, "I totally agree with you, but I won't do it."

"Why not?"

"Because I would lose our defense contracts."

So that was it.

Evolutionary Women do not avoid technology, they attempt to guide it. High Love and High Tech merge for the New Culture of Humanity.

John's son went to Southern Illinois University.

We were invited to a conference there called "Mankind in the Universe. Earl was addressing the student body in the arena, which was like a prizefighting ring with thousands of seats surrounding it. Elegantly dressed, he was totally out of phase with the ragged students in long hair and blue jeans. His speech did not go over well. He called for heroism in the age of the antihero.

Subsequently, I had spent time in small meetings with students; however, it was a time for the radical rejection of society by students. One of the students raised his hand and asked: "Why do you want us to continue

25,000 years of failure?"

An older man, a professor, arose in towering wrath directed at this question. "You would have kept us in the caves! You wouldn't even have dared step into the light."

I began to say in a gentle way, that man had not failed, that we are a young species at a point of transition. Now it is possible for the first time to overcome those terrible lacks such as poverty and disease. Our new tools might transform the ignorance that has forced us into destructive behavior so that we might become a new species

Each one of us is needed.

The longhaired, blue-jeaned, 25-year-old snickered at me. I stared at him and said, "Did I hear you snicker?"

He sank into his seat.

"How dare you snicker at humankind? How dare you condemn the effort of the past? Do you have any idea of the struggle that went into the development of the human species?" I spoke like a mother defending her family.

The Evolutionary Woman has faith in the evolution of humanity no matter what a mess we are.

The next morning Professor Tom Turner, director of special projects for Buckminster Fuller asked John and me to sit with him on the stage. In the audience were several hundred people who had attended various sessions of the seminars. Earl was there too. Tom said, "We would like to make a recommendation that Barbara Marx Hubbard run for the nomination for the presidency of the United States on the Democratic ticket. Her role would be to carry the options for the future into the public arena."

I was stunned; yet amazingly, felt it was a good idea.

The Evolutionary Woman accepts the reality that she is needed for the evolution of the whole culture.

Earl was deeply distressed and said it would kill him if his wife ran for president.

So I did not do it for his sake but felt disappointed.

From the Southern Illinois experiences, John and I realized that some new process was needed. Whenever they discussed the idea of New Worlds on Earth, New Worlds in Space, or New Worlds in the Human Mind, a businessman, for example, would say,

"Yes, I get it but the labor unions won't." Or a politician would get it and say that the public would never accept this new potential.

In a flash of insight, John decided to put apparently opposing forces in a wheel to actually experience each other directly. He said you couldn't make progress when one person is the speaker and everyone else is sitting in a row. "There needs to be a new social structure," he declared.

He drew a new diagram and put functional areas of any social body in the inner circle of the wheel-like pieces of pie facing each other—sections for production, environment, and government, with a coordinating hub in the center where each sector could match needs and resources.

He added a satellite at the growing edge of the wheel to represent new capacities, as in the biological revolution, the physical sciences, psychologies of growth, and information sciences. Finally, there was a far-out satellite for unexplained phenomenon: the intuitive, mystical, and psychic experiences if the human race.

John decided to put a television in every section, with a central open "mission control" where everyone could see everything at once. People could begin to see themselves as one living organism. "Yes," John told her, "We can broadcast the meetings live and call it *the New News*."

Evolutionary Women are inspired by the male creative genius.

I realized he was giving the people their own nervous system. It was the noosphere getting its collective eyes! They called the conference process SYNCON for synergistic convergence. The purpose was to get the broadest possible cross section of people to form task forces in each sector. Each person or group was asked three questions:

What do you want to create?

What do you need to create it?

What do you want to freely give to others?

Then there is the chance for vocational networking. "Vocational arousal" occurs. People are excited to help each other. Instead of win/lose conflict, the process changes to how much and with whom can you co-create to get more of what you want. People merge with corollary but apparently conflicting functions, like environment and business, looking for common goals by matching needs with resources.Finally each sector restates its goals, needs, and resources in the light of the potential of the whole system. The students removed the walls between sectors of the wheel. Participants met in an Assembly of the Whole. A sense of social love infused the group. When astronaut Edgar Mitchell came in he said: "If there had been a spiritual Geiger counter it would have gone off the charts." We called it "The All-Walls-Down Ceremony."

I realized some new form of self-governing process was being born here. This was the beginning of a more synergistic democracy.

John and I begin to join genius to create this new social process to connect people to co-create.

The Evolutionary Woman became a co-creator. The new archetype the Feminine Co-Creator was born in her. Her creativity was an expression of the unique impulse of creation flowing through her.

I could see the pattern of the new society emerging from my life and work. I told my children what was happening and they told me they were with me the whole way, as I included them in everything.

From 1972 to the early '80s, I, and John, did 25 SYNCON conferences throughout the world, from one with gang leaders of Los Angeles to the nation of Jamaica to space scientists in Huntsville, Alabama. They had discovered a new social process to bring separate people and functions together to make a new whole system.

Later in 1985, I began trips to the Soviet Union with Rama Vernon's Center for Soviet-American Dialogue, and did two major SYNCONS in the Soviet Union on the theme of joint projects, bringing Soviets and Americans together successfully to co-create in every sector of the SYNCON Wheel.

But they had neither the resources nor the business skills to continue doing the SYNCONS. I was paying for everything out of the resources given to me by my father, the toy maker Louis Marx, creator of Marx Toys.

I had written a letter to ask to be taken up in the space shuttle. It was my intuition that an Earth/Space Mind Linkage, people in space connected to people on Earth realizing that humanity is being born as a universal species, would create a jump in collective consciousness and the noosphere would "get its collective eyes." Fortunately I was not accepted. This was the shuttle that was destroyed in the terrible accident.

An Evolutionary Woman is inspired by the highest potential within her, acts to discover the reality of her visions and responds to her deepest vocation of destiny.

In 1980 while in Santa Barbara, writing a book on the future of humanity, I had a Christ experience. I had asked the question: *What kind of person can handle all this new power? What is the image of the future human equal to our new powers?*

Jonas had taken me to a biology lab that had *Stamp out physical death* written on the doorway.

With these questions, as I walked in the glorious February day in Santa Barbara, I saw a group of hang gliders jumping off a mountain, floating above the Cross at Mt. Calvary Monastery in butterfly-colored wings.

Suddenly the image of mass metamorphosis occurred to her. I remembered St. Paul's words, "Behold, I show you a mystery. We shall not all sleep but we shall all be changed…in a moment, in the twinkling of an eye, for the trumpet shall sound…"

Oh my God! I thought, what if the whole story of Jesus is true. What if he is the future human!

I entered the monastery to spend a weekend. I picked up the Bible, and turned to St. Paul. As I read I realized it was coded evolution. It could only be understood by the generation who had gained the power to do much of the works that he did and more.

I began to write, without stopping for six months, an evolutionary interpretation of the New Testament. I saw in Jesus the embodiment of the future potential of humanity. He had said, "You will do the work that I did and even greater work will you do."

I realized it's true. We are doing the work that Jesus did without Christ love. When we combine Christ love and new scientific/technological capacities, we shall indeed all be changed!

The Evolutionary Woman is a seminal thinker. She is original.

I sent the manuscript to Buckminster Fuller before it was published. He took her to be alone with him in the garden of the Annenberg Communication Center where they were both speaking. Putting his arms around her and touching her temple with his temple, he said, "Darling, I had the same experience that you did. I was walking down a street in Chicago when I was lifted up. I saw a light that said to me: "Bucky, you are to be the first mini-Christ of Earth. What you attest to is true." Then he told me he went to the New Testament and wrote almost an identical interpretation of the New Testament book that I had.

When I asked him for a comment on the book, he wrote: "Barbara is now the best informed human now alive on the subject of the future and the potentials it brings…"

This was because we both had a Christ experience and actually realized that he embodied the future potential of humanity that we are to become. The ordinary futurists had no idea that this was so.

The Evolutionary Woman is inspired by the higher wisdom of the great avatars and beings to manifest them naturally and humbly as a new norm.

In 1981, John died of a brain tumor. He had inoperable cancer that was terminal. I nursed him until he died.

On his last night he said to me: "Sunshine, I know humankind is born into this universe. I know we will build new worlds. I know you will carry out the mission." His eyes fluttered and he was gone.

"John, where did you go," I asked out loud lovingly touching his forehead, which was rapidly turning cold. I was shocked, never having seen a dead body. He said to me on the inner plane, "I've died to set you free. I have work to do to prepare for what is coming. We will rendezvous again. I will be ready when you need me to build the Great SYNCON in the sky."

Devastated and alone, in 1984, I decided to launch an idea campaign for the vice presidency of the United States at the suggestion of Buckminster Fuller. My campaign was based on the idea of creating an Office for the Future to *scan for, map, connect, and communicate what is working in the world.*

I invited friends throughout the country to give a party for me to raise funds. I joined with Carolyn and Sanford Anderson and began to travel across the country. My goal was to have 200 delegates sign a petition to place her name in nomination for the vice presidency at the Democratic National Convention in 1984. I was told I would be lucky to get one delegate if she were my mother!

It was mission impossible.

Aiming at this goal nonetheless, everywhere I went Positive Future Centers formed. They wanted to create a center for "it." I found that "it" was a center in each person sharing and reaching out to develop a greater community based on the principles of the Campaign.

Each center began to self-organize in what Carolyn and I called The Rings of Empowerment, eventually becoming the Core Group process and *The Co-Creators Handbook.*

The ninety Positive Future Centers all focused on the one goal of the 200 delegates voting for me.

When I went to the convention, I had no media and no passes to the floor. The wife of the governor of Colorado let me in with her little team. I made 30-second speeches, saying, "Vote for me for vice president so I can declare from the great platform of the Democratic Party that our purpose is to identify, connect, and support what is working in the world. And I will then give my votes to Geraldine Ferraro."

So over 200 delegates signed up to give me the power to make the speech, which I did at the Convention. When the guard took her to the great platform he whispered in my ear, "Now honey, they won't pay any

attention to you. They never do. You are saying this for the universe."
And I did.

The Evolutionary Woman speaks far beyond her personal interest for the good of the whole. She is able to give birth to the Unknown Future just as she gives birth to the Unknown Child. No matter how painful.

The people and process had uplifted me during the Campaign. But after the Campaign came the sense of loss. My sister requested that Greystone be returned to her. No one had the strength or ability to organize the ninety Positive Future Centers without the goal of the Campaign. People became critical of me, as though I were failing them. I wrote in my journal, "I have a wound in my etheric body." I realized I had entered into this huge effort with no protection, inner or outer. I was homeless, in debt, and exhausted. I arrived at the home of my friend Kathleen Gildred in Topanga Canyon, California, with all my clothes in a station wagon and no clear sense of next steps.

I said to Kathleen, "I don't know where to go." Kathleen said: "You stay here until you find out." She put me in a little Bucky Fuller type house filled with his books, overlooking the hills. Every day I played *Chariots of Fire*, and asked, *Where shall I live. What shall I do?*

The answer came: ***You are to live in an alternative to Camp David, where the leaders of the old world come to solve problems that cannot be solved in the consciousness that created them. You are to live where leaders of the new world come to tell their stories of what is working, to map it, to connect it, and to discover and communicate the design of the positive future already emerging in our midst. In this center there must be a World Communication Hub, and a Great Library of books, tapes, works.***

The problem was, of course, that no such place existed. My daughters came to help me find an apartment. I said to them, "I don't care where

I live, you find it for me."

So began a period of feeling lost and confused.

Rama Vernon, director of the Center for Soviet American dialogue, came to see me to persuade me to go to the Soviet Union with her. Rama opened remarkable doors with the Soviet Peace Committee and other leaders still during the Cold War. Together we took hundreds of Americans to the Soviet Union as citizen diplomats, as they were called then.

One of the most touching meetings was with Joseph Goldin, a Soviet citizen who had been imprisoned, but now was becoming famous in the citizen diplomacy movement for the development of spacebridges. On their very first trip to Russia I was astonished when at the airport he pulled out a dog-eared copy of one of my old books, *The Evolutionary Journey*, published in 1982. He turned directly to the pages that described the "planetary smile" and told me that was what he was working on! The cosmic birth experience was his goal too!

Later I asked him: "Joseph, is it possible that what you call the 'dialectic,' the inevitable pattern in history leading to a higher order, is what we call the process aspect of God, the implicate order, the blueprint or pattern of evolution?"

"Of course it is," he said, shrugging his shoulders, and going on rapidly discussing his projects.

"But Joseph, if this is true, then those who believe in the quantum jump to Communism in the Soviet Union, and those of us in the United States who believe in a similar jump to a global/cooperative society are natural allies... We are co-creators... Particularly if it is true that you will renounce the use of force and if we will too."

"Of course we are co-creators," he said.

At the Soviet-American conferences we were feeling love, empathy, and friendship.

As Henry Borovik, a major leader of the Soviet Peace Committee told the group: *"Finally, Soviets and Americans are on the same side of the net, while the problems are on the other side. Instead of trying to destroy each other, we're solving our common problems together. We were able to do here at the Summit in a few minutes that would have taken years to do officially."*

We finished the last of the Soviet-American Summits in Washington, DC, in a blaze of creativity. Ted Turner gave a rousing speech. John Denver called in live. Alexander Gratski, the magnificent Russian composer, and David Pomeranz sang together: "It's in every one of us," as a duet. The audience, Soviets and Americans, sang, locked arms, and swayed to the music as the two singers repeated the refrain over and over again:

> It's in every one of us, to be wise,
> Find your heart, open up both your eyes;
> We can all know everything without ever knowing why,
> It's in every one of us, by and by.

I changed the words to: "It's in every one of us here and now."

The Evolutionary Woman sees the pattern of the Emerging World and works toward it.

I saw the 1980s as the time when the nervous system of the body politic began to link us up in consciousness as one living system. Our new planetary nervous system was joining us in people-initiated, nongovernmental, nonpolitical acts of love, celebration, and compassion for ourselves as one human family.

I went to live with the global economist Hazel Henderson in Gainesville, Florida, working on how to tell the new good news. We conceived of a Global Intelligence System and a Global Collegium of innovators, thinkers, and activists worldwide whose work and life successfully manifested the new value system. It would become an interactive global mind.

We couldn't raise the money for it. I moved to different places, not knowing what to do. Often I could hear a flickering inner voice saying seductively, "Would you like to die?" I felt the temptation to sleep and not to have to struggle, but I quickly turned away. "No, I choose to live. I have not completed my mission," I would say, quickly, knowing the power of choice.

I began to realize that in me and millions of others, the Evolutionary Woman was being born through practicing in-depth personal and social evolution.

I wrote in my journal:

"As a woman, I have felt the passion in me being transformed into the drive for vocation, the desire to express unique creativity in service to the world. Within almost every woman I know there is a hunger to give ourselves more fully, not to maintain the world as it is, not only to be equal to men, but also rather to create with men a better world in which all life can fulfill itself.

"Everyone's genius is needed for the evolution of the world, just as every cell's function is needed for the growth of the biological organism. In the past we reproduced the species, lived short lives, and died young. Now, the unique genius of each of us is being called forth, because that is exactly what is needed to solve this extraordinarily complex crisis and move us forward to the next stage of evolution. Nature does not need more bodies. She needs evolved beings! She needs our genius."

Evolutionary Women are becoming co-creators as well as pro-creators. We are extending the love of the Unknown Child into the world as the love of the Unknown Future, toward love of Humanity, and all Life on Earth.

"Instead of separating us from men, co-creation reunites us as partners in nurturing the larger human family, as well as our own social one.

"Each child becomes a chosen child. Every life is cherished. Every individual is needed to do and be his or her best. As we shift from maximum pro-creation to co-creation, the emphasis changes from caring for babies and dying young to evolving ourselves and healing the Earth.

"We have felt the fear of nuclear winter and environmental destruction. We have recognized the pain of social injustice, hunger, disease, and violence. We have felt the stick, but we have not yet fully experienced the carrot. The carrot is the joy of suprasex! The carrot is joining genius to co-create, it is ourselves fully actualized, the world renewed, and the environment restored. If we respond to this call we enter an 'age of co-creation' that has only been envisioned by the saints and seers of the human race. The ecstatic quality of joining together to create goes beyond gender, beyond age, class, or background. It is an endless arc of growth and adventure. It is the fulfillment of our lives."

In August 1988, I was invited to give a keynote speech at John Denver's famous Windstar Symposium in Aspen, Colorado. John had proposed to go into outer space on a Soviet Rocket. (NASA had turned him down—since the Challenger accident, they were not accepting citizen astronauts).

I spoke to John backstage just as I was about to go on to speak. The music of the Olympics was playing as 1,800 people assembled in the big tent. The theme was "Ethics in Action." It was the twenty-fifth anniversary of Martin Luther King Jr.'s speech "I Have a Dream."

Stark King, an Aspen businessman, introduced me, "She lives and works and plays right in that very, very small place where spirit becomes action."

I was buoyant and said:

"At this moment hundreds of thousands of people are gathering in Washington in the memory of Martin Luther King. Let's send them a message from Windstar. 'We are overcoming now…we have the awesome creative power of nature to transform to ever-higher systems with ever-greater consciousness, freedom, and order. This is an implicate pattern in nature. Co-creation is our theme… Ultimately it is a new relationship between humans and God, or humans and evolution.

"The human mind is designed as Buckminster Fuller told us, to penetrate nature sufficiently to understand the impulses of evolution. What we have been doing in the last few hundred years since the Renaissance is learning nature's invisible technologies of creation. Our understanding of the atom, the gene, the brain has put into our hands the power to be co-evolutionary. We can build new life-forms. We can build new worlds. We are inheriting the powers of creation itself. We are at the beginning of a global renaissance."

In 1982, Sidney Lanier, an elegant man of the theater and Episcopal priest, sought me out, having read my book on the *Theater for the Future*. He protected me, gave me a home, and together we explored what it meant to become a co-creative couple. How does it work?

From 1988 to 2017, I have been seeking to fulfill my mission: A Planetary Emergence: Connecting What Is Working World Wide in a Unique Self Symphony in which each person is free to contribute their best into the whole.

In 2012, I initiated with *The Shift Network* a major next step: On December 22, 2012, I became a global voice for "Birth 2012," announcing The Next Era of Evolution. Thousands of people gathered in hubs worldwide.

I taught thousands of students on *The Shift Network*, inspiring them to become Agents of Conscious Evolution.

In 2013, Sidney died of dementia, a sad and tragic death. I cared for him as long as I could, but the fact was, he had lost his mind, leaving me alone again. My Foundation had been launched by a large grant from Laurance Rockefeller in 1993 to publish the Bible writing. Laurance had taken me up to his little spiritual study on top of the Rockefeller Building in New York. He held my hands and said: "I am looking to you to help bring forth the Christ of the twenty-first century." And he gave me one million dollars to cover the next 10 years.

This mission beyond all mental constructs was nonetheless the moving force toward my ever-greater attraction to a planetary birth experience for humanity.

As the understanding of the crises accelerated, we saw we are at the threshold of the collapse of our own life support system, but what to do?

John Steiner, an old friend said to me, "Barbara, why don't you declare victory and retire?"

But I could not, because the flame of expectation was even brighter in me now.

I was lonely but I had faith in that Inner Impulse of Evolution to guide the way.

At just that time, two people appeared that dramatically revived this 85-year-old evolutionary.

Nina Patrick, a former student and business woman came into her life with a passion to build community through her students, to reactivate the Foundation for Conscious Evolution—to connect those who are imbued with the evolutionary impulse, to continue the courses and widen the circle of evolutionary family.

I said YES to Nina who then moved to Berkeley, California, to help grow the Foundation.

My **Mission** is To Connect Co-Creators World-Wide in a Planetary Awakening in Love, in a Unique Self symphony...Time to shift from devolution toward evolution.

Our **Goals** are to offer evolutionary educational teachings to reveal the vast new potential of humanity, while working to establish the Office for the Future in the United Nations and communities worldwide.

Concurrently I have become Co-chair of the Center for Integral Wisdom, co-founded by Ken Wilber, John Mackey, Sally Kempton, John Gray, Walter Farrell, and many others. I have become the evolutionary partner of Marc Gafni, founder of the Center for Integral Wisdom, and a great pioneer in evolutionary thought and action.

I am now working with Marc and the Center joining with the Foundation for Conscious Evolution to found a Great Library of books, tapes and teachings to serve fundamental source code for humanity's evolution.

I am now at the threshold of a new human myself.

To fulfill the dream...

In 2016, I was invited by Ambassador Chowdhury of the United Nations to explore the formation of an Office for the Future at the United Nations, to place the Wheel of Co-Creation and other synergistic processes in the 195 nations to assist them in supporting the UN 17 Sustainable Development Goals. The Foundation is working with Avon Mattison's Culture of Peace and other groups forming small citizens' Offices for the Future, as proposed during my vice presidential campaign. From the US to the UN the process is being developed.

Now, let us join together to realize our potential.

By 2020 on International Peace Day, let us have a planetary event to connect what is working worldwide—with a planetary nervous system, the Noosphere getting its collective eyes, just as Teilhard de Chardin foresaw. Let's have a Planetary Awakening in Love through a Unique Self Symphony shifting consciousness on Earth from fear to love as we move from devolution toward our conscious evolution. ***This is the meaning of our new power that is good!***

Chapter 10

ESCAPING ZOMBIE NATION
Finding Purpose through
Mindful Celebration

Tazdeen Rashid
(aka DJ TAZ RASHID)

I am in the middle of my young adult life. Today I wake up vibrant, grateful, excited about my day and what will manifest as I connect with myself, spirit, and the wholeness of creation. When I was asked to write this chapter, it stopped me in my tracks. How did I get here? How did I find myself living a life of purpose as a DJ facilitating mindful celebrations all around the world? The journey holds wisdom. Looking at our "story" we can pull out the gems of understanding. I share my story of purpose with you in hopes that it inspires your journey of deeper discovery.

I started this life in the country of Bangladesh—comfortable, safe, and well loved. I didn't know fear. I was protected—like Siddhartha, the Buddha, by parents who probably never wanted me to suffer. While I knew that poverty existed, life seemed peaceful and for the most part, predictable.

At five my parents, both doctors, moved the three of us to a small city in Iran—but a year later the political situation became dangerous.

Funny, I probably saw rocket fire and had to evacuate our home in the middle of the night on more than one occasion, but I wasn't scared. My parents were there, and I felt safe. I think I was incredibly blessed because I learned about resilience from the time I was born—there was a way out of everything, solutions would appear.

Using Joseph Campbell's model of the Hero's Journey, my first "Call to Adventure" was this immersion into a foreign culture at the age of four. Though I was safe with my parents, I didn't know the language, so I was challenged to figure out how to create my own world within the bubble of my parents' world.

Only a year later I was sent back to Bangladesh to live with my grandparents—a safer but probably still daunting solution to the danger of Iran. It was the beginning of a bizarre existence. I had my extended family—cousins, aunts, uncles, and so on—but no parents. My life in Bangladesh for the next few years was school and family, with occasional visits to my parents who had moved to Saudi Arabia. Looking back, I was learning the skills I would later need—to be resilient. Challenged but supported by a consisted thread of love and affirmation, I learned to create my own world. I found meaning in reading, collections, music, art and sports—all things I could do on my own.

When I was in third grade, we moved to America. Again, not speaking the language, I had to improvise with nonverbal ways to communicate. Being friendly and somewhat athletic gave me some status in the neighborhood, and I was a good student—except for the learning disability that hadn't been discovered yet. Reading comprehension made language acquisition tough, but the first three months of nonstop American TV helped. I was motivated, so I learned.

My parents were both trained musicians, so when we came to a country where the arts were respected in education, I thrived and my family was right there with me. Despite their heavy leanings toward professionalism and the American dream of big money, their passion included artistic expression—a lucky boon for me. As I grew, I became more and more involved with music—taking piano lessons, singing in the choir, and eventually learning guitar and drums, forming a rock band.

Being an immigrant, I was especially sensitive to the cues of the culture. I was observant, a quick study, and noticed what made people respond positively. I liked connecting with people and found that music was a particular high for me. As I approached and passed through puberty, the harsh reality that I couldn't do music for a living started sinking in. I threw myself into organizational and volunteer activities in high school, honing my leadership, entertainment and organizational skills. I had no idea where I was going—I just did what I loved.

College was basically easy—I had interesting professors and learned about marketing, leadership, and entrepreneurship, and had the "American College Experience" of partying from Wednesday to Sunday. I was still buying into the corporate dream, not wanting to go to medical or law school, and not believing there were other alternatives, I graduated college and the "fun" began.

My college partying became an adult way of life. Clubs, bars, women, and a job. I'd get a job—assume it would be the best thing that would ever happen to me...and then I'd hate it. I started realizing, like a slow burn, that my life was meaningless. I partied more and more, looked for love in all the wrong places and kept switching jobs. Something "out there" had to be the "right fit"—right?

Years passed. Right after college I'd had a crazy stroke of luck after a fire in my apartment—the insurance company basically gave me a blank check. I got all the computer toys, musical instruments, clothes, and books I'd ever wanted with that check. Randomly, I picked out a book called *How to Get Everything You Ever Wanted*, but I never read it. Now, looking back again, I see that at the hand of my Divine nudging me... but I wasn't ready to recognize it.

I moved to Chicago after college and started a string of unsuccessful work efforts. I think I had originally envisioned myself as a business mogul, owning my own hotels or real estate, but the crash began early on as I realized that the people around me were empty—as empty as I now know I was. It was a Zombie life—working empty days for long hours, living for nightlife of partying, clubbing, bar buddies, women..., empty recreation, and distraction. Internally my spirit was trying to tell me to get out but my rational mind couldn't hear that voice at all. I was consciously ignoring it, but subconsciously I was sabotaging my life. I would start with a new job, new fantasies again and again..., each time the reality was empty and miserable, and I would either quit or be fired.

I didn't know there was something to listen to inside of me. My external relationships were short, fast, and furious too, leaving me empty and confused. I didn't know what I was looking for. That's about the time I found a book called *The Secret*.

In 2007, I saw it lying on my roommate's bedstand. Having had so many failed jobs, meaningless relationships and a dying belief in the American dream, I devoured it. The Law of Attraction resonated with me, it made sense. I started to think about what I wanted to attract into my life. The first thing that changed was the rock band. I wanted to bring my bandmates with me on this journey—but they wouldn't bite.

Things started changing at warp speed. I met the woman who would become my wife, a brilliant, creative soul who was deeply dedicated to living a purposeful and clean life. This relationship was based on our conversations, what we wanted to do in the world, our spirituality and sharing conscious time together. She had just gone through her own personal awakening, and I was on the path. There were glimpses, and then I'd slip back into darkness—for about a year.

Most of my lifestyle and my friends had all been about the bars and clubs, and I started to realize that the only thing we shared was hanging out and drinking, playing music, doing drugs. We were destructive but we couldn't see it. I stopped going to bars and clubs, stopped drinking and using, just did it. And I watch my old world fall apart, because it was all based on that. Friends dropped away. One day I walked into a bar but I was sober, and I couldn't believe what I saw. I could see it through sober eyes, and I realized that this is how I must have been—I knew then that I didn't want to be there, be them, or be connected with it... the only way to go back was to get loaded, and I didn't want it.

I got a job working for a university, which felt like a small step forward in terms of my integrity, and I was invited to start playing in a Kirtan band—singing and playing percussion with mantras... I practiced yoga and started studying meditation. I believed I was attracting these shifts with my new attitude and beliefs.

Things kept happening. My fiancé and I were trained to be meditation guides; we did retreats to facilitate forgiveness for everything that had ever happened and hurt us, including ourselves; we became more aligned with our mission and started weekly free meditations at a local Science of Mind church; and finally, a week after I lost my job, we went to India for a month of immersion in meditation, yoga, and awakening.

My conscious purpose had shifted. While I still envisioned material success, the "how" had become the most important aspect of my mission. It was about service, bringing light to people in the form of joy, through guidance and music. Most importantly, I knew I had to completely surrender in trust to the Divine force that had always protected and guided me, and was continuing to respond to my thoughts and choices in an immediate way.

Soul, or my Divine, had always pushed me. I had always fed my creativity and consciousness, despite the more superficial values of the culture around me. Now it was happening constantly, and in my face. I was supposed to come back from India to another sales job, but I couldn't do it. Transformation had locked in, and I connected with my personal relationship with God. I saw myself as a vessel for divine energy.

In 2011, after returning from India, I was talking with a friend who happened to be a transformational life coach. I came to an agreement with myself after that. I was clear that I wanted to inspire and empower human potential through music. I let go of the "how," and just started saying YES to opportunities that presented themselves when they were alignment with my mission. I wouldn't judge, I just stayed connected with the essence of the universe's invitations, and saw them all as pathways on the road to the "promised land" of my purpose, my passion. There was infinite trust.

Many of those opportunities seemed arbitrary and random—but they all connected me to other opportunities that eventually would lead me toward a more fully embodied mission. For example, I started taking on opportunities such as guiding the leadership team of the Sunday services at my metaphysical church, managing a silent auction raffle, using my people skills, focusing on communication, systems, and other skills that would all lead me toward my developing business. Since I was playing in the Bhakti Caravan Kirtan band, I started getting invitations from other kirtan bands and Yoga studios to play for them, making connections that led me to Bhakti Fest, where I started out organizing the festival vendors in the Midwest and eventually taking over putting together street teams in the Midwest, doing a range of at times menial jobs such as ordering porta-potties, setting up and working crew...but learning every aspect of what goes into a successful festival. I was also a regular at night as the Conscious DJ holding down the yoga festival night party!

By 2012, I had started to produce my own local minifestivals—Club Divine—a monthly conscious dance and experiential event that followed our meditations. I connected with other leaders in the conscious community and began partnering and collaborating on event development. In the year that this was building, I now realize that I was building a brand and a set of skills that would eventually go international.

I became more involved in yoga festivals, and was regularly invited to DJ at national events all over the country. I continued to network, and met someone at one of those events who connected me with Greenheart International, where I DJ'd and then became more involved with that organization. I was developing my coaching and consulting skills, able to help others set up conscious events and produce mindful celebrations. This is an emerging genre and in the Midwest there had been almost nothing like this.

My work has taken me around the world and I've enjoyed unimaginable beauty and opportunity, honing my skills, developing a wide network base and staying true to my mission. I'm now aware that I live in the Midwest intentionally; it's my version the Himalayas, my cave. At one point in the past I wanted to be on the West Coast—where the action is, I thought. But that's shifting. I love the identity of being here in the Midwest. My creativity bubble. Maybe this is what was shown to me every time my parents moved around—five years old in Bangladesh, seven years old in Saudi Arabia, then America...in the security of the family, I learned to be resilient and created my own bubble of security—I could leave but always come back. Perhaps my Divine was offering me this model even then.

Today I'm a producer/musician aligned with my passion and my vision. I've created this world, based in Chicago, and it allows me to create from a blank slate. There's no competition or comparison. There's artistic and personal freedom. I look forward to developing music for organizations, festivals, and productions—and continue to create original music for mindful film, television, and media in general. I am loving collaboration on projects that can touch wider audiences and support their alignment with authentic living, mindfulness, and awakening in to a higher consciousness.

Mindful celebrations are key for me, too. We know that celebration—joy—is a crucial component of evolution. We are drawn to what we love. For me, bringing a vehicle for awakening pure bliss, aliveness, and life force—this is my part in drawing the light out in that direction. I believe my piece in this will add a dimension to the "rasa"—the taste of what is unfolding.

As we are all awakened we will be seeking opportunities to come together in a new state—an alternative to the empty, zombie-inducing scene. Bhakti energy is devotional at its root, bringing out spiritually connecting, blissful energy. This is what attracted me initially, and what I'm now offering back on a larger scale.

I believe I've been blessed with my karma in this life, and as soon as I realized everything was playing out for a higher expression, I was in alignment with it—and doors opened. Forgiveness was a key piece in my opening. It cleared the space for my karma to be opened up exponentially. I would see "obstacles" as opportunities, and they would disappear. Deeper love, self-acceptance, and forgiveness were the tools that have supported me through all of this. This was my awakening. I'm grateful, I'm committed, and I am here—open, joyful, and willing.

Chapter 11

THE CONDOR EAGLE CALLING
Purpose and Healing through Indigenous Wisdom

Leela (Lisa) Marie Bergerud

While my quest for purpose has not been intentional, I have been blessed to discover it in my very deliberate quest for personal healing. Healing has been a driving force in my life ever since I became an adult. Quite simply, my pain drove me to seek people and methods that would help me remedy it so I might live a life with some taste of happiness.

As stated in this book in the chapter authored by Ken Wilber and Dustin DiPerna, in order for a Deliberately Developmental Civilization to be established, the following three paradigms must be realized: structures for growing up (largely provided by the Western developmental paradigms/psychotherapies of the last century), states for waking up (largely provided by the ancient Eastern esoteric wisdom practices), and the foundational shadow work or cleaning up (the ugly stepchild of the consciousness movement). The shadow work, while acknowledged in both waking up and growing up paradigms, is a severely malnourished aspect in our current approach to balanced transformation. We are clearly living the impact of our lack of opportunity or reluctance to engage in our shadow work when we look at our current political landscape, for it is here that the shadow element is being played out in full force. While the level of political turmoil we are currently experiencing is truly terrifying, I see this as a profound blessing because the need to do our shadow (and quick-like) can no longer be denied.

We live in a time where we have everything available to us...great lineages of awakening, tremendous tools for personal transformation, technology that will assist us in anything we endeavor to do. And yet, most of us are floundering—wondering what technique or path might be our salvation to jump-start truly discovering and living our purpose. Is it possible that until we clean up our shadow aspects that we will remain Confounded?

In our shadow, we are blind or unconscious to our wholeness and connectedness and we do not feel safe. We quite literally cannot see where we are blind. But those around us bear the impact of our blindness. What has been relegated to the shadow, from a wounded perspective, was simply a means of adapting to survive some form of perceived threat and trauma. When the energy of that shadow is not consciously engaged, it creates a sickness in the individual and the collective. At its most basic, I believe shadow work to be that of healing trauma. And trauma is rampant in our world right now. All you have to do is listen to the news to be overwhelmed by the acute tragedies and atrocities throughout the planet (so much so, that many people choose not to listen to the news because it's so painful). This does not even begin to take into account the personal hardships that each one of us has endured in our lives, as well the impact of intergenerational trauma. From micro to macro, trauma is prolific.

We all know how quick and adept the mind is, and we also know that the body has a timing of its own that often does not match that of the mind. How that discrepancy is resolved depends entirely on our ability to access the unconscious parts of ourselves. Traumatic memories remain active, even if not conscious, and live in the body as implicit memories even if the conscious mind has forgotten. People literally cannot see, hear, and feel specific aspects of the present moment when they are in the grip of unconscious implicit memories [Stanley, 2016]. Furthermore, because the wounds of trauma become deeply imprinted in the soul, imagination, brain, nervous system, organs, and the muscular structures of the body, healing is a complex process that goes far beyond meditation or "a talking cure" [Stanley, 2016]. It requires a very integrated approach.

Our unaddressed trauma not only impairs our perception, it sends out echoes that permeate and influence everything in our life. It colors our reality. In order to collectively evolve as a species, it is imperative that we address the interruptions in our personal development that are no longer consciously available to us. So how do we do this essential work? Where do we go for the help we need? Where do we go that tells the stories of how we got here and how we get ourselves undone, and then start to really imagine forward, together? One way to do this is to go back, to retrace our roots and step into the world of indigenous wisdom and ritual. After all, 99 percent of human growth and development has happened within indigenous cultures [Narvaez, 2014]. The Condor Eagle prophecy helps point the way.

About 14 years ago I attended my first ayahuasca ceremony. I had never heard of ayahuasca and wasn't even that interested, except for the fact that the man whom I happened to be madly in love with at the time had invited me—and was going to go whether I went or not. Apart from taking mushrooms a handful of times and periods of smoking marijuana recreationally, I had never done any psychedelics. I was too afraid! I didn't want to take something and then find myself somewhere in my psyche, or beyond, that I had no way of navigating my way back from. Nor did I want to be that out of control, exposed, and vulnerable. In other words, I did not feel equipped to engage my shadow. Thankfully, I learned that there were going to be designated helpers watching over all the participants and whose sole function was to assist people who needed help during the night. So I decided to take a risk and drink this strange tea from the Brazilian Amazon (commonly referred to as the "medicine" due to its capacity for profound healing capacities).

From the first glass of medicine, I was like a fish to water. There was a felt sense of homecoming. The person serving me the medicine felt it as well and even remarked on it. I had no idea at the time the impact that ceremony would have, but it began a process that would entirely reshape my life's purpose. I was beginning to discover that my life was inextricably linked to this medicinal Condor Eagle way of living.

A few years into my work with the medicine, I met a medicine man from Colombia while in Brazil. I was attending a two-week intensive and he was running sweat lodges after every ayahuasca ceremony. Inside the sweat lodge, a whole new elemental world opened up to me, one that I had read of in books, but had never expected to have a direct experience of. Again, I had the feeling of the sweat lodge being a form of a homecoming. So I spent all my free time in between the sessions, helping this man prepare each lodge. Often he would be shirtless as we were stacking the wood and stones in the scorching sun and I noticed he had these strange scars all over his chest, back, and arms. Eventually I asked him how he got those scars, and he began to share with me, albeit reluctantly, stories of being a Sundancer on the Lakota Indian reservations in South Dakota. He was the first person to tell me about the North American Plains Indians traditions of the Sundance, Vision Quest, and the Inipi (sweat lodge) ceremonies.

It was beyond fascinating to learn from someone who had such direct experience and also strange because he wasn't a Lakota Indian—he was a Colombian medicine man. It was during those many long conversations with him that he shared with me the Mayan prophecy of the Condor and the Eagle. This prophecy states that when the traditions, medicines, and people of the North—the Eagle (archetypically the mind/masculine)—meet and fly together with the traditions, medicines, and people of the South—the Condor (archetypically the heart/feminine)—a new consciousness will be born that reawakens the Earth and reunites the people. A new humanity will be formed that embodies the perfect unity of mind and heart.

In the last decade and a half, I have seen the cross-cultural pollination of indigenous traditions flourish like wildfire. There are many prophecies within various native cultures right now that are directing them to share wisdom that previously would be preserved only for that nation. While I doubt the indigenous people ever lost sight of our overall interconnectedness, they certainly realize that people of the industrialized nations are painfully severed from knowing their connection not only to themselves and one another, but also to the Earth as a whole. This severing of connectivity has brought damage to the Earth in such a way that many indigenous communities now feel it imperative to reach out to us and help us to awaken to the consequences of our largely unconscious choices. However, in order to learn from indigenous and traditional cultures, we must respect each practice within its own context and be sensitive to the misappropriation of cultural practices. It is our challenge to discern the essential elements of traditional cultures while also learning how to expand and enhance our own cultural ways of interacting and healing [Stanley, 2016].

It has been said, that the plant medicines (particularly ayahuasca) appear in times of great evolutionary leaps. I believe this to be true. The more I participate in the ceremonial world, the more I see how vital they are to healing what is ailing on a planetary level. Indigenous ceremonies hold within them the altered states of consciousness indicative of the waking up process, as well as provide strong protocols, which are the developmental structures that foster growing up, *and* they are most vital where we are least willing to look. By providing needed rituals for healing, they enable us to engage our shadow. I think it is precisely the traditions and medicines, which have been generationally preserved and are now being shared by various indigenous nations that are the means for cleaning up and addressing the shadow elements within ourselves and our communities.

From what I have personally experienced and witnessed, I have seen that indigenous ceremonies often involve or require overcoming formidable adversity, but in meeting the challenges we are able to actively transmute our lived experiences, including our traumas, into powerful resources we can then redirect for the benefit of all. These ceremonies are designed to hold deep-seated, intensely chaotic, undifferentiated energies, and allow transformation to occur in a natural communal way, repairing fragmentation and restoring interconnectedness [Stanley, 2016]. In actively participating in and surrendering ourselves to these ancient initiations we are able walk that razor's edge where trauma and vitality coexist, where shadow and illumination dance, and where integrated healing unfolds. Once we begin to undo traumatic knots that keep dysfunctional and entirely unconscious patterns alive within us, we are able to redirect that newly freed energy toward something that can support and celebrate life and our unique purpose. The additional benefit is that our shadow is no longer compromising our structures for growing up and our states of waking up. As a whole we are able to possess more clarity, aliveness, and integrity. We are able to see, hear, feel, and respond to the present moment with revitalized presence and agency.

These rituals, while not originally intended for the maladies of the modern man's trauma, have always treated trauma or sickness in the tribe. They thread us back to the essentials and allow us opportunities to rebuild our foundational fault lines. They reweave bonds with the natural world by providing strong earth-based paths that have been cultivated, upheld, and passed on for generations. The rituals provide a living, breathing connection that is larger than the human experience combined with other worldly means for accessing the grace of the Great Mystery. The traditions, rituals, altars, medicines, prayers, songs, dances are ancient technologies expertly crafted by lineages of elders. Elders that embody the hard-earned wisdom of lived experience and are able to see on the causal planes due to their attuned resonance and interconnectedness with the living world. By design these ceremonies are embodied, relational, and connected with ancestors, animals, the land, and members of the community in order to preserve and protect the health of the tribe [Atleo, 2004].

Perhaps most importantly, they provide an experience of belonging (something so many people hunger for), of a community joined in common purpose that pays attention to and listens to the spiritual realms rather than relying solely on human-initiated disciplines and practices [Stanley, 2016]. Trauma/unconsciousness is not something that can be revealed nor healed in isolation. It must be unearthed and healed by means of the community. Together, these ceremonies take us in that under/inner world and we see what's been left to go feral..., the rampant neglect and disregard of what must be tended to in our bodies, brains, and souls in order for us to evolve. We must return from the diaspora and take refuge in a circle of human souls and beating hearts.

I believe the medicines and ceremonies are literal portals, or doorways, into the darkness that we would otherwise avoid at all costs. These sacred doorways offer a daring invitation to taking a step toward that brave reintegration process. Once you've entered that portal—what is ailing, unconscious, traumatized, is brought to light. Even as it destroys the strongholds, the oblivion, the blindness—the work rebuilds us, gives us new foot-holds, illuminates next steps, and we can see more clearly how to enact our purpose. Evolutionary leaping commences. We remember how to be family to each other, and together we bear witness to where we need to grow up and wake up—simply by being willing to clean up. We also begin to see where we shine and what gifts we have to share. As the shadow is re-integrated into the totality of ourselves, wholeness radiates from our beings and our communities, and this too, has far reaching echoes!

These rituals and ceremonies do not fix us in any sort of passive way. There is a required reciprocity with life itself, for there to be any lasting purification and healing. We have to earn it through demonstrating our commitment over and over. There are no shortcuts or spiritual leapfrog-ging. We resolve to return to our original innocence and in doing so, know that we will have to face and integrate everything unlike that pure state of being within ourselves. Often we have to be willing to die (mentally, emo-tionally, spiritually, even physically) to receive the teachings and blessings these ceremonies possess. Rather than fix us, they reveal our strength and facilitate an integrated wholeness that equips us to meet the challenges of our lives and accept responsibility for the work we need to do. This is an ongoing, lifelong body of work.

Most importantly, these ceremonies and traditions bring us together and unite us in purpose. After all, we are pack animals. We need a tribe to belong to, one that will reflect back to us who and how we are, and an extended family to help and love us. Of the vast array of ceremonies I par-ticipate in—from the various plant medicines from the lineages of Central and South America, as well traditions from the First Nations of North America such as the Sundance, Vision Quest, Inipi, Moon Dance—it is the power of the circle of life that provides the alchemical transformative containment. This work is a collective cleanup. As we mature from being children of our great Mother Earth, we grow to become stewards of all life. So, we come together, we do the work, we chop the wood and carry the water. We empty the buckets and put stones on the fires. We call back, back, back to our ancestors, we call back to the lineage before the confu-sion, we call on the elemental forces, we call on the health and might of that purity and we make our offerings. Offerings of our labor, our sweat, our thirst and hunger, our flesh, our dances, our songs, our stories, our rit-uals. Calling on the wholesome to anchor us as we plunge into the sewage of our minds and the battlefields of our hearts, to untangle and reweave not only our personal story but also our collective chapter as beings on this planet as we turn the page to the new galactic Age of Aquarius. This is what I have signed up to do. This is my personal purpose and it's been a harrowing, humbling, healing, and wondrous journey thus far.

I marvel at the how the medicinal community I have fostered has grown and evolved these last 10 years. Over and over, I see people access-ing who they really are and discovering what they have to give and then of-fering that to the larger circle. Leaders are being born before my very eyes. The more I trust that circle to hold me as I uncover and expose even more deeply submerged layers of my splintered self, the healthier I become. And the healthier we become as a community because we all follow in step and feel safe to reveal even more of who we are, blind spots and all. We continue to raise the stakes and play the game more and more spiritually undefended. I have tasted the possibility of my immediate tribe (all white people) being able to heal itself, with itself, by itself (no apparent leaders) through employing the teachings and wisdoms that we have both earned and learned—and it was one of the best tastes of my life. I think this is the point of the ceremonial work, that it becomes who we are, not what we do a few times a month. We aren't dependent on an actual ceremony for the work and healing to continue—it's been set in motion and there's a con-tainer of people committed to waking, growing, and cleaning up to hold it. It gives me hope and sustains my courage to keep evolving.

But how does my telling you all of this, help you in any way to live your purpose? It is my hope, that you will feel some resonance with the need to truly engage in doing the needed shadow work so you can remedy the barriers that prevent you from shining like a blazing star out in that darkened, confused world. Please be clear, I am not saying that you need to go and drink ayahuasca or commit to putting yourself up on a mountain without food or water for four days and nights to quest for your personal vision (although I highly recommend doing both of those things with a reputable teacher!!)—but I am saying that our great forgetting of how to be connected to one another, the natural world, and the great mystery that animates it all, is relatively new in our time line as a species. I think there is tremendous benefit to be found in retracing back to cultures that have maintained that connection because they can help us restore that within ourselves.

It is my hope that through your own personal commitment to your wholeness via divine guidance you will find the people, lineages, professionals, methods, and ceremonies that you need; may it be a means to resolve the deep seated trauma that lives within. It is also my hope that you will find or create for yourself a community the embodies the Condor Eagle way of life—people that have brilliant minds and truly open spacious hearts that are united in a purpose of making this beautiful water planet a better place for all sentient beings. More than my hope, that is my prayer. Thank you. Aho (to all our relations)!

⊗

References

Atleo, E.R. 2004. Tsawalk: *A Nuu-chah-nulth Worldview.* Vancouver: University of British Colombia Press.

Narvaez, D. 2014. *Neurobiology and the Development of Human Morality: Evolution, Culture and Wisdom.* New York: Norton.

Stanley, S. 2016. *Relational and Body Centered Practices for Healing Trauma: Lifting the Burdens of the Past.* New York: Routledge.

Chapter 12

CIRCLE OF PURPOSE

Susan Lucci

SHE: WE

Kneeling down, coming closer to the edge of a circular pool,
SHE pauses to reflect.
Throwing a stone into the water's wavy center, SHE sets her intention,
Takes a deep breath in, slowly exhales.
Ripples from many stones merge in the middle;
One cannot discern where one begins and another ends.
With the next breath, the water settles more.
Moments after catching a glimpse of her own reflection,
The glassy surface mirrors images of others circling around with her.
Not knowing where one image begins and another ends,
Each reaches for what SHE seeks—
Gracefully genuflecting into the mirror of shared reflections,
SHE dips her entire being into the refreshing water.
After savoring a sense of oneness for some time,
SHE returns to her place at the edge.
Feeling revived, SHE reenters the life she left—more of who SHE is.
Nourished by the satisfying taste of unity,
Knowing SHE will return to reconnect,
SHE leaves—feeling more WE than ME—
With overflowing gratitude for the restorative waters of the WE space.

What's a waking woman to do at life's crossroads, when she's been programmed to do it all and be it all, without the support of tribe, map, or wise guide? Industrious, emboldened—perhaps, even desperate—she seeks to manage the process silently and alone. She volunteers for another project, tries Pilates, experiments with therapists, spiritual mentors and modalities, cleanses, finds an early morning running group, takes up yoga, joins another book club, drinks wine, and once a year or so, escapes to a spa/retreat/workshop. Angsty questions haunt her quiet moments: What am I supposed to do with my life? How can I make my life count and still get all this laundry done? How do I balance all of my commitments? What else is possible? As the internal pressure intensifies, she rationalizes returning to a career she didn't love, ruthlessly criticizes herself in ways she'd never tolerate happening to anyone else, and considers obtaining yet another certification. Little satisfies or distracts her for long. She puts herself last, puts herself down, and forgets where she put her passion. The ache becomes persistent—the whisper grows louder, the inquiry more insistent. Nothing seems to be "enough," least of all, her efforts. Dissatisfaction with her former ways of being and doing—no matter how seemingly successful in the way our modern world measures success—reaches a point where it can no longer be hushed or hidden. Something must change!

Halfway through life, one or more of a woman's roles—wife, mother, daughter, teacher, doctor, lobbyist, graphic designer, activist, realtor, lawyer, or PTO volunteer—no longer becomes her. So used to accommodating, serving, and pleasing others, she has nearly forgotten who she is. She feels increasingly alone, overwhelmed, and disconnected—most of all, from herself. No matter how hard she tries to deny or deflect these feelings, the shoes she's been multitasking in no longer fit. Annoyed by a nagging restlessness or unforgiving angst, she awakens to a relentless longing for MORE followed by a wondering: "What do I want MORE of?" For decades, this condition has been diagnosed a "Midlife Crisis," and its hot flashes often mismanaged and overmedicated, all to her detriment. What if this surge of energy is not tamed or treated and instead, given ample room and encouragement for free expression? What if the response to her symptoms was an invitation to reimagine who she's becoming? What if she had a place to process this threshold with others similarly situated? Fortunately, some of us are realizing how generative this developmentally appropriate awakening can be and experiencing what else is possible when women have the space and support we need to freely express our midlife fire.

I recognize the woman described above—her all-too-familiar fatigue, her overwhelm, her "I used to know who I was" voice, apologizing for nearly every word she speaks. That was my state a decade ago when a series of personal crises and crossroads awakened me. Desperate for meaningful conversations, I responded to my deepest desire for community and re-created the ancient social art form "Circle." (By the way, this was a completely foreign concept in the Midwestern town where I found myself raising three small children.) Nonetheless, Circle evolved herself through ME, a most unlikely candidate—a bulldog of a lawyer who had always had more guy friends than girlfriends and an Olympic multitasker who was frequently referred to as "the Energizer Bunny." In the most unlikely place and time, I became absolutely convinced that, "The Circle is the thing!" More than 500 Circles later, I am privileged to share the alchemy of this WE space—to tell the story of women awakened by so-called Midlife Crises, who chose to make their transitions, transformational and their lives more purposeful! As we learned, it's nearly impossible to become ourselves by ourselves. We need each other to access the wisdom of the WE space to become ourselves. Through it all, I discovered that my purpose is to create safe spaces for us to bravely cross such thresholds, to activate our individual potentials so as to become better together. Because society provides far too few WE spaces, I do.

"Come and sit awhile," I say to the talented, accomplished wife, mother, and community leader, who is fried from doing so much for so many for so long. Driven by her never-ending list, she feels time is racing her by; there is never enough of it, she is never enough. She frequently feels out of control with hurry and worry, and is overwhelmed by caring for the endless needs of others. Her routine can be executed mindlessly; her creativity has been moved to the back burner, if not entirely extinguished. Her "to do" list is zapping her zest for life. Not only has she forgotten who she is, but also why she is here and what matters most. She is stressed, lost, afraid, and embarrassed that she doesn't have it all figured out by now. The critic rules her with its demands of "More! More! More!" Her days are spent shopping, spending, scheduling, shlepping, serving…repeat. She rarely finds what she so desperately seeks: meaningful engagement and impact, a life that matters. Much of women's work still invisible; she, too, begins to feel this way.

We sit in Circle, take a deep breath and conspire together, letting go to let come. We put what matters most at the center of our lives, eager to learn to live from a more grounded way of being. Instead of waiting for retreats or vacations to renew, we gather regularly, right here in our community. And so we begin…with our ritual lighting of the center candle—to remind us of our inner spark and also our ancestors who first met tens of thousands of years ago around a fire—and ringing the singing bowl to come into resonance, setting intentions to focus, and meditating to increase presence. We are all in here and now. It seems simple—being present together in Circle—but the shift feels seismic in contrast to 2017 daily living.

Desperately craving space to catch her so she can catch up with herself, the woman courageously steps off of the moving sidewalk of life and into Circle. For now, no one needs tending to, so the midlife mama puts on her oxygen mask, takes a leap of faith, and begins the process of remembering who she is, so as to reimagine who she can become. Her life depends upon it. This is edgy, risky, uncomfortable work; vulnerability is required. Her relief is immediate. Awash with emotions buried far too deep for far too long and encouraged to be with what is, she lets her tears fall and her feelings be held by the other wise women. Genius meets genius in Circle, comes to the edge, stretches outside of a comfort zone filled with answers to feel into the expansive uncertainty of questions. Learning the practice of being present—instead of long-held habits of dwelling on the past or ruminating about the future—she experiences a welcome homecoming, finding home in her self. Together, in this unfamiliar space, we begin a familiar quest: Who am I? Why am I here? What matters most in this moment?

Setting the Circle container seems simple but it is anything but easy: turn off cell phones (those weapons of mass distraction), close the door (stop the mad dash of busyness), and enter a sense of time out of time—a place where there is nowhere to go and nothing to do—JUST BE. Clearing clutter from our calendars and dialing down the noise allows us to hear our own voices and to remember our own deep desires. Slowing down into this nurturing space, we can become aware of the gifts of the present moment. Attuning to the here and now, we catch up with ourselves to pick up the threads of our lives. Having shed all but what's essential, we make space to notice, name and nurture the essence alive within us. As we intentionally create this distraction-free, judgment-free, expectation-free container to reflect upon what is, we can begin to imagine what is possible. We drop the masks and soften the things that limit and confine us, so we can engage more open-mindedly and wholeheartedly. We give ourselves permission to speak, be silent, struggle, shine, and share in this precious moment. Juicy questions spark rich conversations; our spark returns. Poetry, prose, songs, and stories inspire us. Spaciousness, trust and nonjudgment allow a wide array of feelings to be experienced. As emotions are permitted to flow, we become aware that we are not alone, we share much in common, and we are much more than any single feeling, story, or role. We surprise ourselves by how much WE can hold. The connective tissue creating the WE SPACE between us is the stories we share, making meaning of metaphors that make or break us. Risking vulnerability, we feel into trusting each other—upgrading old stories of painful interactions among women—and see, hear and validate each other. We begin to speak, laugh, and sing from a far more genuine and generous place. We reclaim our inner authority and reflect inner divinity. Reminded of the song that only we can sing, the resonance returns, placing us in the flow of awakening authenticity. Our best selves emerge. Circle after Circle, we realign with our essence and so enjoy being who we are, at home in ourselves, that we want MORE. We discover the MORE that we seek; it is within and among us.

This sacred space is ripe for synergy, mystery, and magic. Accessing the WE space—an ever-expanding space of wisdom and wonder—allows something transformational to happen: time expands, energy increases, imagination intensifies, ideas percolate. Feeling seen, affirmed, and valued by our Circle sisters; we gain clarity and focus, become more creative and expressive. Being reminded of our genius leads to increasing generativity. Becoming ever more present and curious means that new discoveries flow from our open minds and hearts. Our longings to be more authentic, to embrace life more wholeheartedly, and to give our unique talents more generously, deepen. Critical questions open new doors. How did I love to lose track of time as a child? When is the last time I felt most alive? What was I engaged in? How did I love "to be" before my "to-do" list? What one thing would change everything? What stands between me and a life I would love? We harvest wonderings and mine insights, together. The experience truly is too big for words.

By the time we close Circle, we are inspired, energized, and empowered, ready to move more mindfully, authentically, and open-heartedly into the world. As we strengthen the muscle of showing up openly, bravely and fully, we are able to live our genius out in the wider world with greater awareness of our values, strengths, limiting beliefs, and priorities. Emboldened by the clarity, courage, and community experienced in the WE space, we can resume our quest, rediscover what's been lost, reframe old stories, and reimagine who we can become. We step out into the world ready to practice more mindful mothering and more intentional relating by giving ourselves permission to slow down and spend time nurturing ourselves by: taking an art class, walking in the woods, getting more sleep, acting spontaneously, journaling dreams and insights, making music, saying, "No" to "shoulds" and "supposed tos." Along the way, we savor the support of friends, contemplative practices and radical self-care. Knowing our community needs us and our Circle sisters see us, we step back into a life that we love more fiercely and with a more balanced perspective. We give what is ours to give and do what is ours to do…and readily receive the energetic flow of Life in return. Immersed in Nature, creativity, meaningful connections, and fun—Life speaks to us, sparkles, and continues to ebb and flow. We weave together a lifetime of whispers to discern the thread of our unique purpose. Reminded and affirmed, we remember what matters most. By practicing placing our values first, prioritizing our own self-care, and putting our desires on our to do lists, we become even MORE of who we came to be.

After months of clearing—emptying closets, making space on her calendar, and removing relationships that no longer satisfy—Margaret decides to begin a daily walkabout practice of wandering off the beaten path. She and another curious neighbor roam through West Side alleys and into neighborhoods few dare to go. They are rewarded by seeing things and meeting people most of us miss. Her gift (sharing stories and developing uncommon relationships) strengthens Margaret's resolve and grows her community. Increasingly inspired by being in Circle, she picks up the thread of a job she had decades earlier in a school on the South Side, where she witnessed the powerful fail to meet the needs of the powerless. Fueled by her heartache, she remembers her deep desire to shine light on children in the shadows, which leads to creating a peer-based tutoring program in her neighborhood school. As I write, all are flourishing beyond anyone's wildest expectations. The highest measure of her program's success is the long waiting list of teen tutors eager for the opportunity to participate. Not only does Margaret feel more clear about who she is and more empowered to do what is hers to do, but she also empowers others outside of Circle, a fabulous byproduct of a woman on purpose. What I love most about Circle, she says, is this: "We help each other become who we want to be." This mantra also reminds me of Georgia, who was attracted to Circle "to learn a new way of being and to explore becoming someone I wasn't yet." The WE SPACE is the ideal place for becoming.

Belle first came to Circle because she wanted something different; she felt like life was racing her by. Her mind often foggy, she was seeking clarity. She wanted to slow things down to catch up with herself to make sense of the chaos. Circle after circle, she returns to this day: to practice listening, calming, centering, and connecting with other wise women. Many days, it's nearly impossible to quiet her monkey mind. And yet, she persists. One day, catching courage from another woman's sharing her story, Belle remembers hers. An immigrant to this country as a very little girl, she survived struggles of learning another language and culture, matriculating (always the "A student"), repeated abuse, working hard at a career she did not love, marrying later in life, raising children, and then landing in the next chapter.... Now what? By slowing down and sitting down, making space to give voice to her dreams and honor her desires, as well as being seen and heard by other seekers, Belle found her voice and her vocation: to beautify her corner of the world. Her landscape design business just celebrated a major milestone. She loves her unique designs almost as much as her hundreds of clients appreciate her creative expression of beauty in their own backyards!

After only a few months in Circle, Suzanna writes and performs a song she composes on the piano—despite never taking a lesson—as part of a "Story of Self" exercise. As she describes it, the music simply moved through an opening in her broken heart, once she reframed and accepted her role as a child of the world (no longer as an abandoned child), beginning to fill the gaping hole in her adopted heart. She now sits with a literal hole in her heart, with curiosity in place of judgment. Limited physically by a mysterious illness, she dedicates precious time to her new surge of creativity. Suzanna physically comes alive as she sketches, cooks, and writes. As she becomes more calm, creative, and centered, she gains clarity directing her answer to What's Next? Proudly, she reveals that she is taking an online class; she wants to become a therapist. Her newly revealed purpose shines through her satisfied smile when Suzanna shares the news with her Circle sisters.

Nancy returns to a job she was sure she had to leave to survive—renewed by a new metaphor revealed to her in Circle one day, which gifted her with a new perspective on herself, her life, and her role in the world. She is currently thriving at the very same job, feels more energized to travel the world with her husband, and is excited to step into their next "empty nest" chapter. None of us present that day will forget when Nancy experienced a whole body perspective shift!

Alissa came to Circle, intent on discovering her next project: possibly another thesis leading to another master's program, perhaps a new fundraising effort to preside over, or maybe even a part-time job. To her great surprise, her purpose was not "out there" but rather "in here," lying dormant within. Waking up to creativity she first expressed as a young girl, her revelation was awakening to a deep desire to connect to more of herself. She so enjoys "being All-in Alissa" that she's dialed up her creative expression and is committed to gifting her talents daily: by taking on mentoring a young girl from the South Side, hosting thoughtful dinner parties, starting her day with an hour of piano practice, caring for a child who lost his mother, planning exotic vacations for her family, and knitting uniquely designed baby hats. Crafting a formula of self-care, continual learning, and guided reflection that includes constantly challenging herself beyond her comfort zone has been critical to her evolution. Wisely, she now aligns every day's to-do list with "being Alissa," which deeply delights her. Many in her vast network benefit from Alissa being more connected to who she is and her commitment to living fully into the next version of who she is becoming!

Enticed by her future self-calling her into greatness, Lizzie intentionally resigns from her job with a nonprofit educational foundation to seek a more meaningful position to which she can bring more of herself. A variety of opportunities synchronistically appear, each teaching her more about how she naturally contributes. She begins to notice how her presence—just being—shifts meetings, relationships and agendas. Developing a practice of staying present and realizing more of her divinity as it's reflected back to her in Circle, Lizzie courageously steps into new ways of serving her community. As her energy intensifies and becomes more palpable in Circle, she reports more satisfying relationships: her husband accompanies her activist endeavors and a bridge to her estranged brother gracefully appears. Her purposeful self becomes ever more powerful as she continues to claim her unique place on the planet. Lizzie loves being in the generative WE space of Circle, discovering more of who she is, and showing up more authentically in other areas of her life to "make (her) life count." She feels more creative and connected.

Maria works feverishly on discerning her purpose, as intensely as she mastered grad school and her career, committing to both Circle and one-on-one purpose guiding. A highly educated former lobbyist turned environmental activist, she is dissatisfied with politics, wants more from motherhood, feels fearful—and also more fired up!—when her CEO husband loses his job. She has a sense that there must be MORE to life than this. One of her transformative moments occurs on a desert retreat, when she is literally kissed by a hummingbird. We reflect on the encounter and attending insights. Thanks to her diligent journaling, she captures all the sparks of this magical moment. Her vocation is clear to her: connect to everyday nature. Eager to create this "kiss" experience for others, she begins where she is: by creating a green guides group at her children's urban school. Tapping her excellent skills of being a student, she explores and learns as much as she can about Nature in her everyday world, no matter the weather. Inspired by her enthusiasm, many say, "Yes!" to her invitation to guide them, whether it be birding at a local forest preserve, snowshoeing along deer paths in the woods, or forest bathing at the arboretum. Maria is ecstatic about waking up people of all ages to their true nature by immersing them in Nature. At present, she is engaging her vast network with high hopes of taking her purpose into improving healthcare. She is eager to dream up new ways to connect low-income, high-risk patients with Nature. I can't wait to see how high Maria flies!

In Circle, we reframe our fiery hot, misdiagnosed midlife crises as a kundalini fire of creativity eager for expression. We come into Circle fatigued, frustrated, fed up with the status quo, but ready to transform the dissatisfying fire in our belly. Desperate to make meaning and have an impact, we clear the haze and dive into rich, satisfying conversations that matter. We slow down to the speed of the soul and savor what is good, true and beautiful, what's working, what's wonder-full. We change the conversation, deepen connections and put ourselves in the way of miracles. We become safe enough to get brave enough to stretch into new places with new perspectives where new possibilities unfold. We open our collective eyes to new futures possible only with new questions: What do I love? What do those who love me see in me? What do I see in Nature, dreams and daily living that shines a light for me? Where do I shine my light the brightest?

As each woman creates space for discernment, sets new intentions, reestablishes her priorities, and places her values front and center, she reaps increasing clarity about her purpose, as well as the necessary courage and support to become more. Returning home to herself and claiming the divine power she finds there provides insight and energy to narrow the gap between what is and what is possible. Walking into an expanded identity— more herself than ever before —dissipates previous limitations, blesses and buries tired beliefs, and reframes and upgrades old stories. Attuning to her inner guides and accepting her inner genius hushes the denigrating voice of doubt. She sings a different tune now, often harmonizing with others and bringing great joy. As she makes her music, the awakened woman attracts her tribe. Her Circle widens, her commitment to her work deepens and her energy increases. She is more of who she came to be. "Circle makes me think about the most important parts of me; it's the best gift I've ever given myself," a frequent Circler boasts.

A woman on purpose can respond wholeheartedly once her inner angst is quelled, because she is aligned with her true self. Because being in the WE space of Circle feeds her inner life, she now turns within in a nourishing way that is no longer self-defeating. The restlessness that once ravaged her now fuels her passion. On fire with her purpose, she operates from a place of inner calm, as powerful as dancing in the eye of a hurricane. She sees crisis and chaos as opportunities to give her gifts, avoiding overwhelm. Energized by being seen, heard and valued, she knows what has her name on it, what is hers to do, and has more energy to do that. More fully at home in herself but no longer feeling alone, she graciously responds to life with the unique contribution she knows is hers to give, trusting that others in her Circle and in her community are holding up their piece of the sky.

The path is not necessarily any easier now—there are bumps and twists on every journey —but she walks with a certain ease, knowing what makes her heart ache and what makes her heart sing. More at home in herself, a purposeful woman is more at home in her Circle, in her community, and in her world—more willing to wander and also, to wonder. All in all, it is wonderful! In fact, she learns to savor not knowing—the uncertainty that comes with a more adventurous way of living. Her strength lies both within and all around her. When she gets lost—and she knows she will—she has a toolkit of practices, a Circle for support, a clarified intention, next steps, and the necessary courage to continue to discover the path forward. Her transformed angst now feels like evolutionary allurement, guiding her into her destiny—her becoming.

Never before have women been as free and fortified to fully express themselves. It is time, at long last, for HERstory to be lived and told, which is a tale of women waking up together, reimagining what's possible and coming home to themselves. This time, we will meet our needs, satisfy our desires, and realize our dreams. We are far more generative when we care for ourselves first, realize that we are not alone and accept that we are enough just as we are. Women are becoming more visible and vocal because we now know our views and voices are needed. The more we become ourselves, the more we contribute to creating a just, loving, sustainable, and purposeful world that works for everyone. Imagine what WE can do—wide-awake, inspired, supported, on purpose—together I know; I have been privileged to have a front row witnessing the wonder. Watch out world—Women are waking up!

⚮

Note: To date, my work has been primarily with educated, affluent Western women whose basic needs are met and who have access to resources, including time to sit in Circle. My mission is to activate their potential because I witness that women who become more aware of their power and purpose contribute even more to their families and communities; in turn, we all benefit. I appreciate the privileged nature of my work and recognize how critically important it is. All that said, I understand that the context presented here is not yet commonplace, generic, or universal. I am not an expert writing on behalf of all women. Rather, I intend to share themes and patterns I've witnessed as a space holder of hundreds of Circles and individual purpose guiding sessions. This is what I notice as women wake up to reimagine what's possible. I share this good news with tremendous enthusiasm. I hope that the Dalai Lama's prediction is correct and "The world (is) saved by the Western woman!"

Chapter 13

PURPOSE
The Bridge Between Consciousness
and What Really Matters[1]

Nick Seneca Jankel

In the '90s, I went to Cambridge University to study medicine because I wanted to be a psychiatrist. But having been diagnosed with both chronic pain syndrome (fibromyalgia) and clinical depression, which medical science could treat but seemingly not resolve, it dawned on me that philosophy—literally "the love of wisdom"—and not psychiatry might be a better path for me and my career. But I had no clue how to make a career of it. The summer after I graduated, I went on a trip with two friends to Mexico. We spent a few weeks exploring the incredible Mayan temples of the Yucatan peninsula, where crimson enchantment hangs over the vivid green forests. One day I went on a mission to grab some supplies. On my way out of a murky store in the middle of very Mexican nowhere, a Mayan-looking gentleman handed me a scrap of torn paper. On it he had written the words: "Eres el mago." You are the magician. At the time I had absolutely no clue what to make of it. Being a jaded and cynical atheist, I did not think much of serendipities and synchronicities, and so I said "Thank you"

217

and walked on. I clearly was not ready to heed the call of my purpose quite yet. In the vacuum that leaving science and medicine had formed, I ended up working as a strategist in advertising before starting my own innovation agency at the age of 24.

Fast-forward 10 years from that Mexican moment and I was on another extended trip, this time to the Cook Islands in the Pacific to make sense of a full entrepreneurial burnout experience. The pace of life is easy on the islands, coaxed along by a gentle sea breeze upon which Polynesian harmonies float. Whilst I waited for my flight off the island, I went to a salt-corroded cinema to watch a movie. The only movie being screened was The Pianist, a tale of a Jewish musician who survives the German death camps of the Holocaust. It struck me like a lightning bolt. The pianist's father is walking along the streets of Warsaw, just after the Germans have occupied the city in 1939: a city in which some of my relatives possibly died in the ghetto. A German soldier takes great pleasure in knocking off the proud, white-whiskered father's hat and forcing him to walk in the gutter. Something about this needless moment of separation and suffering went deep into my soul. Within seconds I was in floods of tears so hot that they burnt my face, even in that sweltering tropical paradise. Next came an incredible explosion of possibility: I was alive! The Nazis had failed in their grand vision to exterminate us all! My existence on the Earth was a great gift! In that moment, I knew in the deep recesses of my soul that I had to do something meaningful with my life.

After years in the fast lane of high-tech entrepreneurship, I was emotionally frazzled and physically burned out. I was determined to never be like that again. I had spent years helping large organizations find and realize bold business-model innovations and product ideas that were a genuine contribution to society (as well as returning ample amounts of profit). But often, when it came down to it, many companies were not that interested in anything beyond efficiency, productivity, and profit. Most remained resistant to purpose (and so sustainability) as anything much more than sexy wrapping for their brands. Such "purpose-washing" remains rife. So with the logic of self-preservation, we ended up taking the projects we were offered in order to pay for the rapid growth of our business—and the major staff costs and overheads we were taking on as we succeeded. But because our work was no longer entirely aligned with my deepest values and noblest aspirations, it started to grate inside. Over months of reflection and rejuvenation after burnout, I realized the breakdown was less about the stress of running a fast-growing business and managing scores of people (although they both took their toll), and more about the realization that I was running a company that was not 100 percent aligned with my purpose. My heart was broken by my career choices and the business model we had built. My natural loving heart was not able to contribute without limits within the paradigm in which we were operating.

Working with my coach at the time, I grokked—in a moment of inconvenient truth—that I was using the majesty of psychology, neurobiology, and philosophy to help rich companies get richer by inventing stuff that most of us don't need; and then persuading us to buy it with marketing that suggests that we're not sexy/smart/rich/good enough without it. In the middle of this breakdown experience I had a massive breakthrough. I knew, without a shadow of a doubt, that I had to focus on using my skills and talents to use the majesty of psychology, neurobiology, and philosophy to remind us all that we are already enough, and with the resultant sense of abundance, harness our collective creativity to forge a world that works for all. Having since spent years "purifying" myself by healing my own pain, trauma, and patterning so I can serve in this way, the Mayan's pronouncement made a lot more sense. A "magician"—aka a wisdom teacher, "change-agent," and leadership guide—can help people end the relentless suffering caused by the illusion of separation through their own transformation, and the transformation of organizations and systems, so they support human and planetary thriving. It is entirely possible to do this and still make a profit. By helping people to reconnect with the limitless "love" that is waiting for them within their body and within our collective consciousness, a magician can help other people and organizations heal their hearts enough to find their own purpose and express it in the world effectively.

Every one of us has a purpose by nature of being conscious. Purpose exists because we are all part of an interconnected universe that is constantly supporting expansion, learning, and flourishing. Purpose is the actions of the part (the individual) serving the healing and thriving of the whole. There is nothing remotely religious or woo woo about this.

In a complex, adaptive, living system—like our universe—parts will shift, transform, and change so they can relieve suffering and promote thriving. It happens every millisecond all over your body. If we are all connected, all in one field, then if anyone is trapped in separation—and is suffering economically and materially from systems that are driven by separation—then we all suffer. Therefore it is natural for us, once we are switched on, to want to contribute to the world in a meaningful way at all times, physically, mentally, and spiritually. Having lived for a year in rural Africa, their philosophy of ubuntu—we exist because and for others—helps us realize that the concept of a totally separate, rational individual with private needs and private property—upon which our capitalist economic and organizational paradigm is built—does not exist in the same way in every culture. In fact, with ubuntu, people are not born as an essential self-contained subject. They acquire selfhood through relationships as they grow. Purpose is the key determinant in how those relationships play out.

A part of you, that I call Control & Protect Mode (or the Protector archetype)—characterized by neurobiologists as the times you have focused attention and use existing habits and beliefs to solve problems—wants you to cling onto comfortable career beliefs and familiar habits that feel safe and structured. This mode appears to correlate with the Cognitive Control Network in your brain.2 This mode is designed for a serious, sincere, and necessary task: to protect you from uncertainty, ambiguity, and danger. So it will seek to defend against lack and loss with ownership, accumulation, and exploitation. There is nothing wrong with this. It's the design and it works to a degree. However, you have another way of being that we call Create & Connect Mode (or the Connector archetype). This is where purpose emerges and unfolds from. It is characterized by the moments when we are imaginative and improvisational, able to innovate new solutions to new problems. It appears to correlate with Default Mode Network in the brain. In this mode, we thirst for connection and community, long for love, and yearn to find lasting meaning and fulfillment. Neither are better or worse but they do fit some moments well and are a mismatch for others. You must choose yourself, like we all must, which you are ruled by—the aching for connection or the craving for protection—and thus how much of the time you live on purpose and how much off.

Purpose, emanating from the Connector when we are not defended, is the bridge between the inner world of our consciousness and how we change the material world—what really matters—for good. Now of course a materialist atheist—as I was for 15 exciting yet ultimately unhappy years—can't have a purpose beyond passing on their genes because materialism sees no meaning in nature other than evolutionary survival. Materialism only sees the primary qualities as real. But before we dismiss purpose as a made-up fancy, we should know what science is and isn't and what it can tell us and what it can't. Science is the study of what we can see, empirically, outside our hearts and minds in the material world. We turn our brilliant gaze outward, using the scientific method to build up a rigorous body of knowledge about the physical world, including our brains. We study the world through what became known as the "primary qualities": Like weight, length, and wavelength they are clear to see and measure, and they don't tend to change much between different observers. When we want to be an agent of change or purposeful leader, it is these primary qualities we want to change: the number of kids in poverty or being abused; the amount of carbon or pollution in the atmosphere; the scale of social injustice and economic inequality. The wisdom traditions, on the other hand, invite us to turn our gaze inward, through meditation and others forms of self-discovery like ecstasy. No less rigorous than science, if we consistently turn within and study what have become known as the "secondary qualities"— conscious experiences like love and fear, joy and suffering—we discover essential knowledge about our own sense of thriving that science has no access to (and never will).

Early scientists like Democritus in Greece and Galileo in Italy were the ones who helped create the split between primary and secondary qualities. But they did not remove the secondary qualities—whether taste, smell, feeling, love, or belief—because they thought they did not exist and were not important, rather than discounted them because they were hard to measure. They were getting in the way of the progress of science in telling us reliable things about the material world. So they downgraded consciousness in order to make the scientific project work, even though most of the early Western scientists were devout Christians (and many of the greatest physicists have been mystically inclined). Now, centuries later, this fudge had become the great delusion at the core of the modern world, which has created a schism within us that has divorced heart from mind and feelings from rational thought. The divided self is now encouraged and incentivized to drive forward profit (primary qualities) whilst ignoring, more or less, purpose, connection, and love (secondary qualities). This schism became too much within me and I imploded in that burnout/breakdown experience.

I am clear that almost all the problems we face as individuals and those we face together as a species, such as political conflict, economic inequality, and environmental turmoil, can all be traced back to the schism within us that separates us from ourselves, from each other, and from the nature that we rely on for everything. The rise of ugly nationalism, the dominance of daily life by consumerism, the pillaging of entire ecosystems in the name of profit—all these come from this split in our psyches. Wherever I go, I meet people who are suffering from it as it starts to become more obvious. Like me, most are suspicious of religion, perhaps downright hostile to it, but also suffer from the same existential suffering I had to deal with when I believed that the love and connection found in the "wisdom traditions" was shut off to me because I believed in science. For years—years in which I suffered unnecessarily every single day—I did not realize that there is a way to enjoy the benefits of both science and spirituality, whilst avoiding the myriad traps of both. Instead of being locked into the limitations of materialist science, we can experience a nondual universe where there is only one thing.

This oneness can be called Tawhid (in Islam and Sufism) or Brahman (Indian Vedanta). In Kabbalah all things come from the Endless Light, or En Sof, the ground of everything. If you prefer a metaphor of emptiness, you can experience it as the void, or sunyata in Buddhist philosophy. One Buddhist patriarch said "to the awakened, the void no longer is such." Fullness or emptiness are in fact the same unity of being. You can think of it as brotherhood and sisterhood if you are a humanist. Science fiction writer Philip K. Dick, of Minority Report fame, called this nondual universe VALIS: Vast Active Living Intelligence System. I think of the nondual universe as an infinite orchestra playing an endless symphony, always seeking more growth, more evolution, and more complexity in the music. If one instrument plays a flat note, other parts of the orchestra will adapt in real time, even if that is inconvenient or unpleasant to us personally. It is never personal because there is no separate individual in the orchestra, even if we all play a different instrument. If a new tune starts to arise, we can either choose to serve this tune that is seeking to emerge and experience harmony (what the Taoist tradition speaks of when it says something akin to "go with the flow"); or, we can fight reality and experience discord. When we act from the Protector (our fear-driven desire to protect, deal with threats, and survive) in appropriate moment, we usually create a nightmare, from the gulags of Siberia to the suicides in tech factories in China.

The symphony is the Tao. It is the entirety of everything that is happening in a dynamic interplay of constant creation. It is not a noun but a verb. It is constant creating: Create & Connect Mode writ large. Notice there is no religion in any of this. No dogma to buy into. No doctrine to conform to. No rules to obey to help us feel that we are "good" and "worthy." No divine revelations from God. No miracles (aside from the daily miracles of life, love, and creativity). There are no priests with privileged access to the truth. We don't need to be a hippy. We don't need to read New Age books. We don't even need to meditate in a particular way. As spiritual atheists, we reject revealed scripture, priestly power, stale rituals, and all godlike figures as any other atheist would. We know them to be a dangerous and deadly nonsense. But we do embrace the world of secondary qualities, our own consciousness, and find a pathway to a rigorous understanding of our own being-in-the-world. What is truly awe-inspiring, and properly awesome, is that every human being can access and engage in this process. As the Upanishads say, connection is "the hidden Self in everyone." Each of us holds within us the potential for our own liberation. People like me—wisdom teachers—can guide, advise, and cajole. But each person needs to go in pursuit of it themselves.

The split between primary and secondary qualities is not in any way essential in nature. A cat or bat does not distinguish between the two. Only we humans do. The split is a man-made construct that has led to both the great successes and failings of both religion and science. In reality, there is no division between god and man (as organized Judaeo-Christian religion has it) nor nature and man (as science depends on). There is no duality. After enlightenment there is only one thing. We experience this oneness as matter out there when we measure it, and consciousness in here when we feel it. The Jewish philosopher Baruch Spinoza suggested a way to make sense of this. An atheist himself, Spinoza realized that Descartes "extending stuff" (the primary qualities of physical matter) and "thinking stuff" (the secondary qualities of conscious experience) are two different expressions, or attributes, of the same single substance. Scientists call this substance "nature," or "matter." Mystics call it "oneness," "consciousness," or "spirit." In Spinoza's time it was called "God." He realized that whether we call it God or Nature, Deus sive Natura, does not matter. The English poet John Donne reminded us—at the time Galileo was formalizing the split —that "[n]o man is an island entire of itself; every man is a piece of the continent, a part of the main."

Many modern-day spiritual gurus teach that consciousness, or "spirit," is the primary reality. They are idealists who believe that everything is mind, first and foremost. This view sees the material world as a compelling experience but one that is ultimately an illusion or delusion that leads us to suffer (because matter is not really real, and so we get caught in craving things and wanting to run away from others things that don't really exist). So they teach people to reject the material world and renounce all worldly goods. The logical end point to this is to become a monk or wandering mendicant and dedicate one's life to spirit. This is the path of the ascetic, although many of said gurus seem to hold on to a predilection for stuff! On the other hand, atheists and scientists tend to be materialists, who believe that matter is primary and so consciousness experience (and with it all spiritual experience) comes after. They are compelling illusions that emerge from neurons firing but which have no real substance. This can lead to prioritizing sensual pleasure, material gain, tangible proofs, and real-world impact over all else. It can also lead us ultimately to carefree hedonism.

Both these positions seem to deny the most fundamental thing about our lived experience: we are both material and mind at the same time. Either idealism or materialism denies one part of our essential being-in-the-world. If we see the world through the lens of scientific rationality alone, all we will see is separate atoms, leptons, and cells. See the world through the lens of mystical intuition alone and all we will see is consciousness, ideas, and mind. We may be connected to the entire universe but that connection exists in our warm, wet, and squidgy material bodies. We may think an individual self exists and peer out at those hands and legs as separate matter, but we also are part of the whole. If we privilege one over the other then we lose essential tools and thinking that we need to thrive in this crazy-beautiful world. We need to master matter (our biologies in the physical world) as well as our consciousness (our psychologies and our "spiritual" world) if we want to flourish. Bring them both together, which is how they are in nature, and we wake up to the real possibility that scientific insights and spiritual intuitions might both be right. One has mastery over primary qualities like size, speed, and density. One has mastery of secondary qualities like love, connection, and purpose. The split, the schism between mind and matter, is the problem itself! It is the delusion that leads us to suffer.

Spiritual atheism is known as a dual-aspect monism in philosophy. Spiritual atheism resolves the double bind of modernity and heals the schism between science and spirituality. In the real world, primary and secondary qualities are one. They are not bisected but part of one reality. The wisdom traditions are the science of each individual's inner experience. Western objective science is the science of many people's external observations and measurements. The inner consciousness (secondary qualities, mind stuff) and the outer material (primary qualities, extending stuff) are two sides of a Möbius strip: forever connected, forever one... although seemingly two. In this moment the double bind, which holds so many of us in its viselike jaws, collapses under the weight of its own internal contradictions. We no longer have to choose a single arbiter of truth we want: either the joy we experience with oneness or the certainty we get with hard science. We can appreciate them both as equally rigorous, yet different, ways to understand how our universe, full of embodied consciousness, works.

Purpose is one of the main places where they touch in everyday life. In fact, purpose is a powerful and practical wisdom "hack" for reuniting our consciousness with matter. It ensures we place love (secondary qualities) at the heart of our work delivering profit, productivity, or impact (primary qualities). Purpose is enlightenment becoming impact. It is love-in-action. It is the experience connection turned into projects and acts that genuinely help others. Purpose connects the outpouring of love we feel within—once we have "purified" and released inner blockages— with the material problems, issues, and challenges in the world around us. We do not get to decide what our purpose is: we just get to choose whether to listen to its logic and the yearnings of the Connector; or to follow our desires and fears, and the urgings of the Protector.

Intuition is how we discover our purpose and live purposefully each day. When we do "inner work," and seek peace within through self-healing, we start to hear the "still, small voice of calm" that is our intuition. But we cannot hear the low, slow whispers above the clamor of "shoulds" and "musts" of our fearful instincts that arise naturally (and helpfully) when we feel separate, lack, and loss. Intuition is the way the symphony tells us what to do next that will reduce suffering in the space. This is what being on purpose is. Instinct is what tells us how to survive threats. By refining our capacity to discern love-fueled intuition from fear-driven instinct, we get guidance on how to make purposeful choices. We get help to understand what is "on purpose" and what is not. I follow this guidance each day as I teach, write, and make business decisions: from what paper I buy for the printer to what products to focus on next. The Connector calls to me when I veer off path and it tells me in no uncertain terms—when I listen—when I am doing something that is out of alignment with my core essence. This is how I dialogue with the orchestral symphony of the universe. If I do not listen, my system finds other ways to get my attention, which tend to not feel so pleasant.

If you listen, a theme usually emerges: a tune unique to you. This is your life purpose, your unique way of being in the world that brings love and liberty into the moment. Then we can discover our leadership purpose: how we take our life purpose into our careers and projects. Each of us must find out how our purpose can most influence the systems we touch, and the people and places we care about, in a way that fits our skills, talents, and situation. But when we have yet to switch on and seek our own transformation out of pain, we can drown out our intuition, and with it our purpose, with exotic drugs and even more exotic holidays as well as sex, work, exercise, extreme sports, and anything else that we use to stay within our comfort zones. I did this for years upon years, first in advertising and then in my own business, as I ignored the call to make meaningful but inconvenient choices. But after breakdown/burnout brought me to my knees and demanded that I listen, I found within the ashes my life purpose, leadership, and enterprise purpose (they are all distinct, something I go deeper into in my forthcoming book Purpose Will Save Your Life and Your Business).

Once we switch on and start to live a path of spiritual atheism, every moment we spend not honoring the call will bring growing existential agony. Nothing is as painful to us, nothing can spark such torment, as knowing that we are "off purpose," once we realize there is a thing called "on purpose" too. This is not about some kind of religious morality to do with being "good." We have to move beyond this old and pernicious paradigm. It's simply a choice. No one can judge us for being on or off purpose. But it will feel very different. Purpose demands that we take our wisdom practices and spiritual experiences and make them count within our organizations and society. This is why the sage Patanjali, in his Yoga Sutras, tells us that if we practice yoga properly it will lead us to change our lives and the world, getting rid of many of our possessions and starting to practice ahimsa, or nonviolence (the core of Gandhi's theory of bringing about social justice). If we don't change our choices, by keeping "spiritual" beliefs compartmentalized away from social, business, and political decisions, not a lot will change in the world. Mahayana Buddhism developed an idea that helps us avoid the trap of self-indulgence so we can lead on purpose. The core of it is that the switched-on person makes a vow to refuse to disappear into their own experience of liberation and bliss until they have brought about the release from suffering of everyone. The pledge we make is called the Bodhisattva Vow.

I am no purist or ascetic and I live very much in this world. I love gorgeous design, fine wines, Michelin-starred food, and the occasional hedonistic excess. But unless we move beyond using spirituality as a way to feel good—and purpose as a tool to feel better about ourselves—the true power of enlightenment to change the world is lost. There is no getting around it. Genuine spirituality is not about being nice or even happy. It is not about having a Buddha statue in the corner of our home or about lighting incense (although these may be part of a genuine wisdom practice). It means doing the hardest work of our lives to heal our hearts so we can find our purpose...and then change our political choices, consumer choices, and career choices to align them with it. This is usually deeply inconvenient. Once I began to unfold my purpose in the months and years after I exited my innovation agency, I had to give up most, if not all, of my old lifestyle in order to focus: a growing pension, the kudos of my friends and family, designer clothes and furniture, the thrill of being a "player" in the entrepreneurial space, and even the ability to say what I did for a living in one simple sentence! As well as refuse to go through an entrepreneurial exit and reap the multimillions I was worth on paper, I went on to refuse project after project that could have made me lots of money as a consultant but would not have helped the world. I still refuse a lot of work, a choice made all the more fun by having to support two small kids. Nobody said living a switched-on life, of purpose and contribution, was easy!

We must pay the purpose premium, which often means giving up respect, security, and money, in order to get the purpose dividend: a life chock-full of meaning, growth, and fulfillment. The purpose premium I have earned from giving up so much material wealth and psychological comfort is priceless. But I'd be lying if I said it has been easy seeing friends who I used to out-earn in my twenties as a fast-moving entrepreneur race past me to buy houses, second homes, and sexy electric cars. There are moments when my Protector gets massively triggered as it watches people get awards, prizes, and fame whilst it feels it does not get the recognition it thought it needed to make up for not being seen and appreciated as a child. Far from the "prosperity gospel" at the heart of advanced capitalism—god (or the universe) shows his love for us through material wealth, which is endemic in New Age spirituality too in the form of ideas such as the "Law of Attraction"—I believe that the symphonic universe will guide us toward thriving with purpose...but this may not mean we ever become rich or famous. The universe works through our organic ecology and biology. The idea of profit growth and capital accumulation within a material economy is an invention of Protectors that seek material wealth as a proxy for safety and love. The Protector in me genuinely worries about my material safety but it is also caught up in wanting recognition and respect. So if I breathe out, switch on, and remember what I am here to do as purpose, I can relax back into my life remembering that nobody's path is better or worse: it is just on or off purpose for them. The universe has always provided for me what I really need, not what my Protector desires.

The key to getting the full weight of the purpose premium is to connect our own transformation and enlightenment to the suffering in the world. If we don't, it is easy to get lost in a New Age bubble. In the last few years there has been a meteoric rise of what I call "tight-butt spirituality": turning profound technologies for personal and social transformation into yet more tools to speed up the materialistic world. In many ways the capitalist episteme has co-opted yoga, meditation, and purpose. Yoga now sells a feel-good, "well-being" lifestyle. Mindfulness meditation is sold as an efficiency-improving tool to make us more productive cogs in the machine and provide us with competitive edge in the job market. Purpose can help be used to consciously or unconsciously hide unethical business and career choices. The wily yet essential Protector is tricky and can hijack even our best intentions and the most powerful wisdom practices. This is especially true when aided by a profit-driven mentality that is untempered by genuine love-fueled purpose. Yoga can give us a tight ass, contoured abs, and positive vibes. Mindfulness can help us chill out, get more stuff done, and excel at work. Purpose can inspire teams to go the extra mile and feel part of a movement doing something worthwhile. Each can also both be great "gateway drugs" to deeper levels of awakening. But if they are commandeered by the Protector we will consume spirituality, well-being, and purpose work in the same way we consume every other material product in advanced capitalism: to fill a deep lack within.

Wisdom traditions and practices were designed to help us practice living from abundance, connection, and contribution. They were created to help us stop feeling separate and afraid, to no longer feel loss and lack, and so be able to live in genuine collaboration and community. Wisdom practices are a means to an end with the end itself being a world that works for everyone, not just the 0.1 percent, 1 percent, or even 10 percent. Our own enlightenment is the gateway into, not the end point of, a life of purpose. As our heart becomes more whole, less energy is taken up with repressing painful memories and protecting ourselves from the world. As we "purify" ourselves, more of our energy can be invested in changing the world around us. Thus the two processes, of self-healing and world-change, go hand in hand. In the Jewish mystical tradition, this repair of the world is called tikkun ha-olam. However, we can only focus on this purposeful work if we are already practiced in tikkun ha-nefesh: healing the soul within us so we are better able to be compassionate, loving, and purposeful in the moment.

Through the act of self-healing, tikkun ha-nefesh, we discover new capabilities that become essential for our work doing tikkun ha-olam. Without the wounds I received from bullying, abandonment, and alien-ation, I would not have gone on the hunt to find a way to heal them and so discover the Switch On Way. Without finding a way to transcend all those interminable days of feeling like a worthless piece of shit, I would not have the insight and compassion needed to guide people on their own pathway toward enlightenment and transformation. If I had not had my heart bro-ken by building a successful business that was part of the problem and had the courage to step away from success, I would not have had the sensitivity and strength needed to help others align their own projects and companies around purpose. If I had not worked out how to transform my leadership style and skills after failing so horribly to lead my first team, I would not be able to stand in front of tens of thousands of leaders and guide them with how to lead. We can only give to others what we have within: what we have learnt from our own Hero's Journeys.

The universe will give us help along our Hero's Journey in the form of people and experiences that give us the "magical" weapons (tools and ideas) and powers (skills and qualities) that we need to progressively unfold our purpose. So it is important to pay attention to what Jung and Pauli called "meaningful correspondences" in the world around us, like the note I was given in Mexico. The universe is the real El Mago! When we do, they can make all the difference. One day I was working on a social innovation project for a client: attempting to transform a deeply challenged social system. I was in a coffee shop and catching up with a dear colleague in Sin-gapore, who is also a change-agent (and leading civil servant in the city). I happened to mention what I was doing and he suggested, over Skype, that I use a neat methodology that he had worked with. By adapting the tool to my specific needs it became something quite different. After a year or so grappling with this new-fangled "thing" and it became the J-shaped curve we now call The Breakthrough Curve. This is the central pathway in the Switch On Way—the philosophy, methodology, and toolkit that it has become my leadership purpose to unfold and make accessible—to guide either individual transformation or organizational change and innovation.

Because we cannot preempt what the magic will be and predict when the guidance will come, all we can do is follow our intuition to keep us on purpose even if it is scares or confuses our reasoning, strategizing mind. We cannot second-guess genuine intuition as it is the direct "will" of the evolving expanding universe. Purpose and intuition will guide us, as leaders, to make decisions that someone has to make, even without perfect data or visibility. This is why leadership is where the rubber hits the road for spiritual atheists. Leadership is about making change in the material world. But to do it effectively, we need to have constant awareness of our consciousness—our purpose—to ensure that the changes we make in matter serve everyone, not just ourselves. This guides us to do things that are on purpose, as opposed to off purpose, as life unfolds. Each day I have to decide whether to write and edit another book chapter or spend that time with my boys. I have to choose which invitations to accept or reject for public speaking, or whether to invest our income into a new app or technique for scaling transformation (that may crash and burn), or put it toward a pension that is, as yet, merely a fantasy.

We need purpose to make sure we don't get pulled into patterns of protection that lead to more suffering for ourselves and others. Purpose is our anchor for all our life and leadership decisions, and will help us hack through lack and loss whenever it is triggered within. A key wisdom hack for this is devotion, one of the core teachings of the Indian classic the Bhagavad Gita (so good that Gandhi called it his "handbook to life"). To avoid suffering, we must offer up our purpose work back to the universe we are part of. Otherwise we will tend to crave the fruits of our purposeful labors—such as promotion or profit—rather than stay true. To stop this, we devote all our actions, all our decisions, and all our projects to others. We move away from desiring profit and into driving forward purpose (whilst still being clear that without income, without a return path for our energies, we cannot go on). This devotional leadership, called Bhakti Yoga, is premised on our feeling love in our hearts—purpose—when we create and deliver projects of any kind.

This is easier said than done because being openly spiritual in the public domain—as a leader or decision-maker—is one of the last great social taboos in the West. I know for sure that I have lost many projects, clients, TV shows, book deals, and press columns, as well as an awful lot of funding, because I emphatically say that I am spiritual and that my work is guided by love. Go figure! Whilst a much-needed separation between Church and State is necessary, and so was enshrined in the core of Western democracies in order to ensure that religious dogma had no place in political life, this has led to the materialist paradigm running rampant. Businesses, communities, and government agencies are obsessed with primary qualities in work—such as evidence-bases, data-collection, and measuring results—but there is little interest in secondary qualities such as purpose, compassion, and empathy whose presence cannot be measured easily. This has resulted in technocratic management that prioritizes efficiency and productivity above all. This is why there is so much suffering—from depression now being the number one burden on health globally to rampant financial inequality splitting apart societies—everywhere we look.

Purpose always seeks to reduce suffering before it looks to increase thriving. It is important that switched-on people always seek to reduce suffering primarily with their purpose rather than focus on creating an abstract notion of the rational "good." This is because the Good has been the cause of so much suffering in human history. Adolf Hitler really thought he was doing the "right" thing by getting rid of the Jews in order to lead the German people away from moral decay and social decline, and toward strength (the Good). Seeking the good of the many can easily become a terrifying assault on human connection and compassion for the few. However, by seeking the reduction of suffering wherever we see it—and we all know what suffering looks and feels like—we can ensure that nobody is subjected to disempowerment as the cost of delivering the good for others (whatever it may be). Suffering is quintessentially a secondary quality, whereas value/the Good has become rationalized by utilitarians into something that can be measured.

Our hearts—the metaphorical organs of connection, love, and so purpose—need to break open with the enormity of the suffering of the world in order for our true purpose to shine through. As our heart tears apart with the enormity of the pain felt by so many about so much—including ourselves—it forces our self-protective conditioning that has tried to keep the world at bay to crumble. This leaves us raw, ripe, and ready to receive the pure light of our own purpose. Our heart needs to expand sufficiently in this way to give enough space for the size and girth of our purpose. Anything less than this heartbreak will result in a partial experience of purpose and not the full power of it. For if we still have patterns stemming from our own fear, lack, and loss, we will not fully give ourselves over to what the universe is asking us to do to heal the whole. The system promotes more growth, learning, and expansion: we must heal ourselves sufficiently of our own traumas and upsets in order to discover our purpose. As we heal more of our own wounds, the actions we take in the world are more aligned with love, truth, and creativity, and less with the distortions stemming from our own separation and trauma. As we live more moments on purpose and less off purpose, we start to feel increasing levels and intensities of genuine and lasting meaning as the "reward" for all that self-healing.

If we do not heal ourselves and go out into the world to act—as we all do at the start of our studies or career—we will create more pain in some way. This is what I did in advertising and then in innovation until I used the same tools, which are always agnostic, to deliver my purpose. Hurt hearts make their mark in blood. If we go out into the world as leaders held hostage by hurt hearts, we will likely use the awesome power of technology, innovation, and entrepreneurship to scale, amplify, and accelerate projects that do not alleviate suffering but cause it, even if they look cool and make a huge ROI (return on investment). Let us remember that the Zyklon B used in the gas chambers of Auschwitz was a disruptive innovation, bringing industrial scale to a task that was, up to that point, inefficiently carried out by bullets. If we have a healed heart, a whole heart, we will make a difference through impact purpose, integrity, and wise leadership. This means that as we build new products, services, apps, social media platforms, and sharing economy businesses, we must walk the fine, palintonic line between purpose and profit—otherwise the logical of turbo-capitalism will distort our ability to drive positive change. We have to be careful about whether we get investment and from whom as a need to return 1.1x, 10x, or 100x can pervert everything we do. If we are dominated by a Nietzschean will-to-power through profits, size, and scale—which is what Silicon Valley and Wall Street are run by—we will almost inevitably end up hurting everyone, including themselves. So we need genuine purpose at the heart every organization guiding every difficult decision and not just pretty words—or the desire for accumulation, acquisition, and exploitation from hearts filled with lack and loss will swamp everything. They are the inherent logic of a disconnected capitalism that was born in the image of materialist science that is cut off from the secondary qualities.

This is what switched on, or "conscious," leadership is about: letting love, connection, purpose, and collaboration take center stage in all our work, without any shame at all (and without pride either). This is radical. Revolutionary even! But absolutely necessary if we want a world that works. Che Guevara, the famous revolutionary of the 1960s said: "At the risk of seeming ridiculous, let me say that the true revolutionary is guided by a great feeling of love." Conscious leadership is about bringing our unalloyed love and wisdom into every business conversation and into every business decision. It is about leading projects and other people rooted in an abiding sense of connection to the whole, whether we see that at Tao, Tawhid, Brahman, Brotherhood, VALIS, or anything else. This is what living on purpose really means. By transcending the schism between science and spirit with a purpose rooted in the metaphysics of spiritual atheism, we get to place where compassion, empathy, and love are in their rightful places at the heart of all company, community, and government decision-making about the material world.

We can still evaluate programs and policies rationally with metrics and mathematics. But we make the decisions using both the data and our intuitive, heartfelt wisdom. We both measure and feel how our ideas and actions impact others. Then we course-correct, improving our actions according to both the smarts of the mind, and the sense of purpose and love in our hearts. With purpose at the heart of enterprise, our apps, technologies, and innovations can serve real unmet needs of the many—such as poverty, lack of meaning, mental ill-health, social isolation, chronic diseases, and so on—rather than be used to help rich people find parking spaces for their Tesla car in crazily expensive urban areas. Technologies and concepts such as social enterprises, cooperatives, mutuals, crowdfunding, wikis, and blockchains all have the power to encourage more of the secondary qualities of conscious subjective experience back into the heart of materialist capitalism. It is my sincere hope that all organizations—government, private, and third sector—become social enterprises that are entrepreneurial, creative, and efficient in the material world in order to deliver their heartfelt purpose emanating from consciousness at scale.

One thing we all know is that our life and leadership skills will be tested in the times ahead. The Digital Age is like no other. Massive global risks such as severe climate change, resource wars, and devastating pollution are here now, in the present. In China alone, 4,400 deaths a year are caused by dirty air alone. These human-made environmental issues—which, we should be clear, are caused by purposeless business and politics—will interact with other human-made social challenges like mass automation. In the United States, the most populous job is as a driver. When driverless cars become mainstream, which seems likely to occur in years not decades, it will threaten to destabilize society in ways we haven't yet figured. What is being called the Fourth Industrial Revolution is happening today. Digital technologies that connect people (and their biologies), places, and products are multiplying and spreading into every corner of society.

Artificial Intelligence (AI), DNA-editing, smart robots, The Internet of Things, and much more besides, will be everyday realities for all of us within a few years. There is understandable fear that technology will replace us, just as cheaper workers overseas have done in the last few decades. Most technologists are materialists who think that AI will be able to match and even outperform human intelligence. But they are only seeing one aspect of the two facets of reality. They see the primary qualities of our brains and try to replicate them in machines. These machines are great at calculating probabilities and choosing pathways based on established rules, whether preprogrammed or learned on the job. This is why AI can already beat human beings at rule-based tasks like playing chess or

Go. Yet machines, as far as we know, are not being developed to connect up and engage in the secondary qualities. In fact I think it is highly unlikely that AI will ever be able to be conscious, alive, intuitive, interpretive, compassionate, and creative. Networked yes. Connected no.

This points to the opportunities for us all within the next installment of the Digital Age as our most human and humane capacities are going to be needed "up the wazoo" to help guide, support, and empower our sisters and brothers to find meaning, mastery, and membership—and perhaps even food, shelter, and medicines—in the years ahead. Each human being's purpose—the bridge between their consciousness and what really matters—will be able to help them thrive in the decades of fast and furious change ahead, as they consciously interpret for the moment, principles of wisdom and well-being rather than merely calculate rules. When we switch on, we can always see opportunities to reduce suffering and increase thriving that lie latent within each of these problems—and any other—as long as we stay true to our purpose.

Plato said that only true philosophers—lovers of wisdom who no longer want to rule but instead seek to see the truth—should be given the power to lead society.3 In other words, only those who have transcended the Protector's constant need to compete, grab, and defend will be able to follow their purpose to sufficiently to lead us through the trials, turmoils, and tests of the Digital Age. Such leaders will palintonically balance hubris and humility and profit and purpose in service of the whole. They will choose to devote their lives, as the Bodhisattva does, to the removal of suffering not because of what they get but because of how much they can give. This then is an invitation—expressly made to you—to heal all and any schisms within you so you can ground every personal, family, social, or political project you lead in purpose (love, connection, and truth). You are the one you have been waiting for: a leader who can confidently bring more love, truth, and creativity into every area of public life without cringing from shame. When your inherently creative, agile, and purposeful consciousness is combined with the power of science, business, technology, and innovation to rapidly and radically change anything in the material world, nothing is impossible.

Endnotes

1. Abridged from *The Spiritual Atheist (Switch On Books*, 2017

2. Rex, J. et al. The structure of creative cognition in the human brain *Front. Hum. Neurosci.*, 08 July 2013.

3. Bellah, R. *The Axial Age and Its Consequences*. Harvard University Press, 2012.

PART III
The Practice

Chapter 14

WAYFINDING OUR PURPOSE

Patrick Cook-Deegan

Introduction // Personal Narrative

I can still remember the feeling so clearly: sitting on my aunt's back porch in a state of existential panic at 19, frantically trying to Google my way toward purpose.

I typed in "Yale law." The admission rate was under 3 percent. I thought *Yeah, let's do that.* It is super hard to get in, lots of people who go there end up being important. Doing that will set me up for the future. Admittance to Yale Law was highly coveted; I knew it would be a notch on my belt, a marker that would help me move up the ranks of elite, liberal circles. There was only one problem with my plan: I had no interest in becoming a lawyer.

At the time, I had just finished my second year of college. Up until that point, I'd accomplished most of the things I felt I was supposed to: I was an All-American captain of a state championship–winning lacrosse team. The year before, I'd gained admission to an Ivy League school. At Brown, I had a lot of friends, I was playing varsity lacrosse, and nothing was "wrong." But deep down, something was not right. The accomplishments and the "shoulds" weren't enough to fend off my deeper existential questions. Instinctively, I felt I was being called to do something very different in my life. But whatever "it" was, I could not fathom it. So, I made a bold choice: I decided to buy a one-way, round-the-world ticket through New Zealand, Southeast Asia, and over to Istanbul.

As I prepared for the journey, I got scared. What would happen if I got off the track? Was I about to derail my life? I almost didn't board the plane in Los Angeles.

On my trip, I slept in unelectrified huts for the first time in Laos. I spent four months living on the couch of 12 wonderfully hospitable Muslim men near a Turkish university. I spent weeks hitchhiking my way through New Zealand, staying with people who lived without money. I began to develop an inner life—doing my first mindfulness retreat in northern Thailand and having conversations with monks and Sufis about the meaning of life.

I came back a changed young man. I quit lacrosse, searched for a whole new group of friends, and switched majors from American history to international relations with a focus on human rights in Southeast Asia. I jumped off the track, landing in an open field with no path forward, but lots of opportunities to make my own way. It wasn't easy; often, I yearned to be back on that prescribed track. Staying there felt more comfortable: everything you must do to succeed is laid out in front of you; all you have to do is work hard and move toward that predetermined target. Being off the track offered something different—equal parts terror and self-doubt mixed with liberation and great excitement.

❦

The journey toward feeling purposeful can be painful. Leading adolescent developmental psychologist, Dr. Kendall Cotton Bronk of Claremont Graduate University, confirms this truth in her excellent book *Purpose in Life*. Dr. Cotton Bronk cites research showing people suffer and endure lower life satisfaction during the journey to discover a sense of purpose. But, the journey is well worth the reward: people who find a sense of purpose have much higher life satisfaction over the course of their lives. And the sooner they set out to find it, the better. People who search for meaning later in life—often catalyzed by the classic midlife crisis—may not ultimately find as much life satisfaction as those who start the search earlier. What's more, embarking on the quest for purpose four or five decades in is much more painful than starting at an earlier age. People in midlife don't have the same flexibility to explore as young people do. Forty- and fifty-somethings have mortgages, jobs, kids, and big responsibilities; some of these responsibilities can turn into opportunities to be purposeful, but in other cases they keep people feeling trapped from necessary exploration. They also don't have the same biological wiring as adolescents, wiring that encourages the exploration and healthy risk-taking intrinsic to adolescent identity formation and individuation.

Dr. Cotton Bronk's research, combined with my own experience, has led me to believe strongly that it's critical to embark on the journey and exploration of purpose during adolescence. Although the journey I made around the world and the years after were often lonely and painful, starting my search for purpose at 19 years old helped me craft a life unimaginable to me before I stepped off the track. If I hadn't gotten off then, I'm not sure I ever would have.

Shifting To Purpose

I have a friend, a human development teacher to high schoolers, who starts his classes with a simple, powerful question: What's most important to you?

Often, students have never been asked. They pause and think, and often say something about what's important to others, or to colleges. Or, they say things that are important to them but that schools don't value: friendships, hobbies, or creative pursuits.

Dr. Bill Damon, professor of Education at Stanford University and author of *Path to Purpose*, defines purpose as "a stable and generalized intention to accomplish something that is at the same time meaningful to the self and consequential for the world beyond the self."

In order for something to really be a purpose, it must be important to you: not to your parents, your friends, your school, your community, or to others. Your purpose is what lights you up deep down in your soul. This may sound obvious, yet so many people spend most of their time dedicated to pursuits they don't care about at all.

According to Dr. Damon's research, only about a quarter of young adults are on the path to developing a sense of purpose. Damon breaks youth into four distinct groups: dabblers, disengaged, dreamers, and purposeful. Each quadrant represents roughly a quarter of youth. Purposeful youth, he says, "Are those who have found something meaningful to dedicate themselves to, who have sustained interest over a period of time, and who express a clear sense of what they are trying to accomplish in the world and why."[1]

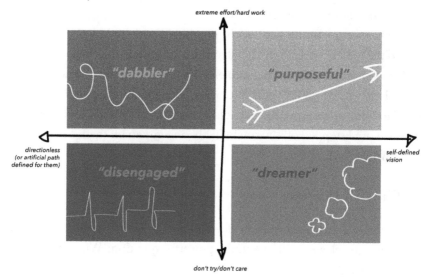

Considering that we do little in our education system to help students move in the direction of purpose, this low number makes sense. How can we expect young people to find a purpose if we don't give them encouragement and meaningful opportunities to explore what that might be during the pivotal years of adolescence and high school?

The journey to purpose begins by helping young people discover what matters to them. Many of us have a hard time figuring this out. This struggle is particularly true of adolescents, who aren't often afforded the time and space to dive into what they care about. They're too busy catering to what their school, college admissions officers, peers, or parents think they should care about. Or, at the other end of the spectrum, disengaged students see no reason to find a purpose, or are simply never offered experiences that ignite their desire to craft a purposeful life. If no one ever asks you to take your own personal journey seriously, it's difficult to arrive at that conclusion on your own.

As an educator trying to help students understand and value purpose, I try to get students thinking about three distinct things: a problem in the world they care about, discovering something they love to do, and identifying the things they're good at or skills they want to acquire. This framework comes in large part from the work of Bill Damon, but if you map it on your own life or the lives of purposeful people around you, the recipe becomes more intuitive and obvious. Purposeful people figure out what they care about in the world, what they love, and what they're good at (or want to be good at), and combine the three to make something powerful happen.

THE WAYFINDER PURPOSE COMPASS

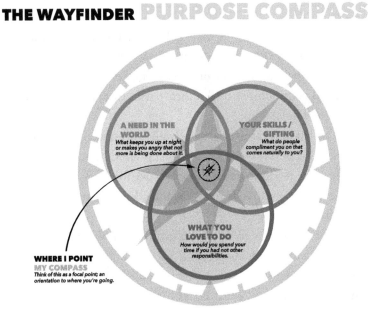

This brings us to the second core component of purpose: consequential work in the world. No purposeful person is thinking solely of themselves. By definition, purpose involves working for the greater good and people beyond yourself. My path to purpose started when I returned from my year abroad and started to brainstorm how I could give back to the world, for the first time in my life.

STARTING DOWN THE PATH TO PURPOSE

When I returned home from my trip, I was confused, lonely, and unsettled. I'd been exposed to so much that was so unjust; I wanted to do something about it. While combing through the internet, again, I got a wild idea: what if I rode by bike the length of Laos to raise money to build a primary school and support girls scholarships in the region?

On my trip, I'd visited school after school in Laos that were nothing more than glorified sheds, and I'd met young woman after young woman who was denied an education on account of their gender. It made me sad, angry, shocked, and guilty. It was the first time I'd been exposed to this level of poverty and gender discrimination, which, to my surprise, resonated on a deeply personal level—I had a younger sister with whom I was very close.

Knowing the project was far too large to take on all on my own, I found an established organization on whose behalf I could fundraise. I chose Room to Read, an organization based in the United States that partners with local communities in Southeast Asia to build schools, libraries, and to provide scholarships.

Even with a fundraising partner, I still had no idea how to move from idea to reality. I'd never owned a road bike, raised money, or built a website. But I had the intrinsic motivation to move forward with the idea; that was enough to propel me to learn what I needed to learn (albeit in clunky and often hilarious ways).

Though I was headed in the right direction, my bike trip was a far from perfect attempt to focus beyond myself. But it was a start. As the first project I ever undertook that was not solely about me, it put me on the path to purpose. For so long, I'd focused on my college admission, my athletic ambitions, my future career, and my life. On my bike trip, for the first time, I was focused on the needs of others instead of those belonging to my future self.

Without a shift to looking beyond the self, purpose remains beyond reach, and even comprehension. Our high school system breeds the opposite of this, a "me-ness" based on competition and class rankings. It is true that many teens still take on meaningful pursuits in high school, but often this is despite high school, not because of it. I have found in my extensive interviews with teens that their most meaningful pursuits come from outside of school. School is something to be survived; outside of school is where personally meaningful projects, relationships, and discoveries develop.

Our current high school system pushes students to achieve blindly or generates little motivation to try at all. It is hard to blame students when they are bombarded with the pressures of class rankings, intensely competitive college admissions, and a narrow focus on standardized tests and GPAs. So much of our system values achievement over exploration and competition over cooperation. So it is little wonder that many students leave high school and continue to drive toward external achievement without a true sense of self or deeper level of motivation.

Purpose Isn't Drive or Achievement

There's a critical distinction to make between purpose and drive. Our education system overemphasizes drive and mostly skips purpose. And the fact of the matter is that many driven people who seem mission-oriented aren't necessarily carrying out a purpose.

At the core of purposeful action is a deep understanding and self-awareness of what's motivating you. It's easy to be driven to do something that you can do—or to prove that you can do it (men in particular often function this way), but this motivation does not necessarily wed action to purpose.

For example, an investment banker may be incredibly driven to close the next big deal to please their boss, reap a financial reward, prove they can succeed, or even because they just really want to do a particular thing. In other words, work ethic and drive shouldn't be confused with having a purpose. In fact in America, Japan, and other industrialized nations where people work constantly, this precise conflation—purpose vs. drive—is ruining a lot of people's lives.

This is not to say that people with a purpose don't have drive—in fact, I don't know a single purposeful person who's not also driven. The difference is that their pursuits aligned with their purpose—their drive originates inside, not as the result of external rewards or accolades. The quality of a purposeful person's drive is very different from the manic investment banker or the overly ambitious young legislative aide who conflates power with purpose. Just think of the high-achieving people you know who can do a lot of things and have achieved a great deal of "success," but they're miserable because their self-acceptance is pegged to external validation (like mine was before my bike trip).

In Silicon Valley, where I now work, or in Washington, DC, where I used to work, folks like this are all over. Often, they're chasing the big five spiritual perils (as I call them): Fame, Money, Power, Intellectual Achievement, and Technological Innovation. Each one has a home city where people flock to accumulate that currency: Fame (LA), Power (DC), Money (NYC), Intellectual Achievement (Boston), and Technological Innovation (The Bay Area). Despite their outward achievements, so many of these people are deeply unhappy. They're driven and successful, but anxious and competitive.

Without a vision for your life and for the world, you can be working incredibly hard but still lacking that crucial element of intrinsic motivation. Understanding one's own motivations for taking action is a deeply undervalued aspect of our culture's achievement-based mind-set.

This privileging of achievement over purpose creates an incredibly small target for success. Think of the person with an impossibly narrow vision of success: I want to be a neurosurgeon at this hospital, by this age, running my whole department, and be widely recognized in my field for my accomplishments.

Many driven people miss their mark by razor-thin margins...and consider themselves failures. Even worse, they continually push themselves toward far-off notions of success that are incredibly hard to achieve and live their whole lives in the future. They tell themselves when they reach that goal, that's when they'll be happy and start to love themselves. And a lot of this behavior is conditioned by the way our education system is currently set up: to reward compliance and blind drive over purpose and self-actualization.

Wayfinding as the Central Metaphor

During my year abroad, I was introduced to Polynesian culture in New Zealand for the first time. It wasn't until years later that my meditation teacher introduced me to the story of Mau Piailug, Nainoa Thompson, and the formation of the Polynesian Voyaging Society (PVS), a group that has led a rebirth of the Hawai'ian wayfinding tradition, and played a role in Hawai'i's cultural renaissance.

I was enthralled to learn that traditional Polynesian navigators, called wayfinders, set out with no maps, or compass to find new lands. Instead, they used the sun, stars, wind, swells, and birds to navigate thousands of miles of open ocean.

The rebirth of traditional Polynesian wayfinding clearly demonstrates that being nonlinear doesn't mean being unfocused, or lacking in purpose. (This is a story that Western colonial hegemonic thinking has perpetuated for the last 500 years: that any culture that wasn't rigid and linear is "less than.") To the contrary, the renaissance of Polynesian voyaging was a huge global event; it reaffirmed achievements of indigenous peoples and celebrated their forms of knowledge.

Being a trained wayfinder is one of the hardest jobs I can imagine. It starts by memorizing more than 200 stars in the sky at different points of latitudes. When wayfinders set off to sail from Hawai'i to Tahiti—a journey of nearly 2,400 miles (imagine walking from LA to NYC without a map!)— they must be able to know where they are within 50 to 100 miles on the largest body of water in the world at any given moment. Leading navigators like Nainoa know where they are within 25 miles or so on the ocean.

The approach taken by these traditional navigators resonated deeply with me. I admired the navigators' skills greatly: their connection with the land and sea, their heightened ability to read the natural world, and their pure stamina (wayfinders only take catnaps on weeklong voyages). These navigators cultivated many skills that I valued—attunement to nature, creative problem-solving, self-awareness, empathetic connection, and risk-taking. My industrialized education taught me these skills were useless, obsolete, and ancillary. In truth, they turn out to be as important as ever, especially in the quest for a purposeful life.

Importance of Crafting a Vision

Before our ancestors set out to find a new island they had to have a vision
of that island over the horizon. They made a plan for achieving that vision.[2]

—Pinky Thompson, quoted in *Hawaiki Rising*

Vision and spiritual seeking are often thing the two things that separate purposeful people from those who are simply driven. Many high-achieving folks have impressive skills but no vision for how to apply them in a way that aligns with their deepest purpose. This is where crafting a vision comes in.

Having a vision for your voyage is an essential part of Polynesian wayfinding culture. Navigators like Nainoa prepared long and hard before heading out to sea (he spent hundreds of hours studying the stars at night and two years apprenticing with master navigator Mau Piailug). Preceding any big journey, navigators had to have a powerful, internal vision, not just the physical and academic training. As Nainoa describes getting ready for his first journey as a navigator, "I had done all my academic study… I was physically strong…but something was missing, my own spiritual preparedness. My own personal journey. It was trying to find my home—inside of me."[3]

Every human needs a sense of spirituality and vision to guide their purpose. It's essential that we each have a bigger vision for the world so that we can orient ourselves according to our own small piece of work within that larger vision (after all, we can only each do a small part). On my bike fundraising trip, I helped try to solve a need in the world (the lack of educational infrastructure and gender opportunity inequality in developing countries). It wasn't quite motivated by a vision, but I did have a desire to solve a specific need I saw. It wasn't until a few years later that I received what I felt like was my first real vision.

After graduating Brown, I still did not know what "my thing" was. At the time, I was working as a volunteer human rights advocate on behalf of Burma, an issue about which I cared deeply. I was also campaigning for Barack Obama in the primary states in New England, and working on launching the Social Innovation Initiative at Brown.

In other words, I was doing a lot of meaningful projects. But again, I sensed there was a deeper "thing" for me out there. And so, I went on another journey, this time to the American West where I drove, backpacked, and hiked 5,000 miles on epic mountain trails in New Mexico, southern Utah, and southwest Colorado. This was, in many ways, the quintessential postcollege graduation What Do I Do With My Life road trip. Later I realized that I was, as one Lakota elder said, seeking a vision, "A vision is a communication from the Wakantanka or a spirit of mankind. It may come at any time or in any manner to anyone… It may come from one giving it, or it may be sent by an *akicita* (messenger). It may come unsought or it may come by seeking it."[4]

I was certainly seeking it and I got one. A very clear one. After doing a 10-day Vipassana meditation sit in Northern California, I went into Yosemite for a week of backpacking in the High Sierra with my little sister. We basecamped for a week and went on day hikes to different lakes. We played in the snow and ate too much tuna fish. But this trip was not about fun or hiking a lot of miles; it was fundamentally about asking myself, *What now?* Not in a tactical, what-do-I-do-next-year kind of way, but in a grander what-do-I-want-the-next-decade-of-my-life-to-be-like kind of way.

It wasn't a cerebral thing; visions rarely come from thinking them to death. Instead, visions come like flowers or plants: they grow up from inside you—your heart and your gut.

I'll always remember looking over the snowcapped Cathedral Peaks on the fourth day of the trip. It was then and there that I had a clear vision, so clear it felt like I'd been stripped bare by a cold wind. It was a vision of leading young people on the exact types of trips that I was on now, adding in mindfulness to backcountry experiences. It was a vision that I could see clearly and feel deeply.

While it was exciting to arrive at such clarity, a vision is still different from an action plan. Even once you have a vision, you can't go make it happen right away. Visions take time to seed and germinate—you can't force them. Often you know what you want to go toward, but you don't yet know how to get there.

At the time of my vision, I'd only done three 10-day long meditation retreats. I'd spent a fair amount of time in the backcountry, but I was in no position to start leading these trips there anytime soon. And furthermore, I had no idea with whom I would actualize this idea. But I held on to it and continued to work on human rights in Burma. Many years later, after moving back from Southeast Asia I was connected to an organization called Inward Bound Mindfulness Education. I moved to California to spread its West Coast operations. Five years later—almost to the exact day of having my vision—we were leading our first group of teens on a wilderness-mindfulness backcountry retreat 10 miles north of the place where I'd looked out at the Cathedral Peaks and seen something important in the future.

Purpose + Vision in Adolescent Education

What would our education system look like if focused on helping students develop purpose, a healthy sense of self, and a vision for their lives?

The first priority would be helping students develop self-awareness and progress on to prompting students to find things in the world they care about, and then giving them space and time to experiment with projects they care about out in the real world.

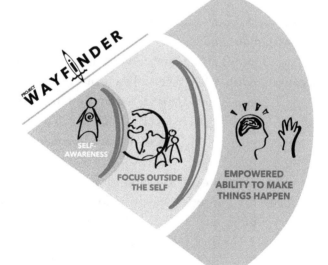

This process would be overseen and mentored by wise, compassionate coaches who don't invoke the constant fear of failure the drives students under our current system. This isn't a radical idea when you think of the principles of human development: first, you focus on yourself, then others, then your wider community, then the world. Finally, you figure out how to synthesize all of this and explore what lights you up and gives you meaning amongst the manifold problems and experiences one can have as a human on this planet. Our education system doesn't support this process. Instead, it mostly squashes real exploration in the areas that would help young people develop a true sense of purpose.

To help young people figure out what they care about, two things need to happen. We need to expose students to many different kinds of things they may care about while simultaneously helping them develop in-depth self-awareness in an iterative, cyclical process between the internal and external, new experiences and reflection, and integration of those learning experiences that translates into action.

As a teen and young man, I repeated this cycle 10 years in a row. Every summer, I'd have some totally new experience, and come home thinking about how it might relate to what I wanted to do with my life. At age 18, I completed six weeks of Officer Candidate School for the Marines in Quantico. Two years later, I spent a summer doing education and public health work in East Africa. I spent another summer backpacking around the American West alone supporting myself with money from Officers Candidates School and speaking about my bike trip at high schools. After each new experience, I'd come back to school and spend the year sifting through my most recent experience. Of course, figuring out through trial-and-error what I did not want to do was as important as finding experiences that tipped me off about what I did want to do. But at some point, you hit a saturation point of exposure to new things. Once you arrive at that point, it's time to dive deeply into yourself and come up with a vision for the next phase of your life and how you want to bring everything you've learned and all that's meaningful to you together to make the world a better place.

So we move from a phase of exploration into a phase of focused experimentation. The research on purpose backs up this kind of experimentation followed by distillation and "course correction." Dr. Cotton Bronk says that purposeful people share four traits: dedicated commitment, personal meaningfulness, goal-directedness, and a vision bigger than self. She also cites three things that foster the finding of purpose: an important life event, serving others in a meaningful way, and changes in life circumstance (all three of which happened to me on my trip around the world and on my bike trip). I've also collected my own observations about traits shared by purposeful people I've encountered: they all have mentors, they have a rich inner life, and they all care deeply about what they do and the people they're serving. One other thing: all purposeful people have a deep level of persistence and determination. For a project to be purposeful, you have to get to the point where you want to turn around, where you hit road bumps, and you must summon the energy and determination to keep going with your own internal resources.

From One Purpose to Many Purposes

Humans do not have one purpose to find at the end of a yellow brick road. It's a myth perpetuated by linear, rational thinking and a foundational aspect of our high school system: work really hard at something for years and arrive at your immutable career. Then, hold on to that precious job for the rest of your life. We place an outsized and unhealthy focus on a singular goal to work toward achieving in the far distant future. This approach, however, can divert students from finding a purpose.

In turns out that purposeful humans have many journeys over the course of a lifetime. These individual journeys may look very different externally. Think of Gandhi. He spent many years of his life dedicated to human rights in South Africa before moving back to India to campaign for independence. In my own life thus far, I spent five years working as a human rights advocate for Burma before co-leading an organization that taught mindfulness education in the United States. Both experiences offered me a similar sense of purpose, even though the pursuits looked very different externally.

Research cited by Dr. Cotton Bronk shows that once people have tasted that first sense of a purposeful project, it's then transferable to other purposeful endeavors. I see this over and over again in my purposeful friends: same sense of purpose, but a different external manifestation.

Developing a sense of purpose is indeed a journey, not something that can be achieved or handed to you. Nor is it a box to be checked off. Developing a sense of purpose is an inherently spiritual thing, as Richard Leider, author of *The Power of Purpose*, notes, "Purpose is spiritual wisdom embodied."[5] Indeed, no one can ever hand someone else a sense of purpose. As Leider goes on to say, "Because a sense of purpose comes from within, only we know if we have it."[6] No amount of money, power, fame, intellect, or technological achievement can deliver purpose as a reward. This is one of the great draws and power of the spiritual journey: the fact that purpose, possibly the most powerful of all human feelings other than love, can never be bought, sold, or handed down. It is always earned through one's own journey through life.

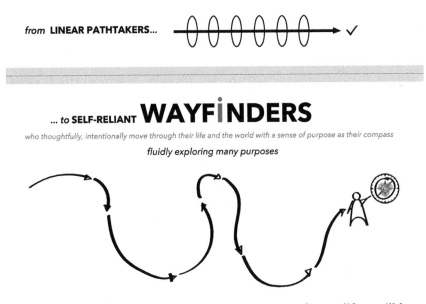

from **LINEAR PATHTAKERS...**

... *to* SELF-RELIANT WAYFiNDERS

who thoughtfully, intentionally move through their life and the world with a sense of purpose as their compass

fluidly exploring many purposes

As I explain to my students, over the course of your life you'll have many arcs to your journey. Each one of the arcs could be a different part of your life: living in Africa in the Peace Corps, being a father of young twins in Milwaukee, or the start-up period of launching own business. You could also think of each arc as a different voyage that you go on in life. Each voyage may lead to a different destination and involve a different crew, but you'll likely use some of the same skills, feelings, relationships, and knowledge that you've accrued over your past journeys to get yourself there.

I like to think the purpose of education is to prepare young people to be navigators of their own lives. The first step is helping students change their mind-sets and getting them comfortable with the reality that life is a series of long, unpredictable voyages, not a straight shot on the freeway using GPS. Ideally, at the center of each of these journeys is the intersection of a need in the world you care about, what you love to do, and your skills (our Wayfinder purpose compass).

The Birth of Project Wayfinder

Two years ago, I was given an education innovation project fellowship at Stanford's K12 Lab Network, housed at Stanford's Hasso Plattner Institute of Design (also known as the d.school), to develop and design a purpose-based curriculum for adolescents. This was my moment to gather and synthesize a decade's-worth of experience. My task was to explore how we could shift our high school education from meaninglessness to purposefulness. To start, I—and my colleague Kelly Schmutte, a product designer and lecturer at Stanford's d.school—interviewed dozens of Palo Alto teenagers about developing a sense of purpose and meaning. We found that students didn't respond well to this language. For many, purpose just felt like "another thing" to achieve (the last thing we wanted).

So, we shifted from talking about developing a sense of purpose to talking about wayfinding. Wayfinding was a perfect metaphor for what we wanted to teach our students. Our ideal student-wayfinders understand what matters to them and in so doing, become confident, intentional navigators capable to tackle the issues they care about most.

As we delved further, we started to see the power of drawing upon the wayfinding tradition to inspire our students. Take the journey from Hawai'i to Tahiti to see what I mean: When navigators set off from Hawai'i they don't aim precisely for Tahiti. Rather, they aim for a series of islands 400 miles long near Tahiti called a "cone of error." When they hit one of these islands, the navigators reorient themselves and navigate toward Tahiti. This approach gives wayfinders a margin for error and takes the pressure off, though it's still an incredibly challenging feat to hit that string of islands at all.

We want to develop highly capable, deeply attuned students who have a sense of where they want to go and why, but are willing to give themselves some room for experimentation, error, and adjustment along the way. Indeed, when Nainoa Thompson was navigating this journey for the first time, he had to make a number of critical adjustments. But he didn't go into autopilot (pretty tough without GPS), nor did he panic or head for home. By the time he set out, he had the confidence, training, and persistence to contend with the inevitable mistakes and moments of doubt that popped up along the way. But there were still moments of deep fear that brought up deeper levels of knowledge, including one moment in the dreaded doldrums.

At one point Nainoa was on the brink of giving up. He thought he had failed, "Then something strange happened. I gave up fighting to find a clue and I settled down. Then, a warmth came over me. I felt the moon on my right shoulder. All of a sudden, I knew where the moon was. I couldn't see the moon…but I knew where it was." As he explained further, "There was a connection between my abilities and my senses that went beyond the analytical, beyond seeing with my eyes. It was something very deep inside. Before that happened…I didn't know how to trust my instincts. My instincts were not trained enough to be trusted. That night, I learned there are levels of navigation that are realms of spirit… It's like new doors of knowledge open and you learn something new. But before the doors open you don't even know that such knowledge exists." Using this deeper knowledge, he course corrected and eventually navigated his crew successfully within 40 miles of his determined destination after voyaging over 2,400 miles of open ocean, a margin under 2 percent.

∞

We hold Nainoa's accomplishment up as an example to our students as the alternative to floating around aimlessly at sea hoping to hit islands, or heading straight to Tahiti in a fancy boat on autopilot using GPS, missing the beauty of the voyage. Instead, we want students to develop focus, intention, and a destination in mind, but also flexibility as to how they get there and the skills they need to course correct. Most importantly, we want students to pay attention to the journey as it unfolds and develop this inner sense of knowing and trusting of one's self.

Finding their own way is something all adolescents crave, and something we rarely teach them how to do. We can never tell a young person what they should do, but we can equip them with the internal and external skills, mind-sets, and behaviors, to figure it out on their own, with the support of strong mentorship and guidance.

Project Wayfinder offers support in three ways: a series of well-designed activities for students called our Wayfinder Navigation Toolkit, teacher trainings on how to teach our curriculum, and finally offering high schoolers transformational programming, or what we call "purpose-provoking" experiences. But more than that, Project Wayfinder is a call to deeply reimagine adolescent education. I am not talking about school reform, or "fixing schools," but offering a vision for a more human-centered and more meaningful way to educate our youth. We need a new generation of purposeful, students who know how to navigate their own lives and deal with an increasingly complex and unpredictable future. It is both deeply practical and incredibly practical at the same time.

For me this is a journey come full circle. After a decade of exploring my own purpose, and often feeling isolated, estranged, and crazy along the way, I want to offer students opportunities to develop a sense of belonging to themselves and our Earth. At the forefront of our education system, we must ensure that students have the space and time to develop themselves and not feel isolated in their experiences. We must give them the experiences, tools, and mentorship to wake up. We must provide them with what I was so desperately craving during my years in high school: guidance on a path to purpose. And so my own path to purpose continues with helping the next generation discover theirs.

❧

Endnotes

1. Bill Damon, *Path to Purpose* (2009), p. 60.

2. Sam Low, *Hawaiki Rising* (2013), p. 201.

3. Ibid, p. 226.

4. Vine Deloria, *The World We Used to Live In* (2006), p.15.

5. Richard Leider, *The Power of Purpose* (2005, 2010, 2015).

6. Ibid., p. 216.

   Credit for all of the graphics in this chapter: Kelly Schmutte

Chapter 15

DISCOVERING YOUR DIVINE DHARMA

Cortney Love, PhD

1. Awakening

Have you ever had a dream and done whatever it takes to achieve it? I thought I had finally "arrived" when I was an assistant professor at a top 10 medical school. I felt confident, overconfident in fact, on the day that my department chair entered my office for my tenth annual review. As he flipped through my academic file, he reviewed my grant funding and publications. He looked up and said: "What the heck have you been doing?" I felt my jaw inadvertently drop.

"What have I been doing? All I've been doing is working!" I replied in utter shock as I thought about how I had been working seven days a week, evenings, and weekends. This was my dream and I had done, and would continue to do, whatever it took. I didn't even have a partner or a family because all of my focus had been on my career.

"Well, you need more grant funding and more publications. You have to at least double your output, or you're not going to survive."

And there was truth to what he was saying, but at what cost? And for what? I felt that somehow, I had lost my way. Why was I constantly striving to meet what felt like an ever-rising bar of an academic institution? I was doing research that was intellectually stimulating, I loved teaching, and my colleagues were some of the best in their field and incredibly supportive. Yet, for some reason it felt like I wasn't where I wanted to be. I felt off-purpose and out of alignment. It was terrifying given how much I had invested and all that was at stake in terms of my career.

I've always felt I had a purpose in life. I worked my entire life to try to achieve it, over 20 years in higher education to get a PhD in biomedical engineering so that I could help impact people's lives in a positive way. I even did research with NASA, which enabled me to go on a microgravity research flight, or "the vomit comet," which was certainly the opportunity of a lifetime! I accumulated a laundry list of accolades, honors, and awards. Yeah, I know what you're thinking: "OK, I get it. You're smart. Big deal." But you would be missing the point.

The point is the underlying thread that pulled me on that path was my life purpose. My driving force was that for each step of the way, I would be one step closer to fulfilling my purpose in life. If I could just become valedictorian at my high school, then I could get a scholarship for college. If I could just get good grades at my undergraduate university, then I could get a graduate school fellowship to a reputable university, and so on. One of my last big hurdles while climbing the academic ladder was if I could just get that big grant, then I will be promoted to assistant professor and can do biomedical research with clinical applications that have the potential to actually improve other people's lives. Not to mention I could also teach medical students and hopefully enrich their lives. Maybe I could actually make a positive impact.

Oh the blood, the sweat, and the tears. The times I almost quit because I just didn't know if it was worth all the sacrifice. Yet, I stayed the course because something bigger than me was pulling me forward. I knew, no matter what, that I wanted to help people in some way, to make a difference and make the world a better place. I knew deep down that all the sacrifice was worth it.

And yet, the institution I had so identified my life purpose with said it's not enough. Suddenly I was in a whirlwind. I felt uprooted from my path and bewildered by this unexpected crossroad. How could this be happening to me? His remarks made me doubt that I should even be there despite the fact that I had sacrificed ALL. I confided my feelings with a few people, who thought I had lost my mind for even considering leaving my position. From an outsider's perspective, I had a dream job and I was about to throw it away. I felt so lost—like I had made a mistake and somehow managed to go down the wrong life path. I was so driven up to this point because I felt it was my life purpose. Perhaps I went down that path before I really knew who I was and what my life purpose was. Regardless, I knew I had to make a decision.

Was I really going to abandon my formal education? I ignored the voice in my head for a while until it got louder and louder. I reprimanded myself: *Stop this nonsense! Don't be ridiculous! You can't throw away over twenty years of education and hard work! If you leave, you won't be able to come back! You're probably just having a midlife crisis. Don't screw this up.*

At rock bottom I asked myself: *In five to ten years from now, will I regret it if I don't leave academia to try to figure out what my life purpose is and live it to the best of my ability?* My answer was: *YES, absolutely! I would most certainly regret it.* So I left academia to become an entrepreneur. I struggled for over two years trying to unveil my life purpose and figure out what to do next. I wasn't making any money and I had drained all of my savings. I floundered doing the wrong things for my business and lacked direction. I lost thousands of dollars and fell flat on my face. I desperately wanted clarity about my life purpose and abundance in my life, which for me meant more happiness, fulfillment, and being able to support myself financially doing work aligned with my life purpose.

Why do I tell you all of this? Because maybe you're at a similar transition in life and can identify. Maybe your story has different circumstances, but has the same underlying thread of the search for meaning in life. I also tell you my story so you can understand my impetus for exploring what life purpose really meant for me. As a result of my search for meaning, I learned several tools to discover my life purpose and live a purpose-driven, spiritually fulfilling life. What I discovered has become the content for this book chapter. I hope it serves you as well as it has served me.

2. What is Dharma?

"Why am I here?" is probably one of the most common questions that we all face. I believe everyone has a purpose in life, a unique gift to give to others. You manifest in physical body to fulfill a life purpose only you can complete—your Dharma. The Sanskrit word *Dharma* comes from the root *dhr*, has a meaning of "to hold, maintain, keep." The word *Dharma* originates from the ancient Vedic religion. Its meaning has and continues to evolve.

Dharma has many definitions and is different depending on whom you ask. For Buddhists, Dharma means "cosmic law and order," and applies to the teachings of the Buddha. For Hindus, Dharma is the "right way of living," which is characterized by conduct, duties, laws, rights, and virtues. Jains refer to the teachings of tirthankara (Jina) and view Dharma as the path of purification and moral transformation. For Sikhs, the word *dharm* means "the path of righteousness and practicing religion." For me, someone who considers herself spiritual but doesn't practice a specific religion, I loosely define Dharma as "life or soul purpose," although it really is so much more.

Dharma brings you purpose, happiness, and fulfillment. It is the reason you feel a "pull," or a calling, to do something bigger than yourself. It is the drive that you feel deep within to make the world a better place, make a positive impact, or leave a legacy. It is that voice that keeps insisting you leave the 9-to-5, soul-sucking job that leaves you unhappy and unfulfilled. That said, although Dharma may be fulfilled through your job or career, it can be something else entirely.

3. Why Does Dharma Matter?

I believe, first and foremost, that discovering your Dharma matters because it gives you clarity—a crystal clear vision for a purpose-driven, spiritually fulfilling life. It is the global positioning system (GPS) that provides direction when you feel lost. It helps you make decisions when you come to a fork in the road of your life path and can't decide which way to turn. It provides the impetus and gives you the drive needed to take steps forward when you feel you can't go on. When you take a bad fall, it helps you get up, dust off your knees, and keep going.

I believe that once you step into the flow of your Dharma, the Universe co-conspires with you however it can to help you make it happen. Life supports you in ways you never expected. Opportunities present themselves to direct you on your path. Doors of opportunity open and you have that deep knowing that you should just walk through even though you may not know exactly where it may lead.

4. The Ikigai Venn Diagram

The basis or starting point for discovering your Dharma is *ikigai*, defined as:

> ***ikigai*** *(n.): A Japanese concept meaning "reason for being," to enjoy the meaning of life, passion, purpose, something one lives for.*

Finding your ikigai sounds simple but in actuality it isn't always easy, and often requires a deep journey into one's self. A tool that I have found useful for discovering your ikigai is often represented using a Venn diagram. As shown in Figure 1, to find your ikigai you should consider four things: what you love, what you are good at, what the world needs, and what you can get paid for. The intersection of what you love and what you're good at is your passion, what you love and what the world needs is your mission, what you're good at and what you can be paid for is your profession, and what the world needs and what you can be paid for is your vocation. The sweet spot where you most want to be is your ikigai, in the intersection of the four circles, or where they overlap. In this chapter, I utilize this concept of ikigai as a starting point and expand it to create a model for my view of Dharma.

[*continued next page*]

Figure 1: To find your ikigai, or "reason for being," find the overlap of what you love, what you are good at, what the world needs, and what you can be paid for.

5. Dharma: The Lotus Flower Model

What resonates for me when I consider life purpose is the concept of Dharma. I have been inspired to take the older concepts from Indian religions and expand it for a modern interpretation. First and foremost, I believe the core of our Dharma, loosely defined as "life purpose," is made up by the energies that we want to experience in this lifetime. The energies can be emotions, sensations, or states. This is where we should begin when it comes to discovering our Dharma, since without knowledge of our Dharma core energies, we may lack clarity and feel off-purpose. I believe our Dharma core energies are the foundation for discovering and living our Dharma. Anyone can start at this core and gain some clarity about why they are here. I love this quote by author and inspirational speaker

Mastin Kipp:

Your purpose is an emotion that you cultivate within yourself and then give away to others

These Dharma core energies are your unique energy blueprint that you are meant to experience and express in this lifetime, which is achieved by cultivating them within yourself and sharing them with others using a vehicle, defined as something used to express, embody, or fulfill something (more on this later!).

The ikigai Venn diagram is certainly an illuminating and useful tool for self-exploration, nevertheless I propose to expand it to allow for an even deeper journey into one's self and self-realization. I created a tool for discovering your Dharma by taking the ikigai Venn diagram concept, expanding it, and using the concept of a lotus flower. I chose it because the lotus flower represents rebirth and spiritual awakening. At night, it closes its petals and sinks into pond water. Over a three-day period, the lotus flower slowly emerges from the pond and then blooms over the course of the day, which I believe is a beautiful representation of spiritual awakening and discovering your Dharma.

For the lotus flower model of Dharma (Figure 2), we start with the center, which represents our Dharma core energies. I believe these stay consistent throughout your lifetime, although you may be more tuned in to some more than others during various phases of your life. There are eight petals, which represent the vehicle through which you cultivate these energies within yourself and share them with others. The exact nature of the vehicle can be dynamic, as oftentimes there are many careers, projects, types of volunteer work, hobbies, and so on, that can serve as your Dharma vehicle effectively. The unique energetic blueprint of your Dharma core energies remains consistent throughout your lifetime, however, the exact nature through which you share them may change. Luckily you don't have to worry too much about what the vehicle is per se, as long as it cultivates the Dharma core energies you are meant to experience during this lifetime, although some vehicles may be more aligned than others.

To clarify this concept further, I like to use the example of Oprah.

She is the same energetic blueprint no matter how or where you experience her. She might use different vehicles to share her energetic blueprint to you as a talk show host on television, writer of articles in her magazine, or blogger online. Regardless of how she shares her energetic blueprint with you, she is still Oprah.

In the lotus flower model I have retained the four elements of ikigai: what you love (Love), what you are good at (Talents), what the world needs (Contribution), and what you can get paid for (Valuable). I have also expanded it to include four other characteristics that I believe are important for your Dharma: you're well qualified (Experience), you feel called to do it (Duty), you feel fear/discomfort (Resistance), and it's according to Divine plan (Surrender). The four elements of ikigai can seem simple and straightforward, but it isn't always easy to figure out for yourself, so I've included some questions to hopefully help you gain clarity.

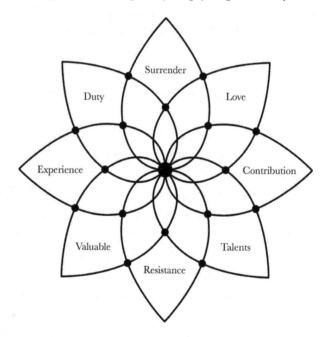

Figure 2: The lotus flower model of Dharma. The center of the lotus flower represents the foundation of your Dharma, or your Dharma core energies. The petals are the vehicle through which you cultivate your Dharma core energies within yourself and share them with others.

5.1 What you love (Love)

The first question about your Dharma vehicle is, what do you love? The answers should be huge motivators in your life. What sorts of things would you do if you had all the money and time in the world, could do whatever you wanted, and could follow your heart? What falls into this petal of the lotus flower brings you great joy and you gravitate toward it. What do you love doing more than anything, so much that you would do it for free? What gives you utmost joy and pleasure? What do you love doing so much that it makes you feel alive?

5.2 What you are good at (Talents)

Identifying all that you're good at can actually be tricky to figure out because some things come so easily that we think it must come easily for others too (and therefore it isn't a unique talent). That said, perhaps there are things that you know you're naturally good at based on your experiences with school, like perhaps you already know you're good at math, science, or writing. Or maybe you're really talented at something nonacademic, like helping friends solve their personal problems. Or you're super resourceful and are able to figure out a solution to a problem when it seems there isn't a way. Or perhaps you have a natural knack for business. Nevertheless, what are you amazing at? What unique skills do you have that come most naturally to you? What do your family and friends often ask you for help with? What talents have you cultivated in your life?

5.3 What the world needs (Contribution)

What does the world need from you? Finding the answer to this question can be more difficult. How can you help others in a way that will make the world a better place? What cause resonates most for you? What do you feel inspired to do here on Earth? What are your core values and beliefs? What would you give your life for? If you created a movement, what would it be about? What breaks your heart or gives you a heavy pit in the bottom of your stomach? What change would you most love to create in the world?

5.4 What you can get paid for (Valuable)

The answer to this question is the most practical, particularly in to-day's world, and can be a profession or vocation but not necessarily. Yet, money is simply energy, and represents the value of your product, service, or solution that you provide for the world. What can you get paid for? If you're struggling to find the answer for yourself, the answer to this question is simply a matter of determining what you can offer that is of value. What do others find valuable about you or what you can do? What would people pay you for? What pain point(s) can you solve for others? What benefit(s) can you provide?

5.5 What you're well qualified to do (Experience)

We all go through things in life that can bring great suffering (abu-sive family life, bad breakup, disability, etc.). Oftentimes this is related to our Dharma, since we can use what we learned from the experience to help others who are going through something similar. Helping others is not only rewarding in an altruistic sense, it can also aid your own healing by bringing meaning to your suffering. To clarify this further by example, it is the woman who had an abusive parent and unhealthy romantic relation-ships throughout her life that grows up to become a love and relationship coach. It is the man whose childhood was stolen from him because of too many adult responsibilities at a young age that grows up to cultivate fun, positivity, and playfulness in the lives of children.

The hidden beauty of this petal is that the difficult, sometimes even traumatic, experiences from your life are truly life's biggest gifts as they are your greatest lessons that equip and inspire you to live your Dharma. What life experiences have you had that you learned your biggest lessons from? What has happened in your life that caused you to grow the most as a person? What have you experienced that may have been challenging, difficult, or even traumatic?

5.6 What you feel called to do (Duty)

Dharma is actually defined as duty, as it comes from the Sanskrit root *dhr*, which means "to hold, maintain, keep." Dharma is what we were put on this earth to do for our soul's evolution and to support the Universe. This is the reason we feel a "pull," or a "calling," to do something greater than ourselves. What do you feel most called to do in this lifetime? What do you feel a sense of obligation to do? If you died tomorrow, what you most regret not doing as part of your Dharma to contribute to the better of society and the Universe? Once discovered, our Dharma is something we feel we absolutely must do during this lifetime. We must use our unique gifts to serve others and live our Dharma. It is not only our destiny; it is our duty.

5.7 What makes you feel fear/discomfort (Resistance)

What do you feel you most want to do as part of your Dharma, but at the same time it terrifies you? What brings up fear, discomfort, and limiting beliefs when you think about it? What have you perhaps always known you should do, but you procrastinate or find excuses not to start or move forward on that path?

Oftentimes we want to live our Dharma and a purpose-driven, spiritually fulfilling life more than anything. It is often exciting and inspiring, yet at the same time it terrifies us. Fears and limiting beliefs or thoughts set in. Inside our head, we might say to ourselves: *Who am I to live a life of my dreams? What if I fail? What if I succeed? What if I'm not good enough? I'm safer and more comfortable just continuing life as-is. I shouldn't rock the boat since who knows what fill-in-the blank catastrophes could happen.* Change, even when it is positive change, can be stressful and uncomfortable. Many of these fears, discomfort, and limiting beliefs can creep in when it comes to taking a big leap, or sometimes even just a step, toward our life purpose.

As a result, resistance or self-sabotage kicks in. Resistance can manifest itself in a multitude of ways, some of which are hidden or unrecognizable, keeping us stuck and not living our Dharma. Procrastination, limiting beliefs (not enough money, time, talent, etc.), self (lack of confidence, negative self-talk), self-medication (alcohol and drugs), disorders (anxiety, depression, etc.), diseases (cancer, ulcers, etc.), and getting into trouble (road rage, crime, etc.) can all be forms of resistance. I believe Steven Pressfield, American author who writes about the creative process, said it best in *The*

War of Art, stating:

> Look in your own heart…right now a still, small voice is
> telling you…the calling that is yours and yours alone…
> And you're no closer to taking action on it than you were
> yesterday or will be tomorrow. You think Resistance isn't
> real? Resistance will bury you.

Steven goes on to say that common activities that create resistance include but aren't limited to creative endeavors, entrepreneurial ventures, improving your health or spirituality, education, acts of political, moral, or ethical courage, undertakings aiming to help others, acts that require heart commitment, or taking of a principled stand in the face of adversity. Perhaps you already see that many of these endeavors are an integral part of living our Dharma. It's no wonder why we have such a hard time pursuing a purpose-driven life!

As if self-sabotage wasn't enough, resistance can also manifest in others: your family, your friends, your colleagues, your confidantes. Even those you think are there to support you and propel you toward success. Ever seen crabs in a bucket? Whenever one crab crawls on the backs of the others to escape the bucket, the other crabs pull it back down so it can't escape. The same phenomenon happens with us humans. For example, when an artist begins to overcome her resistance and create her art, she may find others begin to resist her progress, saying she is "changing," or "isn't the person she was," or other things to dissuade her from progress. The reason is often because they are struggling against their own resistance. Watching the artist overcome her resistance is simply too painful when they are unable to overcome their own. Human nature, unfortunately, is to pull each other back to mediocrity. So we must be vigilant when it comes to guarding our dreams against resistance not only within ourselves, but also within others. Be careful with whom you share your dreams and aspirations with, especially when your vision is in an early, fragile stage!

There is good news though—a light at the end of this dark tunnel of resistance. Resistance is like a compass that points us in the exact direction we need to go. The more resistance you feel toward pursuing a particular "calling," the more important that calling is to your Dharma, or your soul's evolution. Joseph Campbell most famously said:

Follow your bliss.

I would like to humbly add on to the quote...

Follow your bliss...and your RESISTANCE!

5.8 What is according to Divine plan (Surrender)

Dharma is that which supports the Universe and is according to Divine plan; with Divine being an umbrella term to represent whatever higher power you may believe in. Dharma urges you to connect with the Divine for direction and surrender to Divine plan, since its very meaning is that which supports the Universe. Your Dharma is your reason for being, your Divine soul mission in this lifetime. I believe Divine is within us all and you are an agent of the Divine in your daily life. You have been given unique gifts from the Divine to fulfill your Dharma in a way that only you can.

By following Divine plan, you are able to access messages that stem from the Divine, whether that is through angels, guides, Higher Self, intuition, or even directly from Spirit. Receiving Divine guidance involves getting present and using any or all of your senses to receive messages, which may start most simply as a whispering voice of intuition where your inner wisdom lies. In doing so, you may begin to notice messages in different forms all around you that give you guidance on a daily basis. This Divine guidance is incredibly helpful for keeping us on path for a purpose-driven life, to direct us when we don't know what lies ahead.

Once we've opened ourselves to receiving Divine messages, the next step involves trusting those messages and to surrender. If you can release the idea that you must be in control, you can access Divine flow and experience incredible synchronicities that direct you along your path. Moreover, I believe you'll find that life is even more phenomenal and spiritually fulfilling. For example, I often pray or manifest things by ending with the phrase "this or something better," to ask for what I most desire, but then I release attachment to that particular outcome. The Divine knows us better than we know ourselves, and often has something even better than our wildest dreams in mind. Oftentimes, we may feel we need to know every step of the path. However, some of the most extraordinary, successful people create a vision for their life, take a leap, trust, and surrender. They take a step forward even when they don't know the "how" or every step along the path.

When you access Divine guidance, what does it tell you about your Dharma? What does your intuition or gut tell you that you should be doing as part of your Dharma in accordance with Divine plan? In what direction has the Divine or Universe been directing you to go? Can you surrender control and trust that there is a Divine plan for your Dharma, which will serve your highest good?

6. How to discover your Divine Dharma

The first step to discovering your Dharma is to identify your Dharma core energies. Perhaps the best way to determine these is through a guided visualization that aims to turn off the rational mind, drop into the heart, and receive messages directly from Higher Self. However, for the purpose of you discovering your Dharma core energies right here, right now, I invite you to explore the following and write down your answers in a journal:

- Close your eyes and visualize your three or four happiest memories from your child, teen, and adult years. Who were you with? What were you doing? When was it? Where were you? How did you feel? What emotions did you experience? What adjectives best describe those experiences?

- How you want to feel when you're living your Dharma?

- How do you want others to feel when you're living your Dharma

- Who do you most admire and why? What characteristics do they have?

This is a brainstorming exercise, so simply write down everything on paper that comes to mind without reservation or criticism of any kind. Allow it to be a full brain dump. After you're finished, make a list of the emotions, adjectives, and characteristics, and eliminate any that don't fully resonate. To narrow down even further, consider words that have similar meanings or energetic vibrations, choose the one that resonates more for you, then eliminate the other. Finally, let's narrow it down to your top three to five words. Start at the first word and compare it to the second word. Which resonates more? Choose the one that resonates more between the first two and compare to the third word, which resonates more? Go all the way down the list in this fashion until you find your #1 word and make a note of it. Cross your #1 word off the list and repeat the process to identify your #2 word. Repeat until you have your top three to five words. These are your Dharma core energies, which you most want to experience in this lifetime. These are the energies you most crave to cultivate in your own life and share with others. Fill in the blanks below with your top three to five energies and say to yourself out loud:

I was born to cultivate ___ , ___ , and ___ within myself and others.

This is the core of your Dharma. When you read it, it should resonate deep within and feel like you've come home!

In order to identify a vehicle for cultivating your Dharma core energies within yourself and sharing them with others, revisit sections 5.1 to 5.8. Write down answers to all the questions explored in each section. If you have trouble finding the answers, ask your crew from higher up to give you some insight. Set an intention to receive the answers you need for your Dharma then go outside in nature, meditate, practice yoga, or do whatever gets you present and allows you to receive Divine guidance. Write everything down in a journal so that you can revisit it when you feel you've lost your way. As mentioned previously, your Dharma vehicle may be dynamic, so it is important to stay open to receiving Divine guidance on a regular basis. Once you've written down answers to the eight characteristics of your Dharma vehicle, consider the intersection of all eight. What can you do to cultivate and experience your Dharma core energies that embodies these eight characteristics? This may not necessarily be the one and only, black-and-white answer for your life purpose; however, it is intended to be a starting point for self-exploration and discovery. My hope is that it will give you more clarity about your Dharma than you had before you read this chapter.

7. Conclusion

In summary, I invite you to revisit the questions throughout this chapter and use it to gain more clarity about your Divine Dharma. Start by identifying your Dharma core energies. Once you feel crystal clear about which energies resonate most, explore potential Dharma vehicle(s) by characterizing the petals of your lotus flower. Consider what you love (Love), what you are good at (Talents), what the world needs (Contribution), what you can get paid for (Valuable), what you're well qualified to do (Experience), what you feel called to do (Duty), what makes you feel fear/discomfort (Resistance), and what is according to Divine plan (Surrender). Once you discover your Divine Dharma, use it to create a vision for your life that can be used to make decisions when you come to a fork in the road. Simply refer back to your lotus flower and ask yourself which path: 1) allows you to cultivate your Dharma core energies within yourself and share them with others, and 2) has the characteristics of your eight lotus flower petals. I encourage you to then take the steps necessary to follow that path and create your purpose-driven, spiritually fulfilling life. I can attest to the fact that it is certainly worth the effort as the benefits are beyond measure. I'll conclude with this beautiful quote from the Chopra Center:

> *When you live in the harmonious flow of Dharma, the entire field of pure potentiality opens to you. You're able to create as much happiness and wealth as you want because you're aligned with the domain of Spirit, the unlimited source of all manifestation.*

Chapter 16

YOUR PURPOSE EXPEDITION

Brandon Peele

"I'm getting a divorce," said Ariel.

"Wow. Tell me more," I said with trepidation, as many of my clients want to make radical life changes during their purpose expedition.

Ariel was only six weeks into her journey with me. Like so many of my clients, she came to me with the desire to find a job she loves. And as soon as she started to inquire into the broader purpose of her life, however, she saw that it wasn't just her job that needed to change. She discovered that her marriage didn't serve her and that neither she nor her husband really had the will to make it work. She also saw how disconnected and isolated she was from people, and she came face to face with her lack of self-confidence, and her muted desires to start her own healing center, and to be creatively self-expressed.

She continued, "We love each other, but this relationship has run its course, and my husband agrees. We are both ready for something new."

Of course, I cautioned her not to make any bold decisions before her purpose discovery work was over. However, her growing sense of purpose awareness, and her having overcome many of the obstacles that previously kept her quiet, inert, and disconnected from others, empowered her to take bold purpose-aligned actions. As much as I might have wanted to, it wasn't for me to stop her. She was on fire and wasn't going to play small any more. Over the course of the four months of work together, she:

1. Amicably left her husband.

2. Quit her job.

3. Took a month off.

4. Found a new job with a better work environment and fewer hours.

5. Moved out of her house, and found a new place to live in the hills, overlooking the San Francisco Bay.

6. Took a big risk and shared with a friend her romantic feelings for him.

7. Joined two meditation communities and made new friends.

Not every one of my clients has such a dramatic number of life changes occur during this work. Most folks slowly deepen into the discovery experience and take a few months after our work together to make just one of these big purpose-aligned changes, like quitting smoking, changing jobs, finding love, or launching a purpose-driven venture or project. You might be asking, what is it exactly inside of the discovery process that gives people access to the clarity, confidence, and power to make these big changes?

Your Purpose Expedition

Although every human is unique, most (but not all) purpose discovery journeys follow a similar pattern. An apt metaphor to describe the process is crossing a chasm—moving from one place of stability to another. Your life as it is now and your life fully lit up by purpose are separated by a space that is unknown, complete with hidden obstacles and the exciting possibility that new, even-more-desirable destinations may reveal themselves after you begin your expedition. As Ariel did not know her love life was going to go in another direction, your journey may surprise, challenge, and delight you as well.

On any expedition into the unknown, you have to summon your courage and willingness to make necessary sacrifices, to leave behind that which does not serve you. You'll need your resources, wonder, curiosity, and, if you have it, your faith in yourself and/or your creator.

In short, your life with purpose present will be a new way of life, not an incremental improvement, but literally a new way of being and operating on purpose in each of the key areas of your life (health, romance, family, career, community, finances, and spirituality) that greatly expands your fulfillment, impact, joy, connection, and success.

To make the journey from your current way of being (your current connection to purpose or lack thereof) to your new life expressed by your high-resolution life purpose, a couple of things are required.

First, you have to know that the journey is possible. It has to exist as a real and worthwhile undertaking. Usually this means that at least one person you trust has said that the journey exists and that it is worth it. Reading books like this or connecting with a trained Guide or someone who is on the journey can be extremely helpful in clarifying your understanding of what purpose is, why you should connect with it, how to find it, how it will show up in your life, and whether or not now is the time for your journey.

Secondly, you have to be in possession of two important pieces of information. You must know that 1) your current way of being no longer suits you, and 2) that even if you don't know what it is, you have a bigger game to play in life, a game you can no longer ignore. You must get present to the physical, social, emotional, spiritual, ecological, and economic impacts of being disconnected from your life's purpose. You must also feel, trust, or perceive that finding, living, and leading with your purpose will empower you to play that bigger game.

Once you are clear on the possibility of the journey, as well as the chasm between your current way of a being and your future life on purpose, you are ready to begin your purpose expedition.

Step One - Preparation

You cannot do this alone, so you'll need a trained Guide, proven purpose discovery program to follow, or a group of wise and mature friends who share a commitment to helping you find your purpose. By establishing a solid structure, you will markedly improve your odds of success on the journey and the chances that you will move through each of the parts of your journey with as little confusion, pain, and resistance as possible.

Although it is highly likely that you will discover new horizons and destinations after you begin the journey, you've got to get clear on why you're leaving home in the first place, what the current impacts on yourself and others might be if you stay put, and what the your-life-on-purpose could look like. Odds are that you have a good sense of why you want to find, live, and lead with your purpose (live a longer life, make more money, have deeper relationships, create a better world; research here: http://ScienceOfPurpose.org), but it is up to you what new future you want to put at stake in this adventure.

It will be up to you (and your trained Guide, if you have one) to determine if now is the right time for the journey. Although the impacts of living disconnected from your purpose are no longer acceptable, you must first establish that your life, although unfulfilling, is indeed stable.

Oftentimes folks try to embark upon the purpose journey from a less than stable place. Signs that your current place is unstable might be: you cannot meet your monthly expenses, you indulge in overwork, you are psychologically unstable, you have dysfunction in your home, or you have addictions or other health crises. If any of these are present, your purpose journey is going to be difficult, if not impossible. Beginning your journey with any of these conditions present would be like forgetting to pack or renewing your passport. You have to make sure your current life is stable, so that you are ready to leave it.

To ensure your success, it is important to begin with a baseline of economic, social, psychological, and physical stability by completing the **Systems Check** (see below):

◊ **BIOLOGICAL SYSTEM CHECK:** I am in good health and/or am in action with my known health issues.

> o **If not,** begin a regimen to get in shape, join a gym, see a nutritionist, or see a doctor.

◊ **ECONOMIC SYSTEM CHECK 1.1**: I am able to meet my monthly expenses and feel confident that I will continue to be able to do so for at least the next six months.

> o **If not,** increase your hours or get a job that pays more.

◊ **ECONOMIC SYSTEM CHECK 1.2:** I work and commute fewer than 50 hours a week combined.

> o **If not,** reduce your hours or get another job that allows you to earn a living with less than 50 hours of combined work and commute time and leave your work at work. If this is not possible, then ensure that you are not sacrificing your health or important relationships by taking on your purpose discovery at this time.

◊ **PSYCHOLOGICAL SYSTEM CHECK 1.1:** My home is a peaceful place that allows me to attend to my needs for a good night's rest, physical safety, and downtime.

> o **If not,** create or move to a place that allows for this.

◊ **PSYCHOLOGICAL SYSTEM CHECK 1.2:** I am free from any debilitating addictions, such as drugs, alcohol, gaming, gambling.

> o **If not,** get into a recovery program.

◊ **PSYCHOLOGICAL SYSTEM CHECK 1.3:** I accept and love the people I live with and/or see frequently, such as my romantic partner (if I have one), family.

> o **If not,** get into marriage and family therapy, get psychotherapy, attend a personal development weekend, or sit in a regular men's or women's circle, such as ManKind Project's New Warrior Training Adventure/men's circles or the Woman Within Weekend/women's circles.

Together, these conditions constitute a complete Systems Check, a stable place from which to begin your purpose expedition. Buckle up!

Step Two - The Search

The search refers to the initial phase of purpose discovery, wherein you gain greater clarity on your vision, your optimal states of being, what most fulfills you and how you impact others already. During this phase, you'll do exercises that will uncover hidden pieces of your life's purpose. You'll discover how you show up for people, what you do that already makes a huge impact, and how your life would look if, from this point forward, you lived it mightily and on fire with your life's purpose. You'll use this intelligence to refine your navigation as your expedition continues.

As with any search, initially it will at times be rich and exhilarating, and at other times scary and shaky. You'll waiver. The further you get from home, the more you'll doubt how smart your decision was to go on this expedition. You'll question whether this is what the expedition should feel like. This is normal.

As your new life of purpose begins to come into view, you'll get confronted by it, doubt it, and even try to kill it. This is your resistance—the old ways of being and doing that historically kill off possibility, that take you away from living your life's purpose and have you head back home to safety. Collectively, this is The Trials of your expedition.

Step Three - The Trials

The Trials is a gauntlet of obstacles to living your life on purpose. It is your resistance. It is function of your ego, your personality structure. The function of your resistance is to contain your expression and exploration by convincing you to go back home and play it safe. This is the part of the journey during which you will rely most heavily on your structure— your trained Guide, purpose discovery program, community, or circle of wise friends.

Rather than turning back, rather than cowering from the discomfort of the unknown, of growth, purpose, and the beyond, you will head straight into The Trials. You will work with every voice of resistance, each flavor of the message "Stop this nonsense. You have it good. Go back home." You'll meet, among others, your Critic, Skeptic, Image Consultant, Wounded Child, and Risk Manager (Tim Kelley, *True Purpose*, 2009). Much like any hazard on an expedition, you'll learn about it, you'll discover its contours and its behaviors. You'll learn each voice's origin story, needs, and constraints, and begin to transform these voices into allies on your journey.

The process that Tim and his colleagues at the True Purpose Institute pioneered involves a permanent psychological reconstruction around one's soul/purpose. Tim's process is based on the Voice Dialogue Method (Hal and Sidra Stone, *Embracing Ourselves*, 1989), and resonates with other methodologies offer by Richard Schwartz, PhD (*Internal Family Systems Model*, Schwartz, 1995) and Roberto Assagioli (*Psychosynthesis*, Assagioli, 1965). This process entails deconstructing your ego into its multiple parts. By parsing the ego in this manner, you clear the space for new soul/purpose information to arise. Doing so opens the channel for new information from your soul to surface.

It bears mentioning that your ego is not wrong or bad. It serves a vital function. Your ego is the felt sense that you know who you are, what your name is, what you did yesterday, how you feel about things, and so on. And yet you also have a deeper identity, one that generally lies beyond this immediate ego awareness, beyond your resistance. I refer to this deeper identity this as your soul—a felt sense of truth, openness, imagination, creativity, expansiveness, and unity. Atheists might call this deeper truth or higher self or intuition or flow state. For the sake of simplicity, let's refer to the soul as that part of you that knows your life's purpose (Kelley, *True Purpose*, 2009).

Once you discover and understand the resistance offered by of your ego parts, you'll be clear on the internal narratives and limiting beliefs that have historically stopped you. By navigating The Trials, you will understand your ego and establish the solid and secure foundation required for exploring the unknown. Beyond The Trials, you will be present to a vast field of purposeful possibilities. You will no longer be constrained by these voices or the fear of potentially running afoul of them. You will be free to take in this new vista and chart a new path.

Step Four - Revelation

With luck and grit, you will encounter the 10 aspects of your life's purpose—your core, virtues, vision, mission, story, flow, powers, worldview, craft, and the call (see the Purpose Tree below). You'll pick up the discovery phase of the expedition with a whole host of exercises designed to reveal the remaining hidden or cloudy aspects of your life's purpose. A new destination will be revealed. You'll be clear on your craft, your mentors, your path to mastery, what you will accomplish, how your purpose will move into the world, how you will purposefully interact, create, destroy, and sustain.

Looking back on The Trials and your old way of being, you'll see that you could go back, but you no longer need to. There's nothing for you there anymore. There is only forward, only steps toward your purpose or away from it.

Step Five - The Return

This is the integration phase of your purpose discovery journey. This is the phase where your high-resolution purpose awareness begins to settle into your tissues. This is the phase where you integrate your purpose into each core area of life—your health, love life, career, community, family, finances, and spirituality—and deal with the resistance to change that arises.

During this step, you'll take on creating a life on purpose, beginning with new soul-infused ego. This is a crucial step where you will have another look at each of your ego parts and incorporate the wisdom and self-knowledge you unearthed from navigating The Trials, your resistance. You will make new purpose-driven agreements with each part of your ego such that they are now the steward, agent, and benefactor of your soul's purpose. In essence, you will be developing a "new" you, consolidating what you've learned, going back over what you've discovered and grounding it.

Although you now are fully empowered to continue the purpose exploration, an endless exploration is no fun if it isn't punctuated by periods of repose and integration. Nobody says, "Hey, I want to live out of a suitcase indefinitely." At some point you'll want to pause, put down some roots, and begin to embody and integrate all that you have discovered and achieved. You'll want to celebrate the achievements of your discovery journey, enjoy them, play with them, integrate them, and make them your new normal—the new rules of your life of purpose.

This is where the rubber meets the road, where you will learn first-hand that the price of purpose is leadership, where you will confront what Shakespeare meant when he said in *Henry IV,* "heavy is the head that wears the crown." Purpose awareness is all fine and good, however what really makes the journey worthwhile, the reason why you started this journey, is that you now get to integrate and embody your purpose. You will show up differently, more wise, grounded and sovereign in your career, family, and community. You didn't start this journey to see nothing in the world shift or change. You wanted impact. You wanted results. You wanted to be known by your deeds.

With your ego and soul now more integrated, you can take on the soulful reformation of your life. With this psychic integrity established, your task is to take another hard look at each of your seven key life areas and upgrade them with your purpose. You'll ask, "How would my purpose enhance my fitness?" "What sort of love life is best expressed by my purpose?" "How can my family reach its purposeful expression?" "What is the purpose of my community and how can I evolve it?" "How does my purpose make, spend, and save money?" "What is the relationship between my purpose and my spiritual orientation?" You'll immediately see behaviors that no longer serve you and begin to create more purposeful behaviors and relationships. You'll make promises to people in your family, community, and workplace to take on new purposeful expressions—and you'll be held accountable to them.

Most importantly, during this phase you will also take on a Purpose Project, a discrete project that you will complete in 30 to 60 days. This project will have you enroll numerous people in your life, and many folks who you do not yet know, in completing your project. The result is that the world will begin relating to you as your purpose.

Additionally, the goal of this project is to give you the tactile, tangible experience of seeing how your soul's purpose meets the world, as well as the ways your inner resistance to living your purpose shows up. All of your inner voices will still arise. Your Critic will tell you it's not good enough. Your Skeptic will tell you it's not possible. Your Risk Manager will tell you that you have too much to lose to do the project and that you'll die poor. Your Image Consultant will tell you that you'll look foolish, everyone will leave you and you'll die not just poor, but alone, outcast, and living under a bridge. Your Wounded Child will tell you that it's better to play, avoid your purpose, and numb or zone out. All of these voices would otherwise end your purpose project. That is, unless you use the tools you acquired in Step Three. You'll be able to listen to these voices, examine their concerns, incorporate their valid insights, and continue to take purpose-aligned action toward the completion of your project.

With your Purpose Project complete, you'll have the beginning of a purposeful track record and the confidence and clarity to execute your next mission, and the next one, and so on, until your life, your career and the world becomes the full expression of your life's purpose. Your purpose is a profound achievement that takes commitment, effort and time. It is not all hard work, however. Each step along the path reveals more beautiful, rich, and complex textures in your life. Let's explore now what it feels like to find your purpose.

Purpose Definitions

To step into your higher purpose, you'll need a high-resolution view of it, something more rooted, true, and granular than a simple declared purpose. To fully explore the contours of your higher purpose, I offer The Purpose Tree, a navigational metaphor to unearth and connect all 10 aspects of your higher purpose.[1]

We will now consider the **Purpose Tree** (see below).

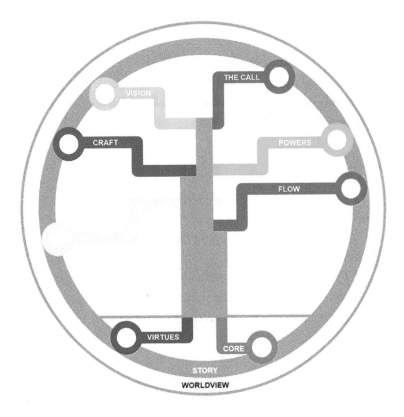

The 10 Aspects of Your Purpose:

◊ **The Call** – What most breaks your heart in the world, calling you to act;

◊ **Vision** – Your picture of the world perfected, pulling you into action;

◊ **Powers** – Your innate gifts, strengths, and talents;

◊ **Craft** – Your highest contribution, your unique way of transforming others, and achieving mastery;

◊ **Mission** – Your declaration to impact a group or dynamic in particular way and by when;

◊ **Flow** – Your most exhilarating, embodied activities resulting in loss of self-consciousness;

◊ **Virtues** – Your most cherished ideals and principles, what you are here to express and perfect, the ways of acting you want your life to be known for;

◊ **Core** – Your naturally radiating qualities;

◊ **Story** – The central themes and lessons you have learned in life;

◊ **Worldview** – Your understanding of how reality works and the manner in which your identity is located within it.

Dynamics:

◊ The Purpose Tree contains a vertical tension along the trunk, creating an upward pull of increasing energy and movement from above by The Call / Vision and generated from below by your Core / Virtues.

◊ The Purpose Tree also contains a creative vs. receptive horizontal tension. On the left are the more creative and ascendant aspects of purpose. On the right are the more receptive and inscendant[2] aspects.

The foundation of your purpose is the tree's root structure, containing the immovable, ever-present, unseen elements of your purpose, your deepest sense of identity as an individual (core and virtues). As the Tree ventures upward and the branches venture outward, you increasingly express the bold, active, and declarative parts of your purpose, how you answer the call, craft your vision, and focus your actions toward a desired impact. These are the unique ways your purpose interacts with, contributes to, enjoys and is rewarded by the world. All of these sit within your narrative of life (story) and your understanding of how the world works.

Endnotes

1. The Purpose Tree is a revised, re-visioned and augmented version of the Purpose Octagon™ created by the Founder of the Purpose Guides Institute, Jonathan Gustin. Jonathan was the first to offer a broad synthesis of eight aspects of soul and purpose (vision, values, core powers, essence, giveaway, task, message, delivery system) based on the work of Tim Kelley, Bill Plotkin, and his other influences. After being trained by him, I added a few other elements I believe are necessary to root purpose in the inescapable context of existence (worldview), to descend purpose into the body (flow) and emotions (call) and create a overarching life narrative (story)—and a navigational metaphor (tree) to relate and express them.

2. "Inscendant" is a word of Thomas Berry's describing the downward/inward movement of soul, more of a receptive, fractal embodiment of soul vs. the creative, ascendant, outward, mission/vision/craft aspects.

Chapter 17

MAKING CHANGE
How to Be an Agent of Transformation

Cassandra Vieten, PhD,
President, Institute of Noetic Sciences

Mica Estrada, PhD,
Assistant Professor, University of California, San Francisco;
Director, Climate Education Partners

Manifesting our global purpose often requires making change—in ourselves, our relationships, our families, neighborhoods, communities, and society. It's inspirational to see how the movement toward a global shift continues to grow and flourish, even in the face of substantial challenges and alarming societal regressions to less conscious ways of being. The worldwide grassroots movement toward higher human potential is undeniable, from the fresh insights of massive numbers of young people, to the elders who continue to hold the flame of hope steady.

Often however, the ways we attempt to make change are ineffective, which can leave us baffled, frustrated, bitter, or worn out. This is in part because the science of change—which spans the range from cognitive, social, behavioral, and neurosciences—does not always inform the actions at the front lines where activism is taking place. Over the last few months, we've launched a task force of scientists, media experts, designers, and advocates who are working together to create a set of knowledge, skills, and attitudes—based on theory and empirical evidence from the science of transformation—that will boost the power of change agents to be more successful in their efforts. Let's look at some of the foundational premises of this effort, and an initial set of powerful concepts/tools that will add some juice to your change-making ability.

The Limits of Information in Making Change

A common misunderstanding is that the best way to make change is to provide people with lots of information that supports what you want them to do differently. This "knowledge deficit model," developed by public attitudes researchers in the last part of the twentieth century, contends that if a little knowledge does not result in behavior change, then the answer is to provide even *more* data, evidence, and education. The idea is that public skepticism or lack of response to scientific findings about issues, such as climate change or health benefits of smoking cessation for example, is based on a lack of knowledge on the part of the public. Makes sense, right? The solution is then obvious—inform the public—transferring knowledge from experts to nonexperts, with the idea that once people fully understand the information their behavior will change. Most campaigns to shift public behavior are comprised primarily of information, education, or awareness-building. The vast majority of our resources go toward the distribution of information, even though information is only a small proportion of what changes people's behavior.

The problem is that information is only one element of what leads to changing beliefs and behaviors, and likely not the most important one. Culture, social norms, economics, upbringing and life experiences, religious and spiritual beliefs, stress levels and biological predispositions, implicit assumptions and biases, and many other factors influence what people believe and how they behave. And, interestingly, self-report data on why a person makes a new behavior choice often is in inaccurate, erring on the side of attributing the change to information, when this is empirically shown to be incorrect. In other words, people think they change when they receive new information, but they really change in response to a host of other factors.

As a change-maker, when you are given an hour to work with an audience, how often do you spend the majority of the hour delivering information to people? It's not strange that you are tempted to do this—in the age of reason, delivery of information has been thought to be the highest form of education. Indeed, most of us likely spent the vast majority of our classroom time throughout our education sitting in rows of desks, listening to teachers lecture, memorizing information from textbooks, and then taking written tests, or delivering oral or written reports, to show that we at least memorized if not comprehended the information we received. It only stands to reason that we tend to use these methods in our efforts to inform others. With technology, social media, and new styles of oration such as TED Talks, we can find more engaging ways to deliver information to people. But to succeed as change-makers, we must do so much more.

Motivation

When information fails, the next change-making approach many of us take is to try to *motivate* people. Motivation is a combination of 1) the reasons people have for doing something, and 2) the desire or willingness to take action. Think about the ways that you have tried to motivate yourself and other people to make changes in their thinking patterns and behavior—in particular, when you were *not* successful. What hasn't worked? Take a moment to write a list of all the ways you typically try to motivate yourself or others. Here are a few that came from participants of a recent workshop we conducted on this topic :

[*see Table next page*]

• Reason with them	• Guilt or shame	• Yell/raise your voice
• Argue your case	• Use graphic images	• Cry
• Cajole	• Scare them	• Withhold affection
• Badger	• Reward and punishment	• Seduce them
• Nag/Use repetition	• Appeal to their ego	• Enlist others against them/gossip
• Verbal sparring/debate	• Bargain	• Ridicule/Make fun of them privately or publicly
• Offer advice and tools	• Tell them they don't care enough	
• Live by example	• Roll your eyes, use body language	• Insult them
• Avoid the topic entirely	• Pout/sulk	• Call them names/stereotype them
• Use peer pressure	• Increase your verbal or physical intensity	• Threaten them
• Create top-down rules and policies	• Express your frustration	• Use physical violence
• Find ways to show how they are wrong		

These are the ways that most of us attempt to increase motivation in ourselves, other people, or societal groups. And many of these can be partially effective. Just as delivering information accounts for a small proportion of lasting change, these approaches to motivation represent another small proportion. The problem is that most of these methods either result in temporary changes, or they are actually counterproductive, resulting in backlash or increased defenses against new suggestions.

The truth is that making people feel bad doesn't make them change their minds. In fact, it can cause people to go into hiding, avoid the topic altogether, or redouble their defenses against future attacks to their current belief system. Making ourselves feel bad doesn't change our own behavior either, though our minds like to think it will. When you step back to consider it for a moment, it's not difficult to believe that barraging yourself or others with information, cajoling, nagging, bargaining, threatening, insulting, or carrot-and-stick approaches do not actually work to encourage long-term changes in how people think and behave. If only accurate information and a desire to change were enough, there would be few people with addictions or behavior-related health problems. But what is the alternative? If information and motivation are not at the root of making change, what is?

Worldview Transformation

If information is about 10 percent of behavior change, and motivation is another 10 percent, what is the remaining 80 percent? Our premise is that it is *worldview transformation*. Long-lasting changes in thinking patterns and behavior spring from foundational shifts in the way people view themselves, the world, and the relationship between themselves and the people, places, and things in their environment. These shifts happen through a natural process that we as change-makers can help to facilitate.

A series of studies at the Institute of Noetic Sciences (Vieten, Amorok, & Schlitz, 2006; Schlitz, Vieten, & Amorok, 2008) has examined how people make significant shifts in worldview that result in long-lasting changes in their thinking patterns and ways of being. For over a decade, we've investigated how people make fundamental shifts in the way they view themselves and their relationships to others and the world. By analyzing written stories of people's individual transformations, focus groups with transformational teachers from a variety of the world's wisdom traditions, in-depth interviews with over 60 masters and teachers who have taught thousands of students, surveys with thousands of people who have made major changes in their lives, and prospective studies following people over time who are engaged in transformative work, we've created a model of transformation that continues to evolve (see http://noetic.org/research/transformation-model). Put simply, our research indicates that there are four interrelated things you can do to foster change:

1. Create opportunities for people to have *direct, personal, and profound* experiences of seeing things in a new light;

2. Provide *scientific evidence* to support and expand the insights from those experiences;

3. Give people *practices, training, and tools* as scaffolding to support the new way of being in their everyday lives;

4. Connect people with *relationships and communities* that support the new way of being. Direct experience, scientific evidence, tools and applications, and community are four key elements to making change.

What we've learned from this work and from the work of other researchers engaged in this field is that **profound transformation in**

people's worldviews is possible under the right conditions, and that this is the foundation of true and lasting changes in thinking patterns and behaviors. In other words, changes in behavior spring from underlying changes in how people view themselves, the attitudes and perspectives they take toward other people and the world around them, and the ways they think in general about reality. This is how religions, spiritual traditions, modern transformative programs, and psychotherapeutic approaches work, each with their own strengths and limitations. The major limit of these programs is that they often require adherence to a particular belief system, set of teachings, or teacher/diety/guru. Our goal has been to develop a cross-traditional model of transformation that can be applied in a variety of contexts, spiritual or secular, to make change.

In short, people make changes in their behavior when they think differently about who they are and the way things are. For example, behavioral changes can arise from changes in how people view time (for example, being able to comprehend the impact of their actions into their own future or future generations), or how they view their connections with others (e.g., being moved by the plight of or impact of their actions on people who are far away, or those who are perceived as different—not the same as me or not a member of my "tribe"). Lasting changes in thinking patterns and behaviors come from seeing oneself and the world in a new way. So, the task of a change-maker is not to deliver new thinking patterns or behaviors directly to people, it's to help people see themselves and the world from a new perspective, and allow new thinking patterns and behaviors to arise from those changes.

Another model of behavioral transformation that relies on essential internal shifts springs from a number of studies on how people create and maintain new behaviors, such as behavioral responses to climate change in and among neighborhoods and policy-makers. Estrada and colleagues (2017) developed a model called the Tripartite Integration Model of Social Influence (TIMSI). The model indicates that the elements necessary for inspiring new behaviors include: the sense that they can do it (efficacy), the sense that the behaviors are consistent with their salient sense of self (identity), and the sense that the new behaviors are consistent with their personal values and the values of those groups that matter to them (values).

Self-efficacy (Bandura & Locke, 2003), or the belief that you actually can do something, has been shown to consistently predict long-term behavioral outcomes and changes in individual functioning across a wide array of domains. Knowing that people like you are also engaged in the new behavior you are working to adopt is also extremely powerful, but highly de-emphasized in our society that focuses on individualism, and routinely underestimates the impact of the social world. A simple example of this is a city that was attempting to encourage its residents to recycle. One set of advertising told people about the problem of plastic and encouraged them to recycle their plastic bottles. The other set of advertising invited residents to join the 75 percent of their neighbors who were already recycling. As you can imagine, the second set of ads were more effective in creating the change. Finally, when behaviors are in strong alignment with our internalized values (both conscious and not conscious), we are less likely to resist engaging in them. So again, to function as a more effective change agent, the majority of your work can focus on cultivating people's 1) identity as someone who acts in the new ways of being, 2) sense of efficacy that they can actually do what is being requested, and 3) identifying with the *values* of the community of people who are behaving in the new way.

Now, we are using findings like this and research from our colleagues around the world to create models and training programs for change-makers who want to enhance their effectiveness. Whether people are working as counselors, therapists, or coaches who support other people in making change, or societal change agents like politicians, activists, or leaders of NGOs, the same principles apply. While a comprehensive treatment of these concepts and tools is beyond the scope of this chapter, and is currently being developed into a book and training program, let's take a look at just a few principles that you can implement today to enhance your effectiveness as a change-maker. Some of these are common sense reminders that tend to elude us when we become passionate or emotional about creating change in something or someone. Others are unexpected, and even paradoxical. Our task force will be elucidating these in a book and a training program for change-makers in the coming year. Meanwhile, we hope that using some of these in your change-making work today will enhance your effectiveness right away.

Creating an Ecosystem of Change

Lasting changes in people's thinking patterns and ways of being and behaving most often spring from a shift in worldview or perspective. Those shifts in worldview and perspective occur within an entire *ecosystem of change*. Behaviors and the worldviews that give rise to them are developed over time in the context of a complex network of relationships between biology, cognitions, emotions, desires, beliefs, life experiences, assumptions, biases, and perspectives that are both explicit (you know about them) and implicit (outside of your conscious awareness). And that is all just *inside* of each person! Behaviors and worldviews are also strongly environmentally and socially mediated, meaning that they are dependent on what is happening in someone's environment (including such things as region, socioeconomic status, and access to food, shelter, and housing) and with whom they come into contact (friends, family, loved ones, acquaintances, communities, neighborhoods, spiritual communities, workplaces, and other societal structures), both over the lifespan and in each moment. No wonder our approaches to change-making must go far beyond simply providing information and stoking a desire to change!

Successful approaches to making change must be comprehensive—addressing multiple levels of people's lives both internally and externally. To affect the complex network of inner and outer systems that determine behavior requires a multipronged approach. You can translate this into practice as a change-maker. Even in the course of a one-hour presentation you can include messages, images, and experiential activities designed less to tell people what they should do and why, and more about helping them link the hoped-for behavioral shift to their preexisting worldviews, efficacy, identity, and values. Or, you can engage in activities that work to shift these to be more in alignment with the hoped-for behavioral shift. Begin to see each person or group you are addressing as an ecosystem rather than an individual. Rather than asking "How much information can I deliver in this one hour?"—ask yourself which aspects of this person or organization's ecosystem of change can be enrolled? As change-makers, we direct our energy toward creating as many of the ideal conditions as we can for the natural process of change to occur.

You've got to create an ecosystem of change. Creating conditions for the natural process of growth and change to occur is sort of like planting a garden—providing the right soil composition, nutrients, water, sunlight, and stakes in the ground, and monitoring each over time to determine which are most conducive to our plants to grow. If you want to make change, you can't address a single issue directly. Here are some ways to create an ecosystem of change:

Nothing Substitutes for Direct Experience

A comprehensive strategy to change your own behavior, or to change the behavior of others, must be deeply experiential. Having a direct experience is the most powerful way to shift someone's perspective. An old adage goes, you can tell someone about what it is like to eat an orange all day long, or you can simply give them an orange to eat. When teaching people about pollution in the oceans, see if you can get them into a boat to witness it for themselves. If you are attempting to increase health through improved nutrition, a visit to a farm to harvest vegetables, a cooking class to prepare them, and a shared meal is much more powerful than a list of nutritional dos and don'ts.

When you can't get people out of their chairs, at times guided visualization can be a good substitute for in-person experiences. Also, the emerging technologies of virtual and augmented reality can effectively "trick" the mind into having a very compelling direct experience. For example, a virtual reality application that introduced students to their elderly selves (by taking their pictures, age-advancing them digitally, and then placing the person face-to-face with their future self in an immersive virtual reality environment), increased their willingness to save for retirement (Hershfield et al., 2014). In effect, this experience shifted their perspective on time, making later monetary rewards more salient in the present.

Direct experiences should engage as many of the senses as possible, be provided in an environment of safety and consent (both ethically, and so that people are willing to be vulnerable and let down their defenses a bit), and ideally, be repeated. Direct experiences that are too threatening or dangerous can backfire, stunning people into denial or dismissal of the event as an anomaly, or increasing their defenses.

Even something as simple as asking an audience to share with a partner or a trio can bring a level of direct experience to a conversation that is quite powerful, and also includes the social dimension. Whatever is feasible, be sure to make each set of strategies you create for the change you are working toward include several elements of direct experience.

Making a Case

We made a strong case at the beginning of this chapter for the limits of information to make change, but while trustworthy information is not sufficient to make change, it *is* necessary. There are some things you should know about providing data, evidence, or information to people that might help you be more effective.

First, each of us is hardwired with certain cognitive biases that are functional for cognitive efficiency (for example, screening out irrelevant information, being able to quickly process new information through categorizing it into buckets, and focusing most of our energy on the most salient parts of our environment, such as those that are most important from an evolutionary perspective including danger, reproduction, or food/shelter). Problematically however, these same functions can make it very difficult to process information that runs contrary to what we believe or implicitly assume is the case. As adult development expert Cook-Greuter (2000) put it, "The ego represents the striving of human beings to understand themselves and the world they live in by fitting new experiences into their current meaning system. Overall, the ego labors mightily to create and maintain coherence and vigorously defends against dissonant stimuli."

As a change-maker, you must work to break through these biases or bring them into the light of day. If you ignore these biases, you can share your information until the cows come home and it will have no impact other than to fortify the defenses of the listener. The strength of the mind to resist a shift in worldview is tremendous, because it is cognitively costly—meaning that everything has to be recategorized. For those of you who remember typing papers, or filing in actual paper filing cabinets, adding a new sentence or a new file meant everything had to be shifted around.

Not only does the new belief need to be instantiated, the existing beliefs all have to be compared to the new one to make sure no major discrepancies are formed. No wonder it's hard to make changes in behavior!

The process of shifting or shedding light on implicit biases and assumptions is most often a long one, requiring repeated intervention and practices. But as a change-maker, knowing that your information may be met with denial, skepticism, or threat-alert may help you change the way you deliver the message. A few things you can do follow:

- Keep it brief, simple, and to the point, and use metaphors, storytelling, symbols or simple representational images, or other nonverbal tools as much as possible. For example, you can tell people who are shifting their nutrition patterns to eat three cups of vegetables, 1/2 cup of carbs, and 1/2 cup of protein at every meal, or you can show them (or better, give them) a plate that has space for 1/2 vegetables, 1/4 carbs, and 1/4 protein. Adding a story, which again is processed by a different part of the brain than pure facts, can also be a powerful way to have information "stick" while circumventing the higher brain's sifting process.

- Make the *immediate* benefits of the change you are proposing clear, as opposed to only the long-term benefits. Long-term consequences, while comprehensible by the higher cortex, are so abstract as to be meaningless to the midbrain motivational system. If the change you are proposing is long term—such as, "if you quit smoking now, you will add 10 years to your life"; or, "if you pay more for solar power now, the planet will benefit in the future by slowing global warming"—you might consider in addition to these lofty goals, focusing even more intently on what it will result in right now. In the climate change world, we call attention not only to the immediate intended benefits but also the immediate "collateral benefits" that are often numerous and under-acknowledged, such as biking to work not only helping the environment but also one's health, energy level, and happiness today. You can frame the conversation with the bigger, longer-term picture, but focus more attention on immediate benefits of the desired behavior—for the head, the heart, the body, the spirit, and current relationships and quality of life. For example, "If you quit smoking now, you will have fewer wrinkles within four weeks"—giving them pictures or video to reinforce that immediate benefit; or, "by going solar now, you join a vibrant community of people who are smart, savvy, and advanced"—giving them ways to know they are a member of that community (even something as simple as a membership card or decal for their car window works) and ways to interact with that community (as simple as being allowed to join a private Facebook page or invitation-only conference).

- On the flip side, it can be powerful to help people pay attention to what is not working, or what is causing dissatisfaction about a particular topic, *right now*. Helping people identify and amplify the discomfort they are experiencing in present time about an issue is more powerful than pointing out how it will have negative future consequences.

There are many other approaches to making your information delivery more engaging, powerful, and participatory. Rather than imagining yourself as an expert who is delivering information to people who need it, consider yourself a tour guide, introducing people to their own journey of discovery. Rather than being a missionary, spreading the gospel of a particular topic, imagine yourself walking beside your target audience, pointing out things in the surroundings that are interesting. Trust that one thing revealed to someone through their own efforts is worth a thousand that you might convey to them.

Training, Tools, and Practices

Instilling new behaviors into people's lives takes almost constant vigilance at first—it's extremely rare that someone has a profound insight and then changes their behavior for good. It's important to realize that even if you facilitate a direct experience that results in the Aha! Moment you were looking for, AND you provide compelling scientific evidence or information to back it up, AND you've got the person on board with you, they will need accessible, feasible ways to integrate the new behavior into their life. The implications of what needs to be done next may be obvious to you, but not so to the person who is ready to make the change. It's incredibly crucial to co-create a simple strategy for making change that people can actually do, rather than telling them what they should do.

How can you blow gently on the flame of nascent motivation for change, without extinguishing it? By giving people feasible, achievable, free or inexpensive, community-supported activities they can immediately integrate into their everyday life. A bit of wisdom from the coaching world is that when working on putting new behavior patterns in place, set initial goals that are 100 percent achievable. This can be something like, "I will exercise for three minutes per day." It sounds silly, and so small as to be worthless, but in fact it provides people with many of the elements that must be in place for behavioral change to occur—such as direct experience, self-efficacy, immediate reward, and when the success is shared with others, social reinforcement. Then these small changes can be gradually built into larger ones. It's important that the person you are working with come up with the strategies themselves, with only a little help from you.

Ideally, new behaviors are presented in someone's "zone of proximal development," a term coined by the Russian psychologist Vygotsky (1987) to refer to what someone can learn to do with just a little help. That little bit of help is what Vygotsky termed "scaffolding": a temporary framework that is put up for support and access to meaning in the early stages of learning a new skill, and taken away once the person secures the ability for themselves. Kind of like training wheels, your job as a change-maker is to identify the next achievable next step for yourself, or assist the person/people you are working with to do the same, and then make sure there is enough scaffolding for them to feel safe to take that next step.

Also, remember that adding a behavior to one's life is often much easier than subtracting a behavior. Your change-making might benefit from mobilizing the "approach" rather than "avoidance" aspects of behavioral motivation. Highlight, emphasize, and demonstrate what people are moving toward, instead of what they are moving away from. The nobility of deprivation or asceticism is motivating for a very small minority of people. Yes, most people are motivated by relief from discomfort or suffering, but you can place the emphasis on moving *toward* relief (rather than what they need to give up to attain that relief). Secondarily, people are motivated by moving toward joy, thriving, belonging, and quality of life for themselves and their loved ones. When working to change the behavior patterns of yourself and others, focus on what people will be adding to their lives, rather than what they must subtract.

Meeting People Where They Are

It seems cliché but, more often than not, as change-makers we neglect this very important principle. Prochaska and DiClemente (1983) identified "stages of change" from precontemplation to contemplation, preparation, action, and finally, maintenance of new behaviors. For example, in the precontemplation phase, people are unaware of their behavior or the problem and resistant to change. In this phase, the task is to increase awareness (remember, not through information alone). In the preparation stage, it's helpful to create a collaborative and achievable plan for change with them. Helping someone in the precontemplation stage create a plan is nearly useless, though that's what we do all the time (think: giving nutritional plans to people who are nowhere near ready to make a change).

The key is to identify where people are in their process, and meet them there. Instead of trying to skip stages, like trying to move someone from precontemplation to action, you can purposely focus on moving them just to the subsequent stage. Notably they include, as a sixth stage, relapse—because the norm in every behavior change is relapse. This stage is not so much about trying to avoid relapse, as embracing the opportunity to learn from backsliding. For change-makers, know that there are stages to change, and that the process is not entirely linear. Acknowledge, recognize, and even celebrate the twists and turns that can occur.

The process of Motivational Interviewing (MI), by behavioral scientists Miller and Rollnick (2012), also holds evidence-based wisdom for change-makers. In MI, counselors are reminded to follow the acronym

RULE: Resist telling them what to do, Understand their motivation, Listen with empathy, and Empower them to take action, setting achievable goals and identifying techniques to overcome barriers. Truly understanding the motivation of another person, rather than imposing your idea of why they *should* be motivated, is one key to cultivating the conditions for change. For example, I worked with a population of pregnant women using a mindfulness-based intervention to help them change health and nutrition behaviors. We discussed with them why they might want to make such changes—including fewer childbirth complications, better health of the baby, better mother-infant bonding. We found that for some of the women, their main goal was to get their size eight jeans back on as quickly after childbirth as possible, to stay attractive. This was their motivator, and going with that despite my wish that their motivations be more noble (and feminist!), was more effective than trying to get them to focus on outcomes that were less compelling and more abstract to them, or seemed out of their control.

Research by Kegan and Lahey (2001) shows that when people are unable to change to more functional ways of being, or have difficult achieving their goals, it is typically because they have competing commitments of which they are not aware. These nonconscious competing commitments often represent deep, survival-level perceived needs that simply overwhelm the establishment of new behaviors. For example, let's say you are working with a CEO who is moving toward establishing green practices throughout her company, and you've worked for a year in an iterative fashion to co-create a set of steps that work for everyone. There will be a slight immediate reduction in profit margin, which will be recouped over five years in energy savings, and the optics of the company will be substantially improved, leading to a projected increase in profit. At your six-month follow-up with the company, you learn that the CEO later drastically reduced the scope of the plan, so much so that it is effectively hobbled, having no impact on intended outcomes and no real change of which to speak.

What happened? What you don't know is that the CEO received feedback from one (just one!) shareholder saying that people wondered if she was going soft, and whether this emotional tree-hugging tendency might impair her ability to be a strong leader. This triggered in her a concern that she herself was keeping barely suppressed—that if she moved too far from the conservative tough business-sense roots she learned during her upbringing and training, she would lose her job, be the subject of public ridicule, and eventually become completely meaningless as a person. This might sound dramatic, but when these competing commitments are uncovered, they are typically quite dramatic. Not a surprise in this case that she was easily swayed toward rejecting the new behavior. What can you do?

Rather than ignoring that people have extremely strong competing commitments, bring them into the light and take a look at them together. Put them all on the table. Respect them, and make room for them. Have compassion for them. And find a way to help people serve those commitments *and* move toward what they really want to do. In this case, you might connect this CEO with other conservative strong business leaders who are going green. You might work with her to test whether it was true, in fact, that if she made these new moves she would lose respect, testing it out by making small moves toward the new behavior and seeing what happened. You might give her extra resilience training, so that she knows she will be thrown into these survival-level conflicts when criticized, and have skills for navigating those moments.

Radical Inclusion

The law of conservation of energy in physics states that the total amount of energy remains constant in an isolated system, and that energy can neither be created nor destroyed but can be changed from one form to another. Similarly, when working to make change, you cannot create or destroy aspects of the essential nature of a person. Patterns of thinking, emotional archeology, implicit biases, and historical perspectives can be de-emphasized and disempowered, to stretch the garden metaphor—composted, through creating an ecosystem of change, but rarely can they be eradicated. As R. Buckminster Fuller said, "You never change things by fighting the existing reality. To change something, build a new model that **makes** the existing model **obsolete**." The best way to de-emphasize an old way of thinking is not to chip away at it with the goal of eventual elimination, but to add new ways of viewing the world that make those story lines less relevant.

We call this radical inclusion. Every part of each person is acknowledged, embraced, and allowed a seat at the table, even the parts we really, really disagree with or don't prefer. The racist parts. The sexist parts. We include the parts that care more about a cheeseburger or cheap television today than about the impact these things have on the environment for future generations. The parts that want more money, that want people imprisoned or killed who might be dangerous. The parts of all of us that have been selected over millennia of evolution to focus on our own immediate survival and that of those in our own tribe, even at the expense of others.

Remember, accepting and allowing in this context are not the same as approving or condoning. This is about meeting things as they actually are, instead of how we think they should be. Instead of focusing on eliminating what we don't prefer, we focus on including and transmuting it. Integral philosopher Ken Wilber (2007) points out that when we move into higher levels of consciousness, we don't leave the previous stages behind, but instead we *transcend and include* them. It makes sense, but in practice it's nonintuitive, and takes a bit of work.

Why would we want to include these parts of ourselves and other people as we work toward change? Because they are actually there, and they are not going anywhere. As Carl Jung pointed out, when we suppress "shadow" aspects of ourselves or other people, pushing them out of conscious awareness, they become *more* powerful drivers of behavior, not less. If our focus as change agents is to successfully suppress or control undesirable thoughts, motivations, or behaviors, our approach will surely fail, and may backfire. In contrast, when we nurture and support the growth of what is positive, this shifts the ecosystem without suppression.

Your Presence as a Change-Maker

Of everything we have said thus far, it's possible that the single most important thing you can work on to enhance your change-making ability is your own state of mind and way of being. The presence you bring to this work is your most valuable tool.

Why? Changing in foundational ways can make people feel vulnerable and scared. Stepping away from what they know can feel unsafe and unfamiliar. By changing, people are often risking loss of comfort, love, social standing, equilibrium, sense of self, sense of control…actually, it's a wonder that anyone changes! Your ability to embody a genuine, authentic sense of caring, respect, and dignity is essential.

As change agents, we must cultivate humility in ourselves—the knowledge that we cannot control the outcome of our efforts. We can only provide as many ideal conditions as we can for the natural process of change to happen. Extending the garden metaphor, making change is about painstakingly cultivating an environment most conducive for a natural process of growth to occur. We don't reach inside the seeds to pull the saplings out; we instead provide the ideal environment for germination to take place. If you have ever tried to make someone (through blunt force or sheer will) to be different, including yourself, you'll know that it is a losing proposition. A guiding assumption here is that given the right conditions, most people grow toward what Maslow called self-actualization (or, a drive that is present in everyone toward the realization of their talents and potentialities). When we work to change people's beliefs and actions by force, we often witness a pendulum effect—where people swing between being on "good behavior" and relapse/regression. Oscillations are to be expected, and are in fact essential to true change, but trying to force change or pushing people too far beyond their current meaning system and capabilities too quickly, almost guarantees a rebound.

In fact, the desire to control other people and situations (which includes employing direct and forceful efforts to change them, even with the best of intentions) paradoxically leads to *less* effective approaches to making change, and also leads to greater burnout for change-makers. Focusing on what we *can* do to provide the ideal conditions under which a new way of being can bloom leaves us knowing in our hearts that we have done what we can, leaves others feeling respected rather than harassed, and leaves a pathway open for future change. Some seeds that are planted germinate for years, with no apparent sign that anything has happened, until they eventually break through the soil. You as a change agent don't always get to know the impact you've had. Two crucial things to cultivate in yourself as a change-maker are 1) trust in the process of change itself, and 2) nonattachment to the outcome of your work.

Make sure your *passion* is tempered by *compassion*. People don't change from being insulted, harassed, shamed, lectured, lorded over, or in response to hysteria or outrage. In fact, when people feel this, they are unlikely to be open to change. When threatened, we perceive an unsafe, dangerous environment that is not conducive openness to change. Unwittingly, we create unsafe environments when we overtly or covertly insult people, their families, their regions, or their people.

In a recent article in *The Atlantic*, Conor Friedersdorf pointed out that "people are never less likely to change, to convert to new ways of thinking or acting, than when it means joining the ranks of their denouncers." He quotes Abraham Lincoln who said, that to dictate to a man's judgment, command his action, or mark him to be despised "and he will retreat within himself, close all the avenues to his head and his heart. And even though your cause be naked truth itself, transformed to the heaviest lance, harder than steel, sharper than steel can be made, and though you throw it with more Herculean force and precision, you shall be no more able to pierce him, than to penetrate the hard shell of a tortoise with a rye straw." Back to our point about radical inclusion: you can *feel* outraged, righteously indignant, and you can have *thoughts* that people who need to change are selfish and stupid. But if your attempts to make change do not afford the other person or perspective respect, dignity, and compassion—conveying what is essentially an invitation to try another way of being and see for themselves how it works—then any change you make is going to be brittle and easily retracted, broken, or damaged.

This is why nonviolent resistance is so incredibly effective. If you watch the speeches of Martin Luther King Jr. or John F. Kennedy, consider the march in Selma, the actions of Rosa Parks, or Gandhi, or countless others—what you see is an invitation to join into a community of dignity and justice. It's inviting people to move toward something, rather than taking something away from them. It's welcoming, and it offers direct experiences, evidence, actual tools and training, and a community of support. It enhances their sense of efficacy, clarifies their sense of identity, and moves them in ways that align with their deepest values. We hope that this chapter has provided some support for your efforts.

∞

References

Bandura, A., & Locke, E. A. (2003). Negative self-efficacy and goal effects revisited. *Journal of Applied Psychology, 88*(1), 87.

Cook-Greuter, S. R. (2000). Mature ego development: A gateway to ego transcendence? *Journal of Adult Development, 7*(4), 227–240.

Estrada, M., Silva-Send, N., Schultz, P.W., & Boudrias, M.A. (2017). The role of social influences on pro-environment behaviors in the San Diego Region. *Journal of Urban Health*, 94(2), 170–179. PMID: 28265806.

Hershfield, H. E., Goldstein, D. G., Sharpe, W. F., Fox, J., Yeykelis, L., Carstensen, L. L., & Bailenson, J. N. (2011). Increasing saving behavior through age-progressed renderings of the future self. *Journal of Marketing Research*, 48(SPL), S23–S37.

Kegan, R., & Lahey, L. L. (2001). *How the Way We Talk Can Change the Way We Work: Seven Languages for Transformation*. John Wiley & Sons.

Miller, W. R., & Rollnick, S. (2012). *Motivational Interviewing: Helping People Change*. Guilford Press.

Schlitz, M., Vieten, C., and Amorok, T. (2008). *Living Deeply: The Art & Science of Transformation In Everyday Life*. New Harbinger Publications.

Vieten, C., Amorok, T., and Schlitz, M. (2008). Many paths, one mountain: An integral approach to the science of transformation. *The Meaning of Life in the 21st Century: Tensions Among Science, Religion, and Experience*, 265.

Vygotsky, L. (1987). Zone of proximal development. *Mind in Society: The Development of Higher Psychological Processes, 5291*, 157.

Wilber, K. (2007). *A Brief History of Everything*. Shambhala Publications.

Chapter 18

TO HAVE OR TO BE?
On Purpose Over Profit

Dennis Wittrock

Looking at the state of the world today, most of us sense that a lot of things are fundamentally off. To pick a representative and prominent example, the major planetary ecological crisis of *climate change* is unfolding right before our eyes and the honest question of a child is enough to dumbfound us on the spot, *"Why can't we stop this?"* *"Well, honey, um…because…um, good question."*

Popular answers to this question mostly feature "capitalism" as the main villain. Somehow, it seems, the inherent logic of a system founded on short-term profit-maximization justifies overriding more rational impulses of long-term survival. But the emperor is naked. We alleged "grown-ups" are behaving ignorantly.

We have unconsciously consented to becoming the effect of a cause, instead of consciously creating new causes that would affect the course of history in a more favorable direction. But there is good news—you can change that, and you can start right now.

Lost in Space: Profit-Orientation

The first step that I suggest is to scrutinize and examine a widespread cultural bias—*profit-orientation*. Early on in life we learn that "money makes the world go round" and—even more magically—that "time is money." Everybody is so serious about money—especially shareholders and corporations. It would appear that their only purpose in life comes down to making more and more money—even at the expense of human decency, dignity, and basic compassion. I am impressed by the ability of the human mind to screen out and ignore any data that is detrimental to one's own comfort and sense of entitlement—even at the peril of extinction.

We have lost something. We have lost the connection to what is alive, real, and meaningful, and we have been looking for it in all the wrong places. Instead, we have accepted a shallow surrogate: wealth in the form of money, an abstraction that is supposed to satisfy our every need.

Money is quantitative and material. You can have it, possess it, accumulate it. Our minds are strapped to the erroneous assumption that if a certain quantity of money is "good," a greater quantity of money is proportionally "better"—ad infinitum. Following this profit-orientation we collectively end up in a bottomless pit of greed and self-deception, dehumanizing each other in the process. Our life compass is broken. We're lost in space. Our inherent *appetite for infinity* was somehow perverted to become an *infinite appetite*—for more things, more stuff, more money. We let profit become our purpose.

It is apparent that an infinite appetite for resources is incompatible with a finite planet. *"Earth provides enough to satisfy every man's needs, but not every man's greed,"* as Mahatma Gandhi put it. The profit-orientation knows no inherent saturation point, no "enough." It is a linear progression of more and more, a "bad infinity," to quote Hegel. The quality of the profit-orientation can be described as mechanical, lifeless, and dehumanizing and unaesthetic. It is inherently dissociating us from each other, from nature, and our own life's purpose.

A Strange Attractor: Living the Purpose-Pulled Life

Let's compare this with a *purpose-pulled life*. When you wake up in the morning you know what gets you out of bed, and when you go to sleep you know what keeps you up at night.

You know what you are burning for. You know what you are destined to do. You chose it and it chooses you. Doing it is joyful, immersive, and effortless. You are just expressing yourself. It feels natural, like breathing. In fact, your purpose breathes you.

Does this sound irrational? Maybe. But only to the uninitiated. Only to the average alienated person plagued by the drudgery of a meaningless existence who out of fear has succumbed to being a replaceable cog in some lifeless machinery designed to extract and squeeze out capital value from his precious lifetime under the verdict of profit-maximization.

Let me tell you this, there is a hidden continent "out there" and "in here" waiting to be explored.

An air of exhilaration, curiosity, and excitement pervades the purpose-pulled life. It is a life ignited by passion, rooted in infinity — a true bottomless infinity within, invisible, immaterial, unexplainable, and mysterious; yet real enough to thrust you forward into the unknown.

The force of evolution itself is pulsing through your veins, yearning to express more beauty, truth, and goodness — through the perfectly imperfect vehicle of your personal existence — if you just let it do its job. Will you?

Purpose provides direction. It is your ever-shining North Star. As such it is unreachable and ever-receding as you approach it. And yet, the purpose-pulled life is like a beautiful fractal — ever-deepening and ever-expanding as you dig into it. There is no saturation-point either. As you are realizing your purpose temporarily, you are circling, or rather spiraling forth, refining every circle of the process on a new level.

So Why Is that Not the Norm in Our World Today?

Only 13 percent of employees worldwide are engaged at work, according to Gallup's new 142-country study on the <u>State of the Global Workplace</u>. *In other words, about one in eight workers—roughly 180 million employees in the countries studied—are psychologically committed to their jobs and likely to be making positive contributions to their organizations.*[1]

Somewhere down the road we took a wrong turn, mistaking profit as being a legitimate purpose of an enterprise.

We're aiming too low, as it were, seeking for the infinite in the world of the finite — a kind of spiritual confusion, where we take our ultimate concern and turn it into an object, a thing, quantifiable, thereby turning money and profit into an "immortality" — or "Atman" — project (Ken Wilber). We can never satisfy infinite longings in a world of finite resources, which is why a mere profit-orientation is an obvious cul-de-sac for the planet. Profit is not a proper purpose, but it is an important metric and a means to achieve a given purpose.

Profit is not valuable in itself, but it has *instrumental* value and helps to realize other "true" values. We all want to be happy, free, enjoy peace of mind, and experience love or human connection. The implicit and explicit suggestion, and predominant cultural myth, is that money is the master key to buy us all these things. Of course this is a simplistic and false proposition, and most of us know it. Still, individuals and organizations act spellbound and accept the counterfeit purpose of profit-maximization. If we stop limiting our thinking to ourselves and our own short-term ego concerns, and consider the fate of the generations coming after us, it is apparent that we cannot afford to maintain such ignorant recklessness in the face of the wicked challenges humanity is currently presented with.

To Have or to Be

In his best-selling book *The Art of Loving* (1956), the German psychoanalyst Erich Fromm likened the ability to maturely love another person to mastering a form of art, which requires continuous dedication and practice along a continuous growth trajectory. Mature love is rooted in a purposefully active mode of *being*, not in *having* or possessing each other in a dead and passive way. In another influential book *To Have or to Be* (1976), a critique of modern capitalism, he contrasted two modes of relating to the world — a dead, mechanical, accumulating, and objectifying mode of "having" and a life-affirming, mindful, appreciative mode of "being."

It is not difficult to map Fromm's characterization of essential modes of *having* vs. *being* in individual humans to the domain of *profit-orientation* vs. *purpose-orientation* in organizations. The point of an organization is not to accumulate dead and abstract values but to foster life itself in its myriad and ever-evolving forms of purposeful expression and to become artful in it.

Allowing Purpose to Pervade Everything

We are being called to create new solutions to simultaneously *work, earn, and live for purpose.* Purpose informs and aligns the organization, the individual, and the collective, and it drives their continuous evolution by exerting an irresistible pull from the future. The leap from profit- to purpose-orientation requires the co-emergence of individual *Purpose Agents, For-Purpose Organizations,* and *For-Purpose Investments.* They all share similar properties:

- They are interested in continuous evolution.
- They view profit as a metric, not as a purpose.
- Their primary concern is realizing and fostering a true purpose.
- Profitability is a secondary concern for them.
- They value aliveness, agility, and self-organization.

We need to create the appropriate vehicles for *people* to express individual purpose, where earning is taken care of, where alignment with an organizational purpose works, where there are collective spaces where we can show up as we are and freely associate with each other.

We need vehicles for *organizations* to express purpose, where work is done that is needed in the world; where work is done that generates value, and enough money for its purpose agents to meet their financial needs; and with legal constructs in place that prevent a hostile takeover of purpose from actors that represent a pure profit-orientation.

We need vehicles for *investors* to enable investment in purpose-driven ventures, where purpose rules and cannot be subordinated to profit and—

last but not least—where a healthy profit is generated as ROI (return on investment).

Encoding a For-Purpose Enterprise

By declaring the profit-orientation obsolete and unfit to express what is required of today's organizations, we simultaneously put into question the generic distinction of *for-profit* vs. *nonprofit* companies. We are better advised to make a distinction between true *for-purpose* organizations vs. *not-for-purpose* (or *just-for-profit*) organizations. The ability to generate profit does not preclude an organization from being *for-purpose* — rather, it is what we would naturally expect to see if its purpose is aligned with what is needed in the world and if it delivered that value consistently. In fact, companies with a distinguished purpose-orientation have been demonstrated to outperform not-for-purpose companies in the long run.[2]

We at encode.org have pioneered our own prototype of expressing the purpose-pulled life — the *For-Purpose-Enterprise (FPE)*.[3] We take existing cutting-edge approaches for the *work to self-organize* around purpose (e.g., Holacracy [http://www.holacracy.org/]) and help organizations to upgrade and integrate their *legal systems* and *people systems* as well. This way we eliminate the influence of personal power-holding and close the neglected legal loopholes where individual ego eventually creeps back in to distort the purpose-orientation of the enterprise in favor of the classic profit-orientation.

It is an exciting time to be alive and to be able to witness and participate in these developments. I encourage and challenge you to follow your own "true north" and to become a Purpose Agent along with thousands of others, contributing to an emerging ecosystem of For-Purpose Enterprises and progressive organizations, supported by purposeful investors — with all of us taking the leap to a richer and more meaningful life where working, earning, and living for purpose becomes a reality.

Let purposeful Being prevail over purposeless Having.

References

Crabtree, S. (2013) *Worldwide, 13% of Employees Are Engaged at Work*, http://www.gallup.com/poll/165269/worldwide-employees-engaged-work.aspx, retrieved on May 6, 2017.

Fromm, E. (1956) *The Art of Loving.*

Fromm, E. (1976) *To Have or to Be?*

Keller, V. (2015). *The Business Case for Purpose*. Harvard Business Review. Boston, MA: Harvard Business School Publishing.

LinkedIn & Imperative (2016) *Purpose at Work, 2016 Global Report* https://cdn.imperative.com/media/public/Global_Purpose_Index_2016.pdf.

Wilber, K. (1980) *The Atman Project. A Transpersonal View of Human Development.*

Wittrock, D. (2016) *How to Work, Earn, and Live on Purpose.* https://medium.com/encode-org/how-to-work-earn-and-live-on-purpose-25c175213030 .

Endnotes

1. Quoted from http://www.gallup.com/poll/165269/worldwide-employees-engaged-work.aspx.

2. Quoted according to *Purpose at Work, 2016 Global Report*, p. 5

3. Also see: Wittrock, D., *How to Work, Earn, and Live on Purpose* (2016).

Chapter 19

TOWARD A LARGER EARTH
Supernormal Capacities and
Our Evolutionary Birthright

Christina Grote and Pamela Kramer

*Like the human heart, the world points beyond itself to something greater
and more beautiful than its present condition. That something attracts us
all, in different ways, and leads many of us to seek transformation. Does
it secretly inform the entire evolutionary adventure? Could it be that the
human heart and the world's heart are one in their self-surpassing? We
believe that they are.*[1]

—George Leonard and Michael Murphy

Humanity and the cosmos are united in common purpose, drawn by
an ineffable pull, to bring forth the beauty and goodness embedded
within. In this chapter we will explore the prospect that there are supernormal capacities within us, as yet undiscovered or undeveloped, and that
these latent capacities express a natural evolutionary progression, that, if
realized, could ultimately result in an evolutionary leap for humanity. By
consciously aligning ourselves and engaging with this universal seeking
through the cultivation of our latent capacities, we are fulfilling our evo-

lutionary purpose. Even our most basic desires to be better parents or lovers, more competent in our professions, or even to make a better lasagna, contain the seeds of this self-surpassing, our deepest yearnings toward an extraordinary life.

Although big picture narratives have fallen out of favor, we see a deep need for a positive and hopeful view of the world that is compatible with our times, one that gives meaning and purpose to life, one that gives us the sense that we are part of something greater. Evolution is the new story of our time and the even newer story is that evolution happens across all domains—not just biological, but cultural, social, and spiritual as well. Although "evolution meanders more than it progresses" as Murphy writes, we can surmise by tracking the increasing complexity of life-forms over time, that evolution is purposeful, that it is going somewhere, and that it is possible and beneficial for us to align ourselves with that evolutionary trajectory.

We will describe an evolutionary worldview, that of Evolutionary Panentheism, fueled by evolutionary love, that provides a basis for understanding our evolving human capacities. We want to demonstrate, as Murphy has, that there is a natural progression of these capacities, and that we, and the entire universe, are predisposed to bring forth the great potentials that were involved at the time of the inception of the material universe. Drawing on the work of Michael Murphy, George Leonard, and others, we will paint a hopeful portrait of our vast potential, as yet largely untapped and unrecognized, and explore ways of approaching its development. We do not intend to provide conclusive evidence for whether or not these various capacities exist but rather to look at them as expressions of humanity's evolutionary potential.

Michael Murphy is the cofounder of The Esalen Institute in Big Sur, California, and author of many books of fiction and nonfiction including *Golf in the Kingdom*, *The Future of the Body*, and *In the Zone*. Traveling to India in 1950 as a young man, Murphy spent a year and a half meditating at the Sri Aurobindo Ashram in Pondicherry. Aurobindo has remained Murphy's main inspiration to this day. George Leonard (1923–2010) was also a prolific author whose works include *The Silent Pulse*, *The Way of Aikido*, *Education and Ecstasy*, as he was also an Aikido sensei, musician, and president of the

Esalen Institute for many years. Both men believed that humanity is capable of much more than is generally believed, and that there could be no worthier goal than the realization of our highest potentials of body, mind, heart, and soul, both for ourselves and for society. Together they created Integral Transformative Practice[2] as a pathway for the realization of these positive potentials and as a launching pad for places yet unknown.

Adam Crabtree, psychotherapist, author and one of the world's foremost authorities on trance, has been developing the concept of Evolutionary Love as first proposed by Charles Sanders Peirce. His work is included here because we feel that the concept of evolutionary love is foundational to the worldview of Evolutionary Panentheism. Both will be described in this chapter.

What We Know About Supernormal Capacities

Most of us have at least heard of, or perhaps even know, people who exhibit unusual abilities, people who for example have deep empathy with others, have precognitive dreams whose foretellings come true in real life, can hear colors, commune with beings on other planes, or experience an extraordinary level of love, joy, and connection with all of life. Supernormal capacities have been experienced and observed in human beings most likely since the emergence of Homo sapiens. Hunter-gatherers needed to find game for the night's meal and used a form of clairvoyance to "see" them, a technique which is still in use today.

Since antiquity, there have been reports of people displaying extraordinary powers. For example, in ancient Indian texts, from the Upanishads to Patanjali's Yoga Sutras, there are descriptions of *siddhis* ("attainments"), or powers, and recommended techniques to develop them, such as meditation to calm the mind. These texts describe many types of siddhis ranging from the ability to see inside one's body down to the cellular level (*animan siddhi*), to precognition, to traveling in other realms. Catholic literature speaks of the *charisms* of the saints, which are considered to be "gifts" of the spirit but nonetheless represent, if true, a higher, or at least different, level of human functioning than is currently evident in our society. Examples here, which have been subjected to considerable scrutiny by the church, include stigmata, luminous phenomena such as halos, extraordinary fragrance emitted by a person's body, and the *incendium amoris*, or bodily heat, generated by ecstatic devotion. There are varying degrees of certainty that these capacities are real but there is enough evidence to suppose that many of them may be. Supernormal capacities such as these can be seen as extraordinary developments of attributes that are already present within us.

In 2013, Dean Radin of the Institute of Noetic Sciences in Petaluma, California, published a book titled *Supernormal*,[3] in which he reviewed scientific studies that were designed to explore the validity of some of these extraordinary powers. He determined that there is good evidence to support the existence of a number of capacities described in Patanjali's yoga sutras such as telepathy, the ability to know another's mind or condition from a distance; precognition—the ability to know events before they happen; and clairvoyance, or extrasensory perception (ESP). He also identified current examples of people with extraordinary capacities such as the Dutch athlete Wim Hof, known as the Ice Man, who holds the world's record for sitting still while submerged in ice water (one hour and forty-five minutes), among other feats.

The Future of the Body, Murphy's magnum opus, was supported by data he collected since his college days and assembled through Esalen Institute's Transformation Project, which was created to study supernormal human functioning. This was the beginning of a collection of over 10 thousand accounts that led Murphy to identify 12 categories of extraordinary human functioning, and to the belief that we are fundamentally wired for these experiences, what Murphy calls "the budding organs and limbs of our latent supernature." These categories include Perception of External Events, Movement Abilities, and Love, among others.[4] Murphy included only soundly verified data, drawing from the natural and human sciences, psychical research, religious studies, and other fields to provide a more complete lens on human development than gained from studying separate domains, an approach he calls synoptic empiricism. As a result of his research, Murphy came to believe that most if not all ordinary human attributes can give rise to extraordinary versions of themselves, either spontaneously or through transformative practice, and that if these were stabilized and mastered throughout society, a new kind of human would walk the earth.

Further, Murphy saw that these human capacities exhibit a continuity, a family resemblance, to capacities inherited from our animal ancestors and created a taxonomy to describe how they may develop, from animal inheritance, through ordinary human development, to products of supernormal development. For example, in the category of Perception of External Events, he uses the example of the eye as a product of animal evolution. Ordinary human psychosocial development of the eye results in improved sensory awareness developed by practices such as martial arts and contemplative practice. Supernormal development could result in extraordinary vision, clairvoyance, and perception of the numinous in the physical world. This taxonomy can provide a road map for the intentional development of these capacities.

One of the benefits of this kind of survey is that it provides us with models, examples of those who have experienced the outer reaches of the human frontier, helping us realize that there is much more to us, and more going on around us, than we realize. We are all carrying a "sack of gold," the old teaching story goes, but most of us have no idea we are carrying it, much less what is in it. These capacities are our birthright. In developing them through integral practice, we move toward the realization of our highest potentials, becoming fully articulated human beings, and in doing so, we help move humanity forward toward a supernormal embodiment, aligned with the universe's evolutionary unfolding. Although we are hardwired for these capacities, from clairvoyance to psychokinesis, there seems to be a difference in their availability, and this may be a good thing. Murphy found that capacities "most crucial to human goodness and growth—namely love, need-transcending joy, and perceptions of oneness with others—are more commonly experienced than potentially dangerous or distracting phenomena such as kundalini arousal or internal clairvoyance... All of us can reach out with love in most circumstances, he says; there are countless ways to perform acts of kindness... We are tilted in the right way toward balanced growth."[5]

The Worldview of Evolutionary Panentheism

The idea that divinity is present in all things and manifesting itself through the immense adventure of evolution helps account for the mystery of our surplus capacities, our yearning for God, our inextinguishable creativity, or sense of grace in human affairs. It helps explain our quest for self-transcendence and humanity's proliferation of transformative practices... Every culture in every age has invented ways to realize their kinship or oneness with divinity.[6]

The worldview we hold must be broad enough to accommodate the kind of evolutionary change we are proposing here. To determine if this is the case, we can ask ourselves questions such as: Do we believe that the universe is purposeful or random? Is the universe against us, supportive, or neutral? Do we have a part to play or are we at the whim of fate? The way we answer these questions has everything to do with how we see our purpose in life and how we act in the world. Such an encompassing worldview has begun to emerge among certain scientists, philosophers, and laypeople. Murphy calls this worldview Evolutionary Panentheism, *Panentheism* meaning literally "all in god," or "in the divine." In his recent white paper on "The Emergence of Evolutionary Panentheism," Murphy summarizes the worldview this way:

> Evolutionary Panentheism is based on just a few fundamental principles, among them: first, that evolution is a fact (though its discovery has given rise to various theories about it); second, that our universe arises from and is constituted by a world-transcending supernature, call it the One, God, Brahman, the Absolute, Buddha-Nature, Allah, Geist, or the Tao; and third, that humans have a fundamental affinity or identity with that supernature, which can be known through immediate experience either spontaneously or by means of transformative practice.[7]

Therefore, our fundamental affinity with the divine can be seen as the basis for the existence of latent supernormal capacities. All potentials are already present.

Rather than a mechanical universe subject only to meaningless random mutations as the strict Darwinists propose, the vision of Evolutionary Panentheism is engaging and unifying: everything in the universe, including ourselves, is evolving and filled with divine spirit and consciousness, and that as we open to this evolutionary flow, the more aware of this inherent divinity we become. It leads us to think about how we can be more active, conscious participants in this journey, aligning ourselves with the drive of the universe to self-surpass, and awakening to the divine through endless creative discoveries. However, In the face of the pain and suffering we see across the world, it can be difficult to believe that there is a divine force working through evolution. Perhaps, our best response to this suffering is to function at our highest potentials: to love, to feel compassion, and to look for ways to be of service whenever possible. In short, to live consciously and fully.

Evolutionary Love

Some have wondered if this hidden divinity, which involved itself in matter, could be none other than an expression of Love—divine, unconditional love—as expressed in the gospel of John, "God is Love." In 1893, Charles Sanders Peirce, one of America's great philosophers (1839–1914), who was inspired by this gospel, wrote a monograph titled "Evolutionary Love." Intrigued by this idea, psychotherapist Adam Crabtree has been developing the concept in a forthcoming book.[8] Stated simply, "Evolutionary love is the heartfelt benevolent desire that everyone—ourselves, others, and all that exists in the universe—reaches their greatest possible fulfillment, whatever that may prove to be. This love is freely given, with no consideration of merit, with no strings attached, with no expectation of return, and it is a love that motivates supportive action in the one who loves." This love object can be a person, an object, or even an idea. When we practice evolutionary love, we are holding the object of our love in its highest possible state of fulfillment. "Love something and watch it blossom," says Murphy. There are many types of this love and on the cosmic level, it could be the telos, or purpose, that drives the universe's evolutionary advance, the very same purpose that is behind humanity's desire to continually self-surpass, and this driving force is nothing less than love, evolutionary or unconditional love.

Unconditional love can also be seen as source of supernormal capacities. When Brazilian psychic and healer Thomaz Morais was asked about his power source, he said the ultimate source of his powers and all human energies is love. "Only by attuning to the ultimate energy of love can we transmute ourselves inwardly...then biological transformation...and then, harmony and peace...there is nothing else of greater value..."[9]

Finally, here are Leonard and Murphy: "We have suggested that cosmic evolution as we know it, from the big bang to the present moment is finally an expression of Eros, of love. If this is so, then can we doubt that love stands as the highest and most fundamental human impulse...a true expression of who we are, a fundamental condition of the path upon which we walk."[10]

Cultivating Supernormal Capacities

Throughout history, human beings have used various means to develop their latent gifts, such as religious practices, magic, psychoactive drugs, vision quests, and recently assisted by technology such as "transcendence tech." Many of these have brought about positive change; however, if one sided, these attempts toward transformation may ultimately fail because they can result in uneven development or only short-term changes of state rather than a permanent positive shift.

From their collective experience and research into human transformation, Murphy and Leonard realized that for true lasting transformation, there must be long-term practice involving body, mind, heart, and soul. We are multidimensional beings, and developing all of our aspects simultaneously creates a kind of synergy that sets the stage for nonlinear, quantum shifts in us and potentially for the arising of our latent supernormal capacities. Other guiding principles include the need for several mentors rather than a single all-powerful guru, and the value of practicing with a community of engaged practitioners to provide context and foster loving support, accepting us as we are, while moving us toward the higher good. From these and other principles, they created Integral Transformative Practice[11] (ITP) to help people reach their highest potentials and explore the frontiers of human evolution. Integral practice helps to avoid the uneven development that comes from exclusive work on one aspect. Of course, in any practice course correction may be required.

There are numerous studies that demonstrate the value of an integral approach, for example combining meditation and aerobic exercise,[12] as well as numerous examples of the dysfunction that can result from developing some aspects of our being at the expense of others: neglecting one's body in the pursuit of enlightenment, or focusing on physical health to the exclusion of all else. Consider also the dangers of highly developed spiritual ability with little or no attention to moral development. We see ITP or other integral practices that involve and integrate the entire being, as a necessary foundation for grounded exploration into expanded human capacities. Involving and integrating physical, mental, emotional, and spiritual health is critical to this effort. When this groundwork has been done, the arising of latent capacities can be seen as a natural outgrowth of evolution, although as Murphy often says, "evolution meanders more than it progresses," and we acknowledge that there are no guarantees.

In *The Future of the Body*, Murphy identified what he called transformative moves or modalities that further the development of the capacities that he identified. The classes of modalities that appear the most often in his survey are: somatic development through sport, martial arts and somatic awareness; mental imagery or visualization; religious or contemplative practice; and psychotherapy, or other types of disciplined inner work. Combining modalities such as these produces a balanced development of our entire being. Much territory remains to be mapped, more effective modalities to be identified, and work in this area continues.

If They Are Natural, Why Don't We See More Of Them?

We really don't know what the limits of our capacities are. Cultures only encourage capacities that they value, and suppress those that they do not. Supernormal capacities, such as remote viewing, can even be seen as a threat to social order. If we give ourselves permission to explore them, however, many more could surface. How many of us were told as children that there aren't colors around people? That we can't possibly be seeing angels?

Most religious and spiritual traditions warn against engaging with these capacities. *"Moksha before siddhi"* is the phrase used in the Hindu tradition, meaning "liberation before powers"; we must free ourselves from identification with the ego before we can be trustworthy. To the founders of most of the world's spiritual traditions, the material world was seen as static and cyclical, a place to escape from, not an arena for life's creative exploration. The Western occult traditions also speak of how easy it is to be seduced by the "glamour" of special powers. Belief in one's superiority and potential attachment to powers becomes an impediment to spiritual development and is potentially fatal to any further advance.

However, we can view the development of these powers differently. Science has given us a new perspective on the universe "as a place of novelty and creativity, firing our imagination with the idea that human possibility is coupled with evolution's dynamism."[13] We want to engage with the world rather than escape from it. We believe that we need healthy ego-strength in order to transcend ourselves. In *The Future of the Body*, Murphy proposes an integral approach "where our world engaging capacities would be cultivated within a deepening spiritual realization, and would be viewed as necessary to our development rather than an impediment to it."[14] We could surmise that humanity has not come far enough in moral development to be trusted with these abilities, but as there are signs that more and more people are discovering some new ability arising within them, any program designed to encourage their development needs to address this. It is crucial to have a theoretical framework for understanding them and sound practices with which to integrate and develop them.

Capacities Important Now and in the Future

The higher gifts of genius—poetry, the plastic arts, music, philosophy, pure mathematics—all of these are precisely as much in the central stream of evolution—are perceptions of new truth and powers of new actions. There is, then, about these loftier interests nothing exotic, nothing accidental; they are an intrinsic part of that ever-evolving response to our surroundings, which forms not only the planetary but also the cosmic history of our race.

—Frederic Myers[15]

No matter our situation or circumstances, we have within us access to infinite resources. Although we have myriad capacities latent within us and capable of being developed, we feel that some have a particularly important role to play, and are needed in both our current circumstances and in those we cannot yet imagine. With many challenges on the horizon such as global warming and the enormous societal disruption predicted as a result of technological advance, what human qualities or capacities will be needed and of value? What will give meaning and purpose to our lives?

To navigate the river of exponential change that is at work in our society and direct it toward a promising future, we will need to further develop capacities, such as a strong sense of our own identity with its unique insights, along with the ability to remain grounded and centered and resilient in difficult situations; clear intentions and focus of will, clear insight into situations, inspired creativity, and creative problem-solving. These are imbued with love and respect for all of existence.

Drawing again from Murphy's work in the *Future of the Body*, here are a few of the capacities that stand out—Cognition, Volition, Individuation, and Love.

Cognition

Supernormal Cognition includes various ways of knowing including analysis and reasoning; intuitive comprehension of another's subjective state; problem-solving that involves visual, auditory, or other imagery; and mystical illumination. Human ingenuity has overcome countless obstacles and there are plenty of reasons to believe that we will continue to do so. Inspirations, such as those of Mozart, whose extraordinary musical works seemed to form all at once, are not limited to such geniuses. They happen spontaneously for all of us in our everyday epiphanies, our "ahas." This occurs, as Murphy writes, because we have a "greater life" in us that we draw upon, both consciously and unconsciously informing our daily activities.

Volition

Supernormal Volition is marked by one-pointed involvement; by disregard for immediate results; by spontaneity, freedom, and effortless mastery; and by a sense that the self is somehow larger and more complex, or conversely, that it disappears into something beyond itself. The flow state, first studied and named by Mihaly Csikszentmihalyi, involving many human attributes, clearly includes an exceptional type of volition. The profound intention and highly focused activity that is part of this state can seem to trigger those startling events that Carl Jung called synchronicities, or meaningful coincidences. These events often reveal a new path to be taken, a long-sought discovery, or something of significance to those who experience them.

The development of volition can take the form of using ongoing self-reflection to recognize our often conflicting and half-hidden inner drives, leading to the integration of our many wills into one single harmonized will, allowing for a strong, single-pointed focus when we want it. We will need this type of will to manifest our intentions, using inner guidance, sensing our way toward what is next for us in an exponentially changing world. The ultimate manifestation of supernormal volition culminates in the Judeo-Christian-Islamic statement of surrender, "Not my will, but Thine be done." We are in harmony with Divine intention.

Individuation and Sense of Self

Quoted in *The Future of the Body*, George Leonard writes, "To be human, it seems clear, is to have a personal identity. This identity is unique and irreversible and it provides our particular viewpoint of the universe. This identity is not the constructed ego but the essence of who we are."[16] This uniqueness becomes more pronounced as our capacities develop. Exercising and broadening the repertoires of body, mind, heart and soul may contribute to the supernormal development of individuality towards "the realization of an ego-transcendent identity that perceives its oneness with all things while remaining a unique center of awareness and action."[17]

Love

All events and persons are the divine in disguise. The Indian greeting *Namaste* brings this recognition to the forefront of social interaction. This greeting, technically meaning "I bow to you," it is often taken to mean "The divine in me bows to the divine in you." Looking back to our earlier discussion of evolutionary love, through that lens we can see all things in the universe as arising from this love and being imbued with love in every particle. With evolutionary love, we are moved to hold each person (including ourselves), idea, or thing in their highest potential, in their fullest flowering, to sustain a fervent wish that they realize that potential, and if possible, to act to help them achieve it.

Love, like all human capacities, grows through its exercise. If we can come to see each one of us as love made manifest, we are more likely to treat each other with respect, work together to achieve common goals, and value all of life, whatever form it may take; we could live from the point of view of love. "If I love the world as it is, I am already changing it," says novelist Petru Dumitriu, "a first fragment of the world has been changed, and this is my own heart."

In summary, the supernormal capacities of Cognition, Volition, Individuation, and Love, as described above, and others that may develop in response to new demands, give us a strong basis for not just surviving but flourishing in what will then be for us "a larger Earth." Supernormal cognition gives us clear vision and openness to receiving inspiration, while supernormal individuation allows us to perceive our oneness with all things and yet to be a unique center of action. Focused will and the flow states that trigger synchronicities can show us the way forward. Love—entwined with the capacities of body, mind, heart, and soul—enjoins us to hold all in their highest possibilities. The development of these capacities will help position us to be of the greatest assistance to humanity and a world in need, and to aid in our mutual evolutionary journey.

Suggested Practices to Open to the More

Integral Transformative Practice (ITP) is a community-based path of practice that engages and integrates all dimensions of our being—body, mind, heart, and soul—providing a foundation for balanced growth over time, enabling us to draw from "the greater life within us." Here are a few guidelines to consider as you engage in the unfoldment of your evolutionary nature:

- Practice being grounded and centered in the present moment.
- Focus on clear intentions and also allow for the workings of grace.
- Identify your gifts and look for ways to serve the world.
- Communicate to be understood and inquire to understand.
- View any given situation from multiple perspectives, holding all in unconditional love.
- Develop the capacities of body, mind, heart, and soul.
- Stay alert, notice synchronicities, and be curious about anomalies, things that seem to happen out of the blue.
- *"Expect nothing; be ready for anything."* —George Leonard

Our Broader Purpose

> *If it is true that Spirit is involved in Matter and apparent Nature is Secret God, then manifestation of the divine in him/herself and the realization of God within and without are the highest and most legitimate aim possible to man upon Earth.*
>
> —Sri Aurobindo

Ultimately, we believe our purpose as human beings is to explore, to grow in love, and express our latent divinity. We do so by developing ourselves through integral practice, contributing talents that most benefit ourselves and the world, and by consciously moving with the power of evolutionary love, that has propelled human beings from the earliest days, toward an ever greater flowering of the richness we embody.

Endnotes

1. *The Life We Are Given*, George Leonard and Michael Murphy (Tarcher Putnam, 1995), Preface.

2. See itp-international.org.

3. Dean Radin, *Supernormal* (Deepak Chopra Books, 2013).

4. The 12 are Perception of External Events, Somatic Awareness and Self-Regulation, Communication Abilities, Vitality, Movement Abilities, Abilities to alter the environment directly, Pain and Pleasure, Cognition, Volition, Individuation and Sense of Self, Love, and Bodily Structures, States and Processes. Since this writing, Murphy has added Memory and Imagination.

5. See: Murphy, *The Future of the Body* (19993).

6. Leonard and Murphy, *The Life We Are Given* (1995).

7. Included in *Panentheism Across The World's Traditions*, Loriliai Biernacki and Philip Clayton.

8. Crabtree, Adam, *Evolutionary Love and the Ravages of Greed.*

9. *Miracles and Other Realities* (Lee Pulos and Gary Richman Omega Press, 1990).

10. Leonard and Murphy, *The Life We Are Given* (1995), p. 194.

11. See itp-international.org.

12. http://www.nature.com/tp/journal/v6/n2/full/tp2015225a.html.

13. See: Murphy, *The Future of the Body* (1993), Chapter 7.1, p, 171-179.

14. Murphy, *The Future of the Body* (1993), p. 174.

15. Myers 1843–1901. Psychologist and cofounder of the Society for Psychical Research.

16. George Leonard, *The Silent Pulse* (2006, Gibb Smith), p. 56, quoted in *The Future of the Body* (1993) p. 143.

17. Murphy, *The Future of the Body* (1993), p. 50.

Author's Bios

Andrea Dennis is a leader in the fields of cultural exchange, fair trade, and service learning, and a committed lifelong student. She serves as the Director of Development, Outreach, Visibility and Engagement for the Chicago based nonprofit, Greenheart International. She also works with the Global Purpose Movement, a project convening purpose-agents to serve our highest purpose. She facilitates workshops and retreats for youth and adults on personal development and social action. Andrea is a certified instructor in Primordial Sound Meditation and yoga, receiving her training from Chopra University and a 200hr course from Yoga Now Chicago. She received her Permaculture Design Certificate at the Earth Activist Training by Starhawk and Charles Williams. Andrea has served on the Board of Directors for the Chicago Social Enterprise Alliance and currently serves with Chicago Fair Trade.

Barbara Marx Hubbard is co-chair of the Foundation for Conscious Evolution and co-chair of The Center for Integral Wisdom. Author of eight books, she is now writing several new books on evolutionary themes. Living at Sunrise Ranch, Colorado, working on "The Planetary Mission: To Connect Co-Creators World-wide," and offering a year long course: The Planetary Awakening Accelerator: to Activate a Planetary Awakening in Love through a Unique Self Symphony with Marc Gafni and Lisa Engles. The prize winning film of her life story "American Visionary" has just premiered at Illuminate Film Festival where she was honored with the 2017 Conscious Visionary Award.

Bill Plotkin, PhD is a depth psychologist, wilderness guide, and agent of cultural evolution. As founder of southwest Colorado's Animas Valley Institute, he has, since 1980, guided thousands of women and men through nature-based initiatory passages. He's also been a research psychologist (studying nonordinary states of consciousness), university professor, rock musician, and whitewater river guide. Bill is the author of *Soulcraft: Crossing into the Mysteries of Nature and Psyche* (an experiential guidebook), *Nature and the Human Soul* (a nature-based model of human development), and *Wild Mind: A Field Guide to the Human Psyche* (an ecocentric map of the psyche—for healing, growing whole, and cultural renaissance). http://www.animas.org

Brandon Peele is a Certified Purpose Guide, and author of *Planet on Purpose* (Hay House / Balboa Press, 2017). Brandon has guided over 2000 people from 50 different countries on their path of purpose discovery, and has worked with leaders of purpose-driven startups (Annmarie Skincare, Dr. Hop's Kombucha, NetDriven/KKR), as well as executives from Fortune 500 companies like Morgan Stanley, Google, Apple and Johnson & Johnson. He lectures and teaches purpose discovery courses at University of California, Berkeley, Northern Arizona University, the Institute of Noetic Sciences and the California College of the Arts. His work has been featured in USA Today, Conscious Company Magazine, Techcrunch and on Fox News.

Bryan Alvarez is an artist, musician, writer and spiritual practitioner living in Chicago. He is the founder of Omnifuture, a blog dedicated to magick, culture, & consciousness. He is also the co-founder of Sweet Aum Chicago and hosts visionary art/music events and workshops throughout the year.

Carly Visk is Partner, Sponsor, and Event Coordinator for Greenheart Transforms and Global Purpose Movement. She is a yoga teacher and has a passion for the mystery of consciousness and transformation. She enjoys creating sacred space that not only fosters inner transformation but also supports the sharing of creative ideas for bringing more balance and peace into our relationships. She studies with plant medicines and ceremonial leaders from Brazil, Colombia, and Europe who inspire her to work towards manifesting the vision of an Earth that can be protected and shared by all living things.

Cassandra Vieten, PhD is President and CEO of the Institute of Noetic Sciences. She is a psychologist, scientist, author, and international workshop leader and public speaker who for over two decades has been studying how people transform their way of looking at the world. She is author of three books, including *Living Deeply: The Art and Science of Transformation in Everyday Life* (2008). Her current projects focus on spirituality in mental health care, extraordinary experiences during or as a result of meditation, and virtual reality approaches to inducing perspective-shifting experiences that change people's lives.

Christina Grote is the board chair of ITP International, a non-profit organization founded in 2005, dedicated to awakening the world to its fullest potential through Integral Transformative Practice (ITP). A practitioner since 2003, she started and ran an ITP group in Columbus, Ohio for seven years. Christina grew up roaming the hills of Marin County, forming a deep connection with the natural world. A life-long interest in healing and spiritual development led to licensure as a massage therapist in 1988 and engagement with healing modalities such as the therapeutic use of sound, color and movement with the Tama-do Academy, and the Genesis Bio-Entrainment Module.

Cortney Love, PhD + Dharma Coach, works with heart-centered, spiritual women who want to design a life and abundant business or career that is directly aligned with their Dharma, or life purpose. She has a Ph.D in Biomedical Engineering with over 15 years experience in research and teaching. She left academia to become an entrepreneur and struggled for several years to discover her life purpose. Fortunately she found the light at the end of the tunnel. As part of that journey, she learned several techniques to live her Dharma, which she now uses to help others gain clarity and live a more purpose-driven, spiritually fulfilling life.

Dennis Wittrock, MA in philosophy, partner at encode.org, founder of Integral Europe, director of the Integral European Conference 2014 and 2016, certified Holacracy® Facilitator, served 5 years as CEO and board member of Integrales Forum and the Integral Academy in Germany. His purpose is to create spaces for the emergence of integral consciousness. www.integral-con-text.de.

Duane Elgin, MBA, MA, is an internationally recognized author and speaker and evolutionary activist. His books include: *The Living Universe* (2009) *Voluntary Simplicity* (1981, 1993, 2010), *Promise Ahead* (2001), and *Awakening Earth* (1993). He has contributed to numerous studies of the long-range future—working as a senior social scientist in Washington, D.C. on a Presidential Commission and then with the futures group at SRI International. Duane received the Peace Prize of Japan, the Goi Award, in 2006 in recognition of his contribution to a global "vision, consciousness, and lifestyle" that fosters a "more sustainable and spiritual culture." He has co-founded three non-profit and trans-partisan organizations using social media to catalyze a citizen-voice movement.

Ervin Laszlo is Founder and President of The Club of Budapest, co-Founder and Director of the Laszlo Institute of New Paradigm Research. Fellow of the World Academy of Art and Science, Member of the International Academy of Philosophy of Science, Senator of the International Medici Academy, and Editor of the international periodical World Futures: The Journal of New Paradigm Research. He is the author or co-author of forty-seven books translated into twenty-four languages, and the editor of another thirty volumes including a four-volume encyclopedia. Laszlo has a PhD from the Sorbonne and is the recipient of honorary Ph.D's from the United States, Canada, Finland, and Hungary. He received the Peace Prize of Japan, the Goi Award in Tokyo in 2002, and the International Mandir of Peace Prize in Assisi in 2005, and the Luxembourg World Pieace Prize in 2017. He was nominated for the Nobel Peace Prize in 2004 and 2005.

Jonathan Gustin, MA, MFT, is the founder of Purpose Guides Institute. He guides people to find and embody their life's purpose, as well as trains those who want to become Purpose Guides themselves. Jonathan has been a psychotherapist and integral mentor for over 20 years. He is also the founder of Green Sangha and Integral Awakening Center. He has taught purpose discovery with buddhist activist Joanna Macy and depth psychologist Bill Plotkin. Currently, he is adjunct faculty at JFK University in the Consciousness and Transformation M.A program, and teaches Purpose Discovery at San Quentin Prison.

Ken Wilber, with over two dozen published books translated in nearly as many languages, Wilber has created what is widely considered the first truly comprehensive Integral Map of human experience. By exploring and integrating the major insights and conclusions of nearly every human knowledge domain in existence, Ken created the revolutionary AQAL Integral Framework. He is the founder of the nonprofit think tank Integral Institute, co-founder of the transformational learning community

Integral Life, co-founder of Source Integral exploring the nature of Integral Society, and the current chancellor of Ubiquity University.

Leela Bergerud is a medicine woman, ordained minister, certified tantra teacher, integrative breath practitioner, and holistic bodyworker. Since 2001, she has been walking the "Red Road" as a vision quester, sun dancer, moon dancer and water pourer for sweatlodges. Her work facilitates embodiment through bridging the body, mind, and spirit.

Dr. Mica Estrada received her Ph.D. in Social Psychology from Harvard University and is an Assistant Professor in the Department of Social and Behavioral Sciences and Institute of Health and Aging at the University of California, San Francisco. Her research program focuses on social influence, including the study of identity, values, forgiveness, well-being, and integrative education. She leads federally funded studies on underrepresented minority student persistence in STEM careers and directs Climate Education Partners, which provides learning opportunities to city leaders about climate change. Her work contributes towards creating diverse and creative solutions to the pressing challenges of our day.

Nick Jankel is a Cambridge-educated thought leader who has spent 25 years cracking the code of breakthrough. As a purpose-driven innovation and leadership expert, he has advised hundreds of organizations from Unilever to Genentech and has lectured at Yale and Oxford. As a professional keynote speaker he has talked at Google, Nike, LEGO and CHRO Summit. As a philosopher he has spoken at Aspen Ideas Festival and The Science of Consciousness. He has starred in his own BBC TV series and is the author of *Switch On: Unleash Your Creativity and Thrive with the New Science & Spirit of Breakthrough* (2015). Nick is co-founder of Switch On (www.switchonnow.com), a leadership and personal development company.

Pamela Kramer is President of ITP International, a pioneering organization that trains individuals, groups and businesses on the extraordinary, well-researched benefits of Integral Transformative Practice (ITP), a long-term program for cultivating lasting personal growth and positive social change. A career specialist and executive coach for the past 30 years in the San Francisco Bay Area, Pam holds a MS in Career and Organizational

Development. She is a frequent presenter at Esalen Institute, IONS and other venues in the US and abroad and provides guidance to people on expressing their fullest capacities to lead purposeful, fulfilling lives.

Patrick Cook-Deegan is a longtime adolescent educator. Over the past decade, he has helped launch or grow a number of innovative youth programs including Back to Earth, Inward Bound Mindfulness Education, and Brown University's Social Innovation Initiative, as well as launching a travel abroad program for low-income high school students. He has taught at public, private, alternative, and charter high schools. In the spring of 2015, Patrick applied for a fellowship at Stanford's d.school, hoping to bring a decades' worth of experience of working with adolescents to develop a program what would answer this question: how do educator's help young people discover and develop a sense of purpose? After being accepted to the fellowship and a year of design work, Project Wayfinder was born.

Susan Lucci, Circle facilitator, Certified Purpose Guide, energetic mother of three individuating teenagers, lifelong learner, community activist and former lawyer, is passionate about: convening space for more meaningful conversations, creating inclusive and purpose-driven communities, and inspiring individuals to become their very best selves. An entrepreneur and thought leader, Susan has facilitated more than 500 transformational Circles and guided hundreds of seekers, all part of her mission to awaken dreams and activate potentials so we can come together to become the Beloved Community. Contact her @ smlucci@sbcglobal.net or see more @ www.2big4words.org.

Taz Rashid has been contributing to and producing mindful events on a global scale since 2011. Also a musician, Taz plays guitar, keyboard, Native American Flute, didgeridoo and hand percussion. Recently he has been performing and DJ'ing at major events including the Yoga Journal Conference, Wanderlust Festivals, Arise Festival, Bhakti Fest, Bali Spirit Fest, Global Purpose, and other similarly intentional gatherings. Taz envisions his work as being a channel for the expansion of global consciousness by giving his audiences a means to tap into their creative wisdom through movement, experience, surrender and awakening. In producing and performing music for yoga and meditation, Taz focuses on guiding students toward developing inspirational music (playlists) for their classes. He emphasizes breath beat sequencing, texture and a wide range of sound sourcing that, with awareness, can be combined to foster a mix of energizing, supportive and healing experiences. Taz also develops his original music for use by mindful brands, tv, movies, events and other media with the vision of spreading an energy vibration of peace, love and unity.

Terry Patten is the founder of Bay Area Integral and a leading voice in integral evolutionary spirituality, culture, leadership and activism. He co-developed Integral Life Practice with Ken Wilber and a core team at Integral Institute and was the senior writer and co-author of the book *Integral Life Practice: A 21st-Century Blueprint for Physical Health, Emotional Balance, Mental Clarity, and Spiritual Awakening* (2008). He hosts the online series, Beyond Awakening, where he has engaged leading-edge conversations with renowned thinkers and teachers. His upcoming book *A New Republic of the Heart: Awakening into Evolutionary Activism* (North Atlantic Press, 2018) which is an a guide to inner work for holistic political change.

CPSIA information can be obtained
at www.ICGtesting.com
Printed in the USA
BVHW051315120120
569208BV00001B/13/P